In the Cross Fire

Explorations in Public Policy

In the Cross Fire

A Political History of the Bureau of Alcohol, Tobacco and Firearms

William J. Vizzard

LYNNE
RIENNER
PUBLISHERS

BOULDER
LONDON

#35830980

Published in the United States of America in 1997 by
Lynne Rienner Publishers, Inc.
1800 30th Street, Boulder, Colorado 80301

and in the United Kingdom by
Lynne Rienner Publishers, Inc.
3 Henrietta Street, Covent Garden, London WC2E 8LU

Library of Congress Cataloging-in-Publication Data
Vizzard, William J., 1944–
   In the cross fire : a political history of the Bureau of Alcohol,
Tobacco and Firearms / William J. Vizzard.
   (U.S. public policy series)
   Includes bibliographical references and index.
   ISBN 1-55587-671-4 (hc : alk. paper)
   1. United States. Bureau of Alcohol, Tobacco and Firearms—
History. 2. Law enforcement—United States—History. 3. Law
enforcement—Political aspects—United States—History. I. Title.
II. Series.
HV8144.B87V59   1997
363.3'3'0973—dc21   96-48456
                                                                CIP

British Cataloguing in Publication Data
A Cataloguing in Publication record for this book
is available from the British Library.

Printed and bound in the United States of America

The paper used in this publication meets the requirements
of the American National Standard for Permanence of
Paper for Printed Library Materials Z39.48-1984.

5 4 3 2

To Diana for all the years

Contents

Preface

In July of 1967 my wife and I packed all our belongings in a Volkswagen and small trailer and headed north from California to a new career and life in Seattle, Washington. Upon receiving my baccalaureate degree, I had resigned my position as a deputy sheriff and accepted an appointment as a special investigator with an obscure federal law enforcement agency, the Alcohol and Tobacco Tax Division of the Internal Revenue Service. I knew little about my new position, except that I would no longer be assigned to night shifts, wear a uniform, or arrest quarrelsome drunks. I chose the position over other options such as the FBI and the Secret Service largely to avoid frequent transfers. Twenty-seven years and five transfers later, I would retire from a controversial and far less obscure descendant, the Bureau of Alcohol, Tobacco and Firearms, to begin my academic career. During those years, ATF was both the center of my life and my greatest frustration. In it I found my closest friends and most bitter opponents, and experienced my greatest satisfactions and most profound disappointments.

Throughout my career, ATF was buffeted constantly by the political winds of its environment. For an insider with an interest, it was a fruitful setting in which to observe the political and policy processes of U.S. government. Unlike the staff of more powerful agencies, ATF personnel never left the details to management. We were never that secure. The agency was small and in a constant state of reaction to outside forces. Although some in ATF displayed the uninterested detachment that is common in many bureaucracies, particularly law enforcement bureaucracies, a significant proportion were always attuned to the outside environment and its influence. As the only law enforcement manager to ever pursue a doctoral degree while in the agency, and as a student of public policy and organizational theory, I was always one of the most intense observers. This book is, therefore, a phenomenological study of a different type than is normally encountered. Numerous key participants were interviewed to clarify critical facts. However, the majority of the observation and interviewing was done informally over many years. In spite of this unconventional form of research, this is not reminiscence, but a work founded in theory.

ATF is engaged in criminal law enforcement, but it is located in the Treasury Department and derives authority from taxation and interstate commerce authority rather than police power. Its jurisdictions are shared with other federal, state, and municipal agencies, and it is internally divided into two very diverse functions. ATF became an independent bureau largely by accident and has been threatened with merger ever since. It is both a captive agency of a powerful but obscure lobby, the alcoholic beverage producers, and the focus of a constant and scurrilous attack by the powerful and highly visible gun lobby.

In short, ATF is not a cohesive, rational, and focused organization but an accident produced by a highly fragmented system obsessed with the dispersal of government authority. The agency did not mature under the focused control of a bureaucratic entrepreneur like Edgar Hoover of the FBI or Gilbert Pinchot of the Forest Service, nor did it enjoy the security of protected turf like the Secret Service or the Park Service. Even its mission, unlike those of the Drug Enforcement Administration or the Internal Revenue Service, has never been well defined.

Because of its unusual history, structure, and environment, ATF is both fruitful and frustrating to study. The agency offers the antithesis of Herbert Kaufman's *Forest Ranger*. It is instead the case study for James Q. Wilson's far more eclectic *Bureaucracy*. Instead of a central theme, such a study offers an opportunity to observe the interaction of structure, leadership, mission, interests, and culture. This interaction has at times produced public service in the highest tradition and even acts of great personal heroism, concurrent with muddled management and self-serving incompetence. To understand how ATF has been shaped by its environment is to understand a great deal about U.S. bureaucracy and the environment in which it operates.

Acknowledgments

This book owes much to the many ATF employees, past and present, who cooperated in my research. In addition, I received extensive support and cooperation from both advocates and opponents of gun control.

I was supported and encouraged in my efforts by my colleagues in the Department of Public Affairs at the University of Wisconsin–Oshkosh and greatly assisted by the department secretary, Mary Blazer. I am further indebted to Cynthia Ragland, whose tireless editing is responsible for whatever readability this book possesses.

My wife, Diana, has been my partner not only in the writing of this book, but through all my years with ATF and my entire graduate education.

Finally, I must acknowledge Chester Newland, Richard Stillman, and Dan McMillin, whose academic mentoring and encouragement over the past twenty-five years are indirectly responsible for this work.

CHAPTER 1

Origins

On April 19, 1993, the Bureau of Alcohol, Tobacco and Firearms (ATF) achieved the widespread public attention that it had pursued for its entire short history. Unfortunately, the attention derived from events that began with the earlier raid on the Branch Davidian religious sect's compound near Waco, Texas, in which four ATF agents and six Davidians died. These events lead to the deaths of over seventy Davidians, multiple investigations, the unscheduled retirement of ATF's senior management, and widespread characterization of the raid and later seige by the Federal Bureau of Investigation (FBI) as inept. For some, the events would come to symbolize the ultimate abuse of government authority and would apparently trigger the most violent terrorist incident in United States history—the April 19, 1995, bombing of the Oklahoma City Federal Building.

Until that date ATF had been well known only in law enforcement circles, among readers of gun magazines, and in the regulated industries of firearms, alcohol, and explosives. How had an agency with responsibility for regulation and criminal law enforcement in such disparate fields ever come to exist in the United States Department of the Treasury, and why was it conducting a raid on an armed, religious cult in central Texas? The answers to these questions are imbedded in a unique organizational history that provides insight into the impact of structure and function on organizational behavior. Concurrently, this history reveals how American political process shapes bureaucratic structure and function. Federalism, constitutionalism, decentralization, and fear of government have all played major roles in shaping the form and function of the federal bureaucracy. In general, the U.S. political system has tended away from rational organization and has created a structure in which agencies are pulled simultaneously among executive, legislative, judicial, professional, and interest group mandates. Structure has been fragmented and is more the result of tradition and expediency than planning. The case of ATF has all of these elements.

Predecessors

Although ATF sometimes traces its origins to 1791, when the first excise taxes were imposed on distilled spirits, its lineage practically begins with the 1919 creation of the Prohibition Unit in the Bureau of Internal Revenue. This organization was granted independent status as the Bureau of Prohibition and was subsequently transferred to the Justice Department.[1] Although not well regarded when it existed, the Bureau of Prohibition since has benefited from the Elliot Ness myth, largely manufactured by Hollywood.[2] It was returned to Treasury by the end of Prohibition and again placed in the Bureau of Internal Revenue as the Alcohol Tax Unit (ATU), later redesignated the Alcohol and Tobacco Tax Division (ATTD).[3] In addition to jurisdiction over alcohol, the agency exercised jurisdiction over the federal narcotics statutes from 1914 until 1930, when the Federal Bureau of Narcotics was formed in the Department of the Treasury.[4] Charged with collecting liquor excise taxes and suppressing the illegal manufacture of untaxed liquor, the agency initially faced a significant enforcement task. During Prohibition the production of liquor in illegal, unregistered stills became widespread and well entrenched. Numerous still operators, or moonshiners, continued their activity, which remained profitable because of the high taxes on alcohol production.[5] This necessitated a national presence in both law enforcement and revenue collection.

Over the next three decades illegal manufacturing of liquor, as a commercial enterprise, virtually disappeared in all parts of the country except the South and a few border states, where it had a long tradition. Agency files and conversations with older agents still serving in the 1960s reveal that large illegal distilleries were operating on the West Coast until World War II and in the urban Northeast until the 1950s. A number of social trends worked in conjunction with enforcement to eradicate moonshining.

Enforcing the Liquor Laws

Commercial stills are large, smelly, and require constant attention. This renders the operators vulnerable to capture. In addition, running stills involves hard manual labor. This was not much of a deterrent in the midst of the Depression or for rural southerners raised on farms, but it has little appeal in the postindustrial era. Liquor is also bulky to transport and offers a far lower profit margin than illicit drugs. In addition to the problem of hiding the still and transporting the product, the moonshiner required large quantities of raw materials, particularly sugar, and produced voluminous waste. The large quantities of sugar and containers could be followed to the still, thus revealing the illegal operation.[6]

Other forces were at work to undermine the moonshine business. National Prohibition had followed the widespread passage of state and local laws prohibiting the sale of alcohol. Many of these laws remained after Prohibition, creating a network of bootleggers who were a natural outlet for moonshiners. Gradually, these laws disappeared, with Oklahoma being the last dry state to go wet in 1959. Cultural traditions and economics also added to moonshine's demise. The consumption of whiskey has steadily fallen as a proportion of alcoholic beverages since the 1950s. Because the excise taxes on wine and beer are far lower than on distilled spirits, there has never been a profitable trade in untaxed, nondistilled, alcoholic beverages. Even those who continued to drink distilled spirits moved progressively to vodka, gin, or high-quality whiskeys. The market for moonshine, which has a very distinct and harsh taste, steadily declined as older, rural, southern populations died off.[7]

Law enforcement likely is most effective when it moves with, not against, social and economic forces. This was clearly the case with liquor enforcement. In addition to all the other dynamics, inflation steadily reduced the impact of the federal excise tax, which remained steady between 1952 and 1986. With no economy of scale, the ability of moonshiners to compete with legal distillers was lost. The seizure of stills by the ATTD peaked in 1956 and began to decline. By 1968, the well-informed in ATTD foresaw the end of any need for liquor enforcement within a few years.[8] In recent years moonshine has sold in small quantities, as a curiosity, for more money than legal whiskey. Curiously, this almost uniquely successful law enforcement effort has been little examined.[9]

During the 1950s and 1960s, ATTD agents, then known as investigators, were the dominate federal enforcement presence in most of the South. Towns as small as 10,000 population had as many as a dozen agents. Most were hired from state police or liquor agencies, the Border Patrol, or municipal police departments, although some were recruited directly from colleges in the 1960s. These agents spent much of their time working in the woods and became experts in such tasks as "cutting sign" and "laying in on a still."[10] Although assaults and even murder of agents were not unheard-of, the majority of agents and violators recognized rules of engagement that precluded violence. The agents were a tough lot who could respond fiercely, if challenged. And the federal courts did not look kindly on assaults or resisting arrest, whereas they often viewed moonshining with some tolerance.

As moonshining faded from those areas of the country outside the South, agents found themselves seeking tasks to justify their existence. As a result, some offices began more active pursuit of the firearms laws. They also pursued small-scale moonshiners, who would have received little attention in the South, and enforced certain other federal liquor statutes. This essentially established two classes of enforcement offices: those that had liquor violations and all others.

Although the Bureau of Prohibition was a highly visible agency, its successor, the ATU, was little known outside of the rural South. While the liquor laws shaped the predecessors of ATF for years, a largely ignored jurisdiction would prove even more crucial in the long run. In 1934 Congress passed the National Firearms Act under the taxation authority granted to the federal government. The ATU did not assume jurisdiction for the law until 1941 and paid little attention to it until the 1960s. Assignment of the law to Treasury for enforcement assured that all future firearms laws would be within Treasury's jurisdiction and eventually would lead to the creation of ATF.

In 1951 the ATU became the ATTD of the Internal Revenue Service (IRS). It would remain a division of the IRS until it became an independent bureau in 1972, although it would be renamed the Alcohol, Tobacco and Firearms Division (ATFD) in 1969. This extended period under IRS control and the division of the agency into distinct functional subunits for enforcement and regulation proved far more influential than Prohibition in molding the agency that would become ATF.

Treasury Law Enforcement

Although the Justice Department has always dominated criminal justice policy, Treasury enforcement agencies rivaled their Justice counterparts in operations for many years. In addition to the ATU, Treasury contained the Federal Bureau of Narcotics (FBN), the United States Secret Service (USSS), the Customs Agency Service, and the Intelligence Division of the IRS. Collectively, they exercised jurisdiction over federal statutes relating to drugs, alcohol, guns, gambling, counterfeiting, forgery, smuggling, and tax fraud. Although Treasury enforcement agencies accounted for a majority of federal criminal prosecutions, they remained relatively small, fragmented, and out of the mainstream of Treasury business.[11] Individually or collectively, they could never rival the FBI's success in dominating the attention of the public and Congress.

The late 1960s was a period of significant change in federal law enforcement structure and policy. In 1968 the Bureau of Narcotics was moved from Treasury to Justice and redesignated the Bureau of Narcotics and Dangerous Drugs (BNDD). The narcotics laws were subsequently rewritten and placed in the criminal code (Title 18) rather than the tax code (Title 26). Treasury had already lost jurisdiction over the Coast Guard. In 1968 the Supreme Court further eroded Treasury jurisdiction when it effectively terminated IRS enforcement of federal wagering statutes.[12] These events marked the beginning of a relative decline in the role of taxation authority and Treasury agencies to implement law enforcement at the federal level.

The one serious effort to unify the various Treasury enforcement agencies into a single bureau occurred in 1936 under Secretary Morgenthau. The authorization bill, known as the Secret Service Reorganization Act, would have merged all Treasury enforcement functions into the Secret Service. The bill was opposed primarily by the drug industry, which had developed a comfortable relationship with the Federal Bureau of Narcotics. Although the interest of the drug industry was simply to maintain an existing favorable relationship, the opposition was sufficient to block the bill.[13] The linkage of the administration of revenue and compliance functions with law enforcement has been a recurrent issue in restructurings and reorganizations of federal enforcement functions and agencies.[14] Some agencies, like the FBI and Secret Service, have resisted any such jurisdiction. Other agencies, like ATF and Customs, owe their existence to such linkages.

After 1968 the magnitude of federal involvement in law enforcement and criminal justice greatly expanded. Although Barry Goldwater had endeavored to make law and order an issue in 1964, his efforts were not fruitful. By 1968, rising crime rates and urban riots had significantly altered the political landscape, and both Nixon and Wallace capitalized on the issue. The Nixon administration authorized significant increases in law enforcement spending as a part of the first war on drugs. Treasury agencies experienced substantial growth during this era. The ATFD nearly doubled its enforcement personnel and the Secret Service continued a buildup that began after the assassination of President Kennedy and accelerated with its assumption of candidate protection after Robert Kennedy's assassination. Customs benefited the most, more than doubling the number of agents in the first two years of the Nixon presidency. Justice agencies, however, experienced even greater growth. This was particularly true of the FBI and the BNDD.

In spite of growth in Treasury enforcement agencies, in the period 1969 to 1971, their relative share of law enforcement turf declined.

New jurisdiction and the resources to implement it would in the future flow predominantly to the Department of Justice. The heyday of Treasury law enforcement, an accident of history and constitutional constraints on federal authority, was at an end. Although Justice would dominate operations as well as policy in the future, the split in law enforcement authority would remain and continue to complicate both. This would impact the future ATF in both firearms and explosives enforcement. In the former, it would be structurally excluded from most executive policymaking, which would occur at Justice, without benefit of ATF's expertise in implementation. In the latter, ATF would be in constant competition with the FBI for jurisdiction. Always, ATF would be peripheral to Treasury executives, who are far more concerned with monetary and tax policy than law enforcement or regulation.

The IRS Years

Among federal bureaus and agencies, the IRS is one of the giants. It employs over three-quarters of all employees in the Department of the Treasury, and the commissioner of Internal Revenue is a presidential appointee, who bypasses the Treasury hierarchy and deals directly with the Treasury secretary. Although it has numerous ancillary missions, the IRS's prime mission of collecting the income tax is both unambiguous and vital to the operation of government. Because alcohol and tobacco excise taxes are second only to the income tax as a source of federal revenue, jurisdiction over collection of these taxes was consistent with the IRS mission. Enforcement of criminal laws relating to drugs, firearms, explosives, and wagering was not. Even regulation of the legal industries, though more in line with IRS skills, was a distraction for IRS executives responsible for collection of income taxes, one of the most daunting and critical tasks in government. This likely explains why the IRS did not commit significant effort to retaining these jurisdictions.

To understand the impact of the IRS on the future ATF and the reasons that ATF would eventually seek to escape from the IRS umbrella requires an understanding of the evolving mission, structure, and culture of the ATTD during its years with the IRS. Although the ATTD's structure changed several times under the IRS, these changes were of minimal importance. The description of structure that follows is the configuration at the time ATF exited the IRS and had been the structure for some time previously. It differed little from earlier variations, and the impact on the future ATF was little affected by the minor variations.

The IRS was regionalized into seven quasi-independent regions. Although procedures were centrally specified in detail, operational management authority was placed in the hands of the regional commissioners and district directors. Regional commissioners had an assistant regional commissioner (ARC) for each major function, one of which was for alcohol and tobacco tax. Unlike ARCs for other field functions, the ARC-ATTD exercised direct line control over field operations. Other functions, such as audit and collection, were operationally administered through district directors dispersed throughout the region. As an example, the Western (San Francisco) Region had district directors in such locations as Anchorage, Seattle, Portland, San Francisco, Los Angeles, Salt Lake City, and Phoenix. The ATTD had a separate field office structure independent of the district directors. This independence from the IRS district structure was the primary key to the ATTD's level of autonomy. ATTD field operations were divided into enforcement and permissive offices, supervised by chief special investigators and supervisors in charge, respectively.[15]

Each of the two ATF branches had a distinct culture. Enforcement, charged with suppression of illegal liquor production, employed primarily special investigators, who were hired from the Treasury Enforcement Agent (TEA) examination and trained in the Treasury Law Enforcement Officer Training School along with agents from Customs, the Secret Service, the IRS Intelligence Division, and the Federal Bureau of Narcotics. Permissive, charged with regulation and revenue collection from the legal liquor industry, employed inspectors and storekeeper gaugers, who were hired from general civil service lists and trained internally. Although the distinction between the two groups appears to have been less in the early 1950s, it had grown to be substantial by 1972.[16] Special investigators hired after the introduction of the TEA primarily came from law enforcement agencies, were graduates of university criminal justice programs, or both. The Southeastern Region conducted substantial hiring for a program dubbed Operation Dry-Up in the early 1960s, and other regions hired extensively as a result of new firearms legislation in 1968 and explosives legislation in 1970. ATF would, therefore, begin as a bureau with two distinct cultures.

Each of the Treasury enforcement agencies had a unique structure and culture, but the ATTD was the most unusual. Both the Secret Service and Federal Bureau of Narcotics had fewer criminal investigators than the ATTD, but each enjoyed independent bureau status. In these agencies, agents dominated the culture and occupied all key management positions. These agencies also enjoyed greater independent identity, particularly Secret Service because of association with the president. All Treasury agencies, however, felt constantly overshadowed by the FBI. Although the Treasury agencies collectively produced more prosecutions for many years than the FBI and were clearly dominant in investigation of organized crime and drug trafficking, they could never match the well-funded and expertly conducted public relations program of the FBI. As a result their budgets and salaries always lagged behind those of the FBI.

Law enforcement personnel of both Customs and the IRS were buried in much larger bureaucracies, whose primary focus was voluntary compliance. This was more pronounced in the IRS than in Customs, as the IRS was a much larger agency. Ironically, the IRS employed more than three-quarters of the Treasury enforcement agents until the formation of ATF as a bureau, yet these law enforcement agents remained a small minority of IRS personnel, with very limited influence on culture and policy. The ATTD was unique in that it was a semi-autonomous division within the IRS. In some regions, such as the Southeast, enforcement clearly dominated. In others, such as the Western Region, the regulatory and licensing functions were clearly dominant.

With the passage of the Gun Control Act (GCA) in 1968, the law enforcement function in the ATTD began to ascend in those regions where it had not been prominent. The division was enlarged and renamed the Alcohol, Tobacco and Firearms Division. Although the size and visibility of the organization increased, some aspects remained constant. The IRS continued to provide all support and administrative functions. ATF, therefore, still had no capacity to hire, fire, pay, or train personnel. It could not prepare or present a budget or procure items necessary for daily operation. Functions as mundane as processing a promotion, adding a telephone line, or reimbursing travel required IRS support. Regions remained independent and unequal in power. Thus, ATF managers did not develop skills or discipline that would later be necessary to administer an independent agency.

ATF was far more influential in the Southeastern (Atlanta) and the Central (Cincinnati) Regions than in the rest of the country.[17] The enforcement function, in particular, was dominant in the Southeast. As late as 1972 Georgia had twice as many agents as California, although liquor enforcement had ceased to be a significant problem. The assistant regional commissioner and later regional director for the Southeast, Bill Griffin, was universally known as the most powerful man in the bureau until the reorganization of 1977. Although all regions retained substantial autonomy, Griffin was known for simply defying any direction from Washington with which he disagreed.[18] Regional distinctions were so entrenched that in many areas employees did not identify first with ATF but with enforcement or compliance and second with their regions. Thus, there was little sense of organizational identity and loyalty such as existed in the FBI.[19] Virtually all transfers and training, beyond the initial phase, were intraregional, enforcing the fragmentation.

Certain problems with the structural nature of ATF began to be apparent in 1969. With the passage of the Gun Control Act in 1968 and the beginning of the Nixon presidency, funds for law enforcement began to flow to ATF. Although ATF grew more slowly than the enforcement function in Customs and the newly created Bureau of Narcotics and Dangerous Drugs, these agencies did not change primary function nor were they as impacted by regionalism. ATF's most significant problem was the uneven distribution of its enforcement resources, experience, and prestige and the lack of relevant experience. Its organizational structure inhibited efficiency in responding to these problems as a national entity.

In the areas where there were numerous experienced agents, neither the agents nor the managers had any experience administering firearms laws, and most resisted the move from liquor to firearms enforcement.[20] In other areas, newly hired agents often outnumbered the available trainers. Many of the senior agents were nearing retirement and little motivated to take on new tasks. In an organization so structurally and culturally regionalized, shifting staff was not easily done. This tendency was exacerbated by the fact that no ATF headquarters existed with authority and funding to move personnel.[21]

The conflict between ATF enforcement and the prevailing culture of the IRS increased significantly as jurisdiction expanded. Enforcement of the liquor laws had not been without conflict, but it was clearly linked with protection of the revenue, geographically limited and supported by the politically powerful legal liquor industry. With the exception of areas in the South and border states where ATF had been well staffed, the existing cadre of agents had limited influence on the large number of former police officers who made up the majority of new agents. These new agents continued to act much as they had as police officers, except that they now had less supervision and more autonomy. The IRS routinely referred to all nonemployees as "taxpayers" and stressed voluntary compliance. The use of criminal prosecution as a means of enforcing compliance was a last resort and seldom if ever involved undercover operations, arrests, or violence. IRS orders prohibited the display of firearms to accomplish an arrest, and all income tax cases were reviewed by IRS lawyers before being submitted to United States attorneys for prosecution. The IRS, as an organization, understood that it was administering a very unpopular law and that maximization of revenue, not arrests, was the goal. Until 1969, IRS regulations required that nonwillful firearms violators be allowed to register their unregistered machine guns or other illegal firearms. Violations were assumed to be nonwillful if the taxpayer had not been previously warned and was not a convicted felon.

ATF agents, particularly those newly hired from police agencies, assumed that a felony mandated an immediate arrest. They spoke of "suspects," "informants," and "witnesses"—not of taxpayers. They assumed that their job was to investigate and arrest. Prosecutors could decide if charges should be filed. They focused their attention on those people they viewed as criminals, primarily convicted felons and drug dealers, and assumed that all arrests were potentially dangerous. Even older ATF agents were surprised that the new agents carried guns while working undercover. Liquor violators were not passive, but the money involved seldom justified robbery. ATF's organizational culture was clearly in transition and becoming less compatible with that of the IRS.

The new agents quickly established working relations with local police and drug agents. They were far more influenced by the expanding war on drugs than either liquor enforcement or the IRS culture of voluntary compliance. By the end of their first year on the job, many new agents had more firearms investigation experience and, in some cases, more law enforcement experience than did veteran agents. In areas where alcohol violations had been numerous, the new agents outdistanced the veterans in firearms enforcement. In many other areas, where enforcement activity had been limited, they simply outdistanced the veterans.

The tension between ATF and its parent organization increased steadily, and ATF law enforcement personnel at all levels expressed the desire to exit the IRS. Many in the IRS agreed. The stakes were raised in 1971 as the result of an incident in Silver Springs, Maryland, a suburb of Washington. ATF agents and Montgomery County police served a search warrant on an apartment occupied by Kenyon Ballew, a life member of the National Rifle Association (NRA) and an employee of the *Washington Post.* Although versions vary somewhat, certain aspects are uncontested. Agents obtained the warrant based largely on information from a local police informant. Agents broke down the door. Ballew's wife screamed, and Ballew responded with a revolver. The agents and police shot and permanently disabled him. The primary point of contention was whether the agents and police adequately knocked and announced their presence and intent. The NRA magazine, *American Rifleman,* published a series of articles highly critical of ATF that were primarily focused on Ballew but extended to other alleged ATF activity.[22]

The incident proved critical in framing the gun control debate in future years and in molding NRA tactics.[23] The mismatch between ATF's evolving enforcement culture and the culture of the IRS became far more visible as a result of the Bellew incident.

Divorce

Although opinion among IRS administrators was divided regarding the future retention of ATF, external forces would decide ATF's fate.[24] According to Rex Davis, who served as both the last director of the Alcohol, Tobacco and Firearms Division and the first director of the Bureau of Alcohol, Tobacco and Firearms, the decision to separate ATF was made in the White House to provide John Caufield a position. Caufield, a former New York City Police detective, had developed ties to Richard Nixon after he lost the California gubernatorial race and moved to New York. Davis states that Caufield was to be director but that senior executives in Treasury resisted and Davis was allowed to remain on the condition he accept Caufield as assistant director for law enforcement.[25] Eugene Rossides, the assistant secretary of the treasury for enforcement at the time, states that the decision was made by John Connally, secretary of the treasury, to facilitate control of ATF.[26]

Caufield began to act with total independence once he was appointed, bypassing Davis and communicating directly with the White House.[27] This subsequently fueled widespread speculation among knowledgeable persons that ATF was to become a private investigative arm of the White House, which was not receiving the cooperation it expected from the FBI or the IRS. Regardless of the intent, little came of the effort. Caufield was soon caught up in the Watergate investigation and was forced to resign.

The full reasons for ATF's creation are likely more complex than many now remember or are willing to state. There was an organizational culture and mission conflict between ATF law enforcement and the IRS. The Ballew incident had created a political issue and provided at least a justification, if not a reason, for separation. The creation of a separate bureau enhanced the status and power of the position of assistant secretary.[28] ATF management, particularly law enforcement, had long desired independence and the prestige and autonomy that accompanied bureau status. If more sinister forces were involved, they did not prove important in molding ATF, and evidence of them likely died with John Connally.

In a pattern that would be repeated in almost every administration, a political problem, born of policy conflict, was addressed as an oversight and management problem. The solution was to change

structure and oversight. This likely reflects the potential cost of ac-
knowledging the underlying conflict and the relative ease of symbolic action by changing structure or leadership. Both these strategies would be used in the future.[29] There was apparently a
last-minute effort by the IRS to retain the alcohol and tobacco functions. This was rebuffed when the alcoholic beverage industry lobbied to keep all ATF functions together, apparently because they
feared that a division charged only with alcohol regulation could
not maintain independence within the IRS.[30]

The lack of a well-defined policy and mission, particularly in
the firearms area, and a resolution of turf issues between Treasury
and Justice would plague the new bureau. Those responsible for the
policy decisions that created the agency displayed little command
of the details and quickly moved on to other issues, a pattern that is
recurrent in U.S. government.[31] As a new bureau with little political support, ATF stood little chance of being able to resolve policy
issues, particularly when faced with forces as formidable as the gun
lobby and the FBI. Even more fundamental, there was no well-
developed conceptual link among firearms law, policy, technology,
and desired outcomes.

The linking of the what, how, and why of policy is widely overlooked and misunderstood. This is best illustrated by the assumption that a nation that can build a nuclear bomb and go to the moon
can perform any task if the resources are available. In fact, both of
these tasks were engineering problems that utilized existing theory.
Problems such as poverty and crime have proven far less tractable.
In the case of firearms, the law was not crafted around specific policy goals, and little attention was paid to technology.[32] In such a
contentious policy area, agency action is limited severely by the law
and thus is dependent upon its underlying logic. In one sense, the
application of the gun laws to the crime problem was parallel to the
application of counterinsurgency to Vietnamese nationalism. Given
the task, the agencies developed routines and applied them. Policymakers assumed these routines would in some way impact social
trends but had little or no understanding of how. The agencies went
forward with much observable activity to which they linked output
reports; however, outputs were never closely linked to outcomes.

Entrepreneurial politics is often associated with the creation of
new agencies, bringing ideologically committed constituency groups
together with highly motivated and committed staff to focus on a
program of mutual interest.[33] Even in the best of cases such commitment is, however, often short-lived.[34] In the case of ATF, the only
constituency group was the legal liquor industry, which was hardly
ideological. The firearms mission had, at the time, no organized

constituency, and Congress had played no part in the creation of ATF. The new bureau, therefore, had several disadvantages. It did not attract the bright, young, committed employees who are often associated with new efforts, nor was a significant constituency formed in Congress as a by-product of its creation. Although it had the advantage of an existing structure, it lacked any administrative infrastructure, was highly fragmented, and lacked extensive experience in the very functions that would become most crucial in coming years. In addition, the budget estimates for its operation were dominated by IRS administrative staff who had a vested interest in minimizing estimates of cost, since the IRS would be losing budget in proportion to ATF's gain. For the first year, the IRS provided all administrative support for the new bureau. The factor that would most influence the nature of the new bureau, however, was not structure or resources but jurisdiction.

Notes

1. Arthur Millspaugh, *Crime Control by the Federal Government* (Washington, D.C.: Brookings Institution, 1937) 70–72.

2. Ironically, Ness's birthday is April 19, the date of the Waco fire. Before Waco, numerous ATF offices established a tradition of hosting Elliot Ness parties on that date.

3. Millspaugh, 72.

4. John C. McWilliams, *The Protectors: Harry Anslinger and the Federal Bureau of Narcotics, 1930–1962* (Newark: University of Delaware Press, 1990) 39.

5. The term *moonshiner* refers to the operator of an unregistered distillery, the form of which varied with locale. In the South, stills were almost exclusively closed or pot types, located in the woods or farm outbuildings. In the industrial Northeast, they were often column or continuous-operations types located in warehouses. *Bootlegger* refers to those who sell liquor without a license. The liquor can either be tax-paid or moonshine.

6. Contrary to the popular image, corn whiskey was not common among moonshiners in this century. Mash made from sugar and water bypasses the steps of breaking down the grain, or malting, and converting the starch to sugar. By beginning with sugar, the entire process was greatly speeded up.

7. In addition to the taste, there was always the issue of safety. The use of old automobile radiators as condensers was not uncommon, making blindness from lead poisoning a potential risk. Moonshine was not interchangeable with "bonded whiskey," but was a unique drink with a unique following, which was predominantly comprised of poor rural southerners, both black and white.

8. While addressing a Basic Special Investigator Training class in June 1968, the chief of enforcement stated, "Don't worry men, we will have something for you to do when liquor is gone."

9. It seems apparent that law enforcement supported by cultural and economic trends is more likely to shape social behavior than enforcement

that runs counter to these forces. Drug prohibition, over the past three decades, provides an example of the difficulties in attempting to overcome these forces.

10. In many areas of the South, woodcraft was as important a skill as interviewing or evidence handling. Stills were normally located outdoors or in outbuildings, such as barns. A successful investigation involved capturing the still operators, or still hands, at work and conducting surveillance to tie in financiers and transporters.

11. For fiscal year 1935/36 Treasury agencies accounted for over 67 percent of all federal arrests and the ATU accounted for almost 95 percent of these. The entire Department of Justice accounted for less than 12 percent (Millspaugh, 255).

12. In the Grosso and Marchetti cases the Court ruled the requirement for bookmakers to register was self-incriminating. Until this time the Intelligence Division of the IRS had actively investigated bookmaking violations. Additional federal gambling laws were passed under the interstate commerce authority but assigned to the FBI for enforcement.

13. McWilliams, 90–91.

14. Ultimately this derives from the lack of federal police power and the piecemeal entry of the federal government into narrow enforcement issues. The recurrent question has been whether to structure around a specific commodity, such as alcohol or drugs; a function, such as border control; or a technology, such as law enforcement or regulation. This has been most pronounced in the area of drugs. The first of numerous efforts to consolidate drug enforcement into the FBI occurred in 1935 but faltered over the issue of licensing and regulation of the industry (see Chapter 2). The same issue impacted the assignment of authority over the Explosives Control Act of 1970 (see Chapter 3), and in 1982 the alcohol industry blocked the merger of ATF and the USSS to assure continuity in the regulation of the Federal Alcohol Administration Act (see Chapter 7). Also see Millspaugh, 36–37 and 280–281.

15. The Southeastern Region differed slightly from all other regions in structure. The two operational entities within ATF and its predecessors have changed titles several times but retained their essential character. The law enforcement function has been designated "enforcement," "law enforcement," and "criminal enforcement." The revenue and regulation function has been designated "permissive," "regulatory," "regulatory enforcement," and "compliance."

16. During the Korean War the excise tax on liquor was raised and all existing inventories, or floor stock, in possession of wholesalers and retailers were assessed. Additional permissive employees added for this task were offered the option of transferring to enforcement, and many accepted. The earliest of these received no formal training, but those that transferred after the establishment of the Treasury Law Enforcement Training School received eight weeks of basic training. In the main, a cultural gulf existed between these former permissive employees and agents hired later from the Treasury Enforcement Agent examination roster. Although the former permissive employees exercised little influence in regions with liquor enforcement activity and large enforcement staffs, they predominated in others. Prior to 1968, for instance, they occupied almost all enforcement management positions in the Western Region.

17. Interviews with former directors Rex Davis and Steve Higgins.

18. When experienced agents from the Southeast were given the option of transferring to the understaffed Western Region, Griffin was ordered to send all existing personal equipment with them, including vehicles. Those who transferred reported that they were required to give up newer model cars and in some cases even their issued firearms. They were then given equipment that was barely serviceable and ready for surplus to take with them. Although former director Rex Davis stated that he did not remember specific details such as this, he confirms that the Southeast Region and Bill Griffin were very independent of authority from Washington.

19. Several years after ATF had become an independent bureau, a young agent who volunteered to move from Tennessee to California was approached by his special agent in charge (SAC), who asked why he would move to a place filled with "drug users and hippies." Trying to be politic, the agent replied that he would probably associate mostly with other agents and thus be little affected by California culture. The SAC replied, "I am talking about the other agents."

20. The lack of priority and attention can best be illustrated in the story told by an agent who worked for years in Virginia and transferred to Seattle in 1965. He described how numerous agents had followed a major liquor violator across the state line on a regular basis attempting to locate his still. The suspect, who was a convicted felon, always carried a rifle in open view in his pickup. None of the ATTD agents realized that this was a violation of the Federal Firearms Act, although they were charged with enforcing it. The agent telling the story realized the oversight only after transferring to an office were liquor violations were not common, forcing him to pursue firearms investigations.

21. Under the IRS, the ATTD (later ATF) had a director in the IRS national office, but field operations were controlled from the regional offices. ATF's budget was intermingled with the regional IRS budget and thus under the control of the IRS regional commissioners. Although the Southeast Region had about five hundred enforcement agents in 1968 and the Western Region, which included the nine western states, had less than seventy, action to shift staff was very slow. The lack of central control over budget constituted as much of an impediment as organizational culture and tradition to reallocating agents.

22. *American Rifleman* (July 1971, August 1971, September 1971, October 1971, November 1971), see Bibliography.

23. Although Bellew was unsuccessful in a suit against the government, the incident was primarily reported in the firearms press hostile to ATF's version of events.

24. Interviews with Rex Davis and former associate director William Drake.

25. Davis's contentions are supported by the statements of G. Gordon Liddy, who stated in his autobiography, *Will*, that he pursued the position of ATF director while he was a political appointee at Treasury, but was told that the job was reserved for John Caufield. In addition to Liddy, former commissioner of the IRS Randolph Thrower described a continuing campaign by the Nixon White House to place Caufield, whom Thrower describes as clearly unqualified, as director of the ATFD. See Margaret Shannon, "Before Watergate: Randolph Thrower vs. the Nixon White House," *Atlanta Journal and Constitution Magazine* (April 7, 1974).

26. Former assistant secretary of the treasury Eugene Rossides told the author that there was little or no discussion regarding the movement of

ATF. Secretary Connally simply called him in and advised him that ATF would be removed from the IRS. Rossides did not believe that the White House played any role in the decision. When asked about the appointment of Caufield, Rossides stated that Caufield was never considered for the position of director but was well qualified for the job he got, although he did not remember what job that was. Caufield was a former New York City Police detective with no policy or management experience. John Connally also attempted to place another political appointee, a former small-town police chief, in a high-level law enforcement position in ATF. The agency successfully resisted placing the appointee in law enforcement but did accept him into an administrative position at a management level. This appointee was later arrested and convicted of theft from the government.

27. Interview with Rex Davis, former ATF director. This was also a rather open secret in ATF at the time.

28. Although the assistant secretary for enforcement and tariff affairs exercised policy supervision over the IRS and Customs law enforcement operations, the commissioners of these agencies were presidential appointees and not under his direct line of control. The Secret Service has enjoyed more independence than would be expected of such a small bureau, due to its close relationship with the president. Thus an independent ATF and the new Federal Law Enforcement Training Center created entities directly subordinate to the assistant secretary that enhanced the status of that position, which has since been elevated to undersecretary.

29. The Carter, Reagan, and Clinton administrations would all follow this same pattern. None seemed to fully comprehend that the political conflict resulted primarily from opposition to firearms regulation by a powerful and sophisticated interest group that used ATF as a means of attacking those laws. Although the NRA reacted favorably to the ATF reorganization at the time (see *American Rifleman* [May 1972] 45), they soon resumed their attack (see Chapter 6). The underlying issue was, and remains, the legitimacy of firearms control as a government policy and not its administration.

30. Tanna Pesso, "Gun Control (B): The Bureau of Alcohol, Tobacco and Firearms," an unpublished case study prepared for the John F. Kennedy School of Government, Harvard University, Boston, 1981. Former assistant secretary Rossides did remember some agenda by the liquor industry but did not remember the details.

31. Hugh Helco, *Government of Strangers* (Washington, D.C.: Brookings Institution, 1977) 102–110.

32. For an in-depth discussion see William J. Vizzard, "The Evolution of Gun Control Policy in the United States: Accessing the Public Agenda," DPA dissertation, University of Southern California, 1993; "Practical Implications of Crafting for Compromise: The Case of Assault Weapon Legislation," unpublished paper presented to the Academy of Criminal Justice Sciences, Boston, March 10, 1995; "The Impact of Agenda Conflict on Policy Formulation and Implementation: The Case of Gun Control," *Public Administration Review* (July-August 1995) 341–347.

33. James Q. Wilson, *Bureaucracy: What Government Agencies Do and Why They Do It* (New York: Basic Books, 1989) 189.

34. Ibid., 250.

CHAPTER 2

Law and Jurisdiction

James Q. Wilson, in an argument heavily influenced by James Thompson, contends that task is a key factor in molding virtually every aspect of a bureaucracy's behavior.[1] The history of ATF supports Wilson at every turn. ATF's most unique characteristic is its unusual overlay of jurisdictions. The agency administers federal law regulating the manufacture and wholesale distribution of alcoholic beverages under the Federal Alcohol Administration Act (FAA), collects all federal excise tax on alcohol and tobacco, and regulates the manufacture and distribution of firearms and explosives at both wholesale and retail. It has primary jurisdiction over all federal criminal statutes relating to firearms and shares jurisdiction over criminal statutes relating to explosives with the FBI. The explosives statutes give it jurisdiction over arson of any business engaged in interstate commerce. It also has exclusive jurisdiction over interstate smuggling of cigarettes to avoid state taxes and all federal criminal statutes relating to alcohol. Over the years, the unusual combination of jurisdictions has even frustrated efforts to rename the agency. Although there have been several efforts from within ATF and in Treasury to devise a different name, nothing acceptable has been arrived at and the efforts have repeatedly been abandoned.

To understand ATF as an organization, one must first understand that it operates in several distinct task and interest environments that derive from its fragmented jurisdiction. And to understand how ATF came to have such a fragmented jurisdiction is to understand something about the impact the political structure and tradition of the United States have on formulation and implementation of public policy. Martha Derthick has observed that the political process is not conducive to effective and orderly administration.[2] In the case of ATF, administration is aggravated not only by policy but also by structure.

The underlying causes of much of the peculiar organizational structure and fragmented jurisdiction in the federal bureaucracy are the absence of police power from the authorities granted the federal government by the Constitution, federalism, and a tradition of opposition to strong central government. These factors precluded development of much of any federal government for a century and a half. As a need for a more active central government was perceived, problems and issues were addressed piecemeal, and agencies grew up in response to narrow political initiatives. Agencies involved in law enforcement are among the least rationally structured in the federal government and have been targets of repeated recommendations for reorganization from the 1920s to the present.

For almost a century the United States had virtually no organized law enforcement at any level. Those officers who did exist, such as sheriffs and United States marshals, were primarily officers of the courts. The first professionalized law enforcement organization at the federal level was the Secret Service, organized after the Civil War to investigate counterfeiting. It assumed the incongruous task of protecting the president after President McKinley was assassinated because it was the only agency available. The Justice Department did not have a true law enforcement arm until the powers of the FBI were expanded in 1934.[3]

Congress passed the first narcotic laws in 1914, but these were more focused on commerce than policing, and they were assigned to the Bureau of Internal Revenue for administration. Prohibition really marks the first broad application of federal law enforcement jurisdiction. Interestingly, expansion of federal authority in law enforcement predated much of the New Deal's expansion into social welfare and economic activity. In the decade between 1924 and 1934, the FBI was granted arrest powers, the Federal Bureau of Narcotics and the Border Patrol were formed, and the laws granting federal jurisdiction over bank robbery, kidnapping, and firearms were enacted.[4] Although the postal and the taxation authorities were used rather cautiously for expanding federal law enforcement authority, the shift to the interstate commerce authority, beginning in the 1930s, effectively removed almost all constraints on federal jurisdiction.[5]

Essentially two traditions developed in federal law enforcement structure. Initially enforcement grew from functions such as tax collection and control of the borders. Later this tradition was expanded, using functions such as taxation to justify expansion of federal authority into more general law enforcement. These laws were enforced by specialized agencies whose jurisdictions were tied to function or commodities. With the extension of law enforcement jurisdiction to the FBI, the federal government began to develop a general law enforcement agency that was organized around a technology, criminal investigation. The FBI has expanded until it has approximately as many agents as all the other more specialized agencies combined.

The last significant uses of the taxation authority as a justification for federal exercise of police power were the wagering statutes and the National Firearms Act (NFA). The latter was not assigned to the ATU until 1941, but its passage would both lay the groundwork for the creation of ATF and shape its history as a bureau. Firearms regulation would prove far more difficult than liquor regulation.

Symbols, Myths, and Paradigms

The issue of gun control has persisted as a periodic national controversy in the United States for over half a century. The inability to reach consensus on public policy relating to gun control is a reflection of both our political structure and process and the ambiguity with which the population conceptualizes the issue. Gun control has been conceptualized in four basic paradigms by both advocates and opponents. The most persistent of these in the United States has been as a mechanism for crime control. Akin to this paradigm has been that of social order or sovereignty. More recently, sociologists have conceptualized the issue as a symbolic conflict over values and world view, and most recently the issue has been cast in the language of public health. Each of these paradigms has components of reality and myth, and each emphasizes different language, values, and assumptions. Clearly, these paradigms overlap. Both the crime control and social control paradigms emphasize restriction of access to instruments of force and violence. The crime control paradigm, however, focuses on individual acts of violence, while social control focuses more on the right of the state to maintain a monopoly on legitimate force. The greater the willingness to rely on government for social order, the greater is the acceptance of gun control as a legitimate mechanism of social control.

The struggles between opponents and proponents have been directed as much at controlling the language and presumptions of these paradigms as at the direct control of the political process. As such, the issue of gun control offers a look at the policy process in the United States from a unique perspective. This has not been a conflict over who gets what, when, and how, as Lasswell characterized politics. This has been a conflict over ideas, values, perceptions, and most of all the role of government. It also has not been an area that has lent itself to compromise. To examine the history of gun control is to come to understand that sometimes ideas matter more than assets. This has been a struggle over what Robert Reich has called "public ideas" more than over process, power, or re-sources.[6] Underlying this entire issue are powerful American myths.

The importance of the gun as a mythical symbol in the United States can be demonstrated by any review of popular culture. The frontiersman, cowboy, soldier, private detective, and policeman have provided this country with most of its mythical heroes, and each has been conspicuously armed. No other object is so common in the popular culture. At times dogs, horses, airplanes, and auto-mobiles have rivaled firearms, but firearms always seem to return. As such, the firearm has taken on cultural importance in the United States unrivaled in any other industrialized nation. Because the firearms controversy is so infused with symbolism and myth, it of-fers a vehicle for understanding the importance of these elements in the government policy process.

The Paradigms of Gun Control

Each of the four paradigms that have dominated U.S. thinking, dis-cussion, and ultimately public policy in relation to guns has at least two alternative conceptual orientations with its own presumptions, values, and language.

Crime Control

The crime control paradigm is essentially built on the assumption that easy access to firearms either encourages crime or exacerbates the level of violence associated with crime. This has been the most common paradigm invoked by advocates of stricter controls, and it has been the paradigm most attacked by opponents. The advocates are clearly influenced by the widespread use of firearms in crime and the far greater incidence of this phenomenon in the United States than in countries with more restrictive firearms policies. Al-though it has occasionally been argued that the availability of guns exacerbates the attitudes that motivate crime, most argument is fo-cused on the escalation of violence facilitated by firearms.[7] When proponents utilize this paradigm, they focus primarily on handguns, "Saturday Night Specials," or other categories of firearms believed particularly suitable for only criminal purposes.[8] The language is often cost/benefit in orientation, with advocates attempting to reduce costs through narrowing their proposals to "reasonable controls."

Opponents respond primarily in the same language, with the em-phasis on benefit. Their arguments focus on the inability to obtain

compliance with the law from criminals. They stress the impracti-
cality of controlling 200 million firearms, point to the 20,000 existing
firearms laws that "do not work," and generally attack the cause-
and-effect argument.[9] When dealing with the general public, opponents are less likely to emphasize cost, although this is done for ardent followers. Cost generally consists of inconveniences for some
gun owners that would not be fully appreciated by the general public.

Cultural

In 1972, the *Wall Street Journal* portrayed the battle over gun control
in the United States as a symbolic conflict between two identifiable
social groups. The advocates were characterized as the cosmopoli-
tans and the opponents as the traditionalists. The former are urban,
educated, and internationalist in their orientation. They look to
Western Europe as a model for governance and tend toward liberal
democratic values on most social issues. The traditionalists are rural
or small-town in orientation, their frame of reference for governance
is domestic, and they are less tolerant in their social values. This
theme has been pursued by several academic writers who have examined the gun control field.

   This paradigm has been invoked more by scholars than by advocates or politicians, but efforts on both sides of the issue are focused on influencing the public parameters of this paradigm. Bruce-
Biggs picked up this theme in his 1976 essay, as did historians
Kennett and Anderson, who characterized the widespread gun
ownership as embarrassing to the internationally oriented, cosmopolitan United States.[10]

   Other writers have gone beyond simply characterizing the advocates and opponents of gun control. Tonso concurs with the characterization of the groups, but criticizes the advocates for the practice
of "sagecraft" based on their personal biases rather than any utili-
tarian purpose.[11] Kaplan has argued that the movement for gun control parallels the Prohibition movement and is primarily symbolic,
with a goal of declaring some people less worthy than others.[12] Zimring and Hawkins have couched their perspective of this concept in
crime control language. They portray advocates as seeing crime as
an outgrowth of social forces while opponents perceive sharp quali-
tative distinctions between ordinary citizens and criminals.[13]

   Likely, many people come to their positions on gun control
based primarily on their perceptions of its utility. Many more likely
come to their positions based on self-interests or innate acceptance
of or distaste for guns. No doubt both of these elements influence
some who have strong ideological leanings. But repeated interviews

with persons having strong views on the subject of gun control reveal certain defined and consistent ideological patterns. Advocates are more collectively oriented and more disposed toward governmental solutions, while opponents are far more suspicious of collective decisions and solutions and more likely to look to the individual for solutions. Ultimately, gun control may be more a test of libertarianism than of liberalism versus conservatism.

Three cultural influences have contributed to a highly individualistic and libertarian strain in American cultural tradition. The first of these was a tradition of suspicion of authority born of revolution and independence. The second was a vast frontier, offering space and free land to all who would claim it. The third was Protestantism of the most decentralized type, which placed the maximum emphasis on the individual relationship with God. Historian Richard Hofstadter traces the routes of the American obsession with firearms to both the frontier and the Lockian tradition that looked to an armed populace.[14] Although he does not consider the gun issue, Robert Dahl attributes the lack of European-style class conflict in the United States largely to this independence spawned by philosophy and the opportunity for land.[15] Evidence of this persistent national trait appears in the resistance to national health care, the absence of a national identity system, resistance to mass transit and land-use planning, and some tendency to resist urban lifestyles.

Benjamin Barber has characterized American political thought as being heavily anarchist. He also saw strong elements of minimalism and pragmatism that combine with suspicion of authority to produce two distinct approaches to government.[16] When minimalism is combined with anarchy, the result is Madisonian restraint on government. When pragmatism is combined with anarchy, the result is focused on preservation of rights through government action. In both cases, however, the focus was seen as individual rights and the restraint of government, not collective rights and the action of government.[17]

This historical American focus on the individual provides an explanation as to why gun control advocates have been less than successful in advancing their world view and why they have often focused on particular "evil guns." In American political values, the individual is supreme and the state must justify every intervention. Clearly, narcotics were demonized to justify the type of strict control and intervention that has been imposed.[18] With over 200 million firearms in the United States, most of which are not being unlawfully used at any given time, the task of outlawing them would be daunting. In addition, the historic reverence of Americans for the

Constitution has generated an added burden for control advocates by way of the Second Amendment.

As with all issues in the United States, ideology and world view do not entirely dominate the cultural paradigm. Guns themselves are apparently perceived as either positive items of recreation and healthy activity or foreign and dangerous instruments of destruction. Both gun ownership and attitudes toward guns and gun ownership are apparently highly influenced by early exposure to recreational use of firearms.[19]

Sovereignty and Social Order

The hesitancy of advocates to pursue their world view publicly is closely associated with their reticence to characterize gun control as an issue of social order and state sovereignty. Although periodic references can be found to this concept in the testimony of some advocates, in the main they avoid the subject. No such hesitancy is found on the part of the most ardent foes of gun control.[20] Even more scholarly opponents such as Don Kates trace the origins of most gun control efforts to the desire of a dominant population to control political or social unrest.[21]

It is not surprising that advocates tread lightly on the issue of sovereignty and social order. The underlying question is one of legitimate control of power. Americans have long been ill at ease with this issue. The concern can be clearly found in the discourse on control of the militia during the debate over ratification of the Constitution.[22] Although the issue was largely resolved by the Civil War, the subsequent decline of the state militias, and the creation of a standing army, it does not appear to be an issue with which Americans are fully comfortable. This ultimately may be because, as John Rohr argues, the concept of the state, in the European sense, does not exist in the United States.[23] If the ultimate legitimate authority is the Constitution, who then has a legitimate monopoly on the use of force?

It is in these areas of order, control over legitimate use of force, and sovereignty that Barber's paradigms of American political thought become most significant. The minimalist seeks to disperse power and its means through limiting government, thus opposing controls on weapons by the state. The pragmatist seeks controls that will protect one citizen from another and thus looks for "reasonable controls." The issue of state sovereignty is essentially avoided because of the character of the political value system. Even the pragmatist can be expected to be less than enthusiastic in actually implementing sanctions to enforce controls, particularly against those who cannot be seen as immediately and directly threatening others. This pattern, in fact, is common.[24]

Although many Americans are uncomfortable with the sovereignty and social order paradigm, it is likely at the heart of the gun control issue. Unlike the issue of crime control, for which the practical utility can be debated forever, sovereignty and control of force are value issues. As such, positions can be pursued on principle as opposed to research and evidence. This would not essentially lead to compromise, but it does provide a clear basis for positions.

Public Health

The diametric opposite of the sovereignty paradigm is the public health paradigm. Although occasional references to accidents and suicides can be found in the arguments of advocates in the period before 1980, the public health paradigm as a distinct concept applied to guns developed in the 1980s. By the last of the decade, a variety of articles began to appear, primarily in medical journals, that focused on the public health implications of the presence of firearms in society.[25]

The public health paradigm is still in the process of developing. It differs from the crime control paradigm in that it focuses essentially on the effects of guns on people regardless of the causes. Deaths by accident, suicide, or intentional killing are viewed as costs of equal impact, as are injuries. This presents a challenge for opponents of gun control that is very different than other paradigms. Here the analysis is clearly cost/benefit, and the ability to demonstrate benefit is limited by the structure of the paradigm. Although there has been some response to this paradigm by the opponents of gun control, the response is not yet well defined.[26] In a nation focused on health costs, this new paradigm may present the greatest challenge to the opponents of gun control.[27]

Options for Gun Control

Conceptually, the approaches to gun control are limited. The simplest is prohibition. This is essentially the approach of the Japanese, who prohibit private ownership of virtually all firearms. Such an approach clearly has to be national in scope and requires very little specialization to administer, as there is little regulation. This approach did not eliminate alcoholic beverages from the United States, though it did reduce consumption, nor has it eliminated narcotics.

Firearms might well present a far different case than liquor or drugs, as they are not consumable items that build a repeat-customer base. However, any analysis of the potential reaction to this approach in the United States is supposition. A related approach is limited prohibition, in which certain classes of firearms are prohibited. We have come close to this with machine guns and certain models of assault weapons. In the case of machine guns, the prohibition appears to be reasonably effective, but not with assault weapons. The difference is largely linked to the unique nature of the items controlled.[28]

A second approach is to license firearms. Licensing can be permissive, in which all applicants are presumed to have a right to a license unless cause is shown that they fall into a prohibited class, or restrictive, in which discretion is vested in the licensing authority. Some states practice permissive licensing and the state of New York has a system of restrictive licensing for handguns. Licensing systems, by their nature, require more regulatory apparatus than does prohibition.

Closely akin to licensing is registration. Registration requires that firearms ownership be recorded with a government authority and mandate either prior approval or at least notification of all transfers. Like licensing systems, registration systems require substantial administrative action by the state. Licensing and registration models tend to be mutually supportive. Licensing of owners allows for rational approval of transfers and registration supports and reinforces licensing by restricting transfers. Although the federal law governing machine guns functioned more like Prohibition, because of the associated taxes, it was for many years a registration and permissive licensing system. Since 1986 it has become a partial prohibition.

A lesser level of control than any of these is the prohibited-class approach, which prohibits certain classes such as felons from possessing firearms but provides no administrative mechanisms to reinforce compliance. Since this system depends solely on prosecution of offenders, it requires little or no administrative support. This final system can be combined with a system of dealer licensing or sales reports. These limited controls on firearms commerce are designed to police transfers by commercial sources. They assure commercial records and can provide the state an opportunity to prevent transfers from organized commerce to prohibited classes of person. The level of administrative support necessary depends upon the level of control exercised and the complexity of the law. These approaches offer the appeal of only impacting commercial sources and thus avoiding state intervention in most private behavior.

Finally, control can be asserted on the carrying or use of firearms. This function provides the state no mechanism, other than
catching the violator in the act. It requires administrative support if
licenses to carry are issued, but little or none if they are not. This
has been wholly the purview of the states and local governments,
except in specified locations where the federal government has exercised police power, such as aboard aircraft.

Each of these approaches has specific costs and benefits. Each
requires a different role for government and some clearly are a better fit with the traditional federal role than others. In general, conversations regarding gun control in the United States have been
highly charged and have not defined what particular model was
being discussed. Opponents in particular have assumed that all controls were simply efforts to impose prohibition. In addition, gun
control discussions in Congress and elsewhere have paid little heed
to the type of administrative and enforcement mechanisms necessary to implement them. Thus policies have been drafted with little
concern for the underlying theory and the mechanics of implementation. The results have consistently been driven more by political
compromise than policy objectives.[29]

Gun Control Attempted

In 1927 Congress, after several years of debate, passed the first national firearms control legislation when it banned the shipment of
handguns to individuals by mail.[30] The issue of mail-order sales of
handguns would not be resolved for another forty-one years, as
Congress did not address the shipment by common carriers. Although this was clear at the time, Congress was willing to settle for
a largely symbolic action.[31] This pattern of debate, followed by action characterized by its advocates as inadequate to solve the alleged problem but the best that could be accomplished at the time,
would repeat itself for years to come.

With the election of the Roosevelt administration came the first
executive initiatives to pursue gun control at the federal level.
Franklin Roosevelt had previously demonstrated a predilection to
support gun control as the governor of New York, where he vetoed
a bill to rescind the Sullivan Law and supported the prohibition of
private ownership of machine guns.[32] The Department of Justice,
under the direction of Attorney General Homer Cummings, began a
concerted effort to pursue serious federal legislation.[33] Cummings's
proposal was modeled on the Harrison Narcotics Act and utilized
the federal taxing power as a mechanism of control. Transfers of

handguns over .22 caliber between individuals were to be taxed at a rate of one dollar and would require approval by the secretary of the treasury. Other so-called gangster weapons, including machine guns, silencers, and sawed-off rifles and shotguns, were to be taxed at a rate of $200. Transfers to dealers were exempted if they paid a special occupational tax.[34]

Hearings were held in the Senate to concurrently consider two bills introduced by Senator Royal Copeland of New York along with the administration proposal. Copeland's proposals were based on the interstate commerce authority and proposed limiting the shipment of concealable firearms across state lines to licensed dealers, prohibiting the interstate shipment of machine guns, and requiring a library of test-fired bullets from all new firearms.[35]

Opposition to the proposed legislation focused primarily upon the inclusion of handguns and primarily came from the firearms industry, sport and hunting groups, and the NRA.[36] Both the NRA and the firearms industry had responded to past legislation with improved organization.[37] The opposition was able to achieve the removal of handguns from the proposed act before it was reported out of both the House and Senate committees.[38] Additionally, definitions of a machine gun that would have included modern semi-automatic assault weapons were considered and discarded by the committee.[39] The resulting bill was quickly passed by the Congress and signed by the president.

In the 1934 congressional hearings, the crime control paradigm was clearly dominant in the testimony of both advocates and opponents.[40] Advocates alluded to the low violent-crime rates of Britain, and the NRA argued that laws could not prevent criminals from obtaining firearms. One unusual characteristic that appeared in the Senate hearings, particularly as they related to Senator Copeland's bills, was the focus on firearms laws as a mechanism of law enforcement. Although Copeland's proposals for manufacturers retaining sample bullets and for marking bullets were not practical, they did seek ways of utilizing firearms laws to aid police. Later hearings would largely ignore such concepts and focus solely on the ability to deny firearms to criminals. Clearly the NRA was not impressed with the concept of firearms laws being a useful mechanism for law enforcement.[41]

The passage of the NFA did not end the discussion of firearms legislation by Congress or the efforts of the Justice Department to pursue more strict legislation. In 1937, the Justice Department again proposed the placement of handguns under the National Firearms Act.[42] The result was a compromise largely written by the NRA that utilized federal authority to regulate interstate commerce for jurisdiction. The product of the compromise was the Federal Firearms Act (FFA), passed in 1938.[43] The FFA included all firearms but provided for very limited controls. Persons dealing in firearms in interstate commerce were required to obtain a one-dollar license, but the fingerprints, photograph, and police reference required for NFA registration were not included. Some restrictions were placed on the interstate shipment of firearms in violation of state laws, but no mechanisms were provided for enforcement. Dealers were required to maintain records, but no usable penalties were provided to sanction a failure to comply. In effect, the FFA was a symbolic effort with little effect.[44]

Curiously, the original legislation proposed the Department of Commerce as the agency of jurisdiction. During the hearings it was pointed out that the Department of State already had jurisdiction over international commerce and Treasury had jurisdiction over the NFA. The NRA proposed consolidation in the Department of Commerce, a department with no law enforcement structure. A compromise was reached with assignment of both the NFA and FFA to Treasury. There was no discussion of the structure or resources necessary to enforce the law, thus giving the distinct impression that not much enforcement was contemplated.[45]

By the time of the 1937 hearings, it was apparent that the NRA was the primary force in the lobby opposing firearms legislation. The NRA had adopted the tactic of endorsing alternate legislation whenever legislation capable of significant impact on unrestricted possession of and commerce in firearms threatened. In addition to the FFA, the NRA had cooperated in the drafting of a uniform firearms act for adoption by states.[46] Ironically, this model legislation began the concept of the waiting period for firearms purchasers, one of the goals of the Brady Bill. Although the NRA advocated such legislation as a compromise, they apparently had little faith in its usefulness.[47]

Although the passage of the FFA marked the end of a cycle of interest in firearms legislation, the momentum was likely gone by 1934. The administration clearly had many higher priorities and the forces of opposition had proven themselves capable of forcing compromises that would prevent policy from impacting the majority of firearms and firearms owners. In addition, the murder rate and crime rate in general had taken a sudden downturn during the middle 1930s.[48] As a confirmation of the thesis that gun control was primarily viewed in a crime control paradigm, the issue did not get serious national attention for thirty years, when crime rates again began to rise steeply. Although there were periodic proposals for new legislation, none was seriously considered until after the assassination of John Kennedy in 1963.

The Gun Control Act of 1968

Senator Thomas Dodd of Connecticut had introduced a firearms bill, S. 1975, requiring affidavits from purchasers of mail-order handguns and restricting the importation of surplus military firearms in 1963. This bill received support from both the firearms industry and the NRA.[49] Dodd, who chaired the Juvenile Justice Subcommittee of the Judiciary Committee, amended his bill to extend the affidavit requirement to long guns shortly after President Kennedy was assassinated with a mail-order rifle. Although these bills were supported by the NRA staff, a core group of members was opposed and an internal revolt began within the NRA.[50] Eventually this schism would lead to a coup, in which the more libertarian forces would take full control of the NRA. A key component in this process was the development of a specialized gun press that was intensely opposed to all forms of gun control laws and provided the primary source of information on the issue for avid gun enthusiasts.[51]

The House and Senate held repeated hearings between 1965 and 1968 on the issue of gun control, and several bills were considered. The center of activity was Dodd's subcommittee, which focused its attention on a succession of bills, introduced by Dodd but largely written by the administration. Dodd's original bill was reintroduced by the ranking Republican on the subcommittee, Roman Hruska of Nebraska, and was endorsed by the firearms lobby as an alternative to a succession of bills introduced by Dodd.

Dodd's 1965 bill amended the Federal Firearms Act by prohibiting interstate mail-order and over-the-counter sales of handguns by dealers, raising dealer license fees to $100 per year, setting age limits for purchases from dealers, and restricting destructive devices.[52] In 1967 Dodd reintroduced this bill as S. 1 and later introduced Amendment 90 to S. 1 at the request of the administration. The bill, as amended, differed from the earlier version in replacing rather than amending the FFA, extending the prohibition on interstate transfers to private transactions, including long guns in the mail-order restriction, eliminating ammunition controls, and reducing dealer license fees to $25. The bill also placed destructive devices under the NFA rather than restricting them under the interstate commerce power.[53]

On June 6, 1968, the day after Robert Kennedy was assassinated, the House passed Title IV of the Omnibus Crime Control and Safe Streets Act, essentially a slightly modified version of Dodd's bill.[54] Before Title IV could be implemented, Congress passed the Gun Control Act of 1968, which superseded Title IV.[55] The Gun Control

Act made it to the floor only after two proxy votes in the Senate Judiciary Committee were changed in response to the assassination of
Martin Luther King.[56] After years of hearings, events moved so
swiftly that few participants knew exactly what was happening.
Title VII of the Omnibus crime bill was inserted without hearings
and largely as a favor to Senator Long. Title VII prohibited the "possession in commerce" of firearms by a felon. Although little noted
or discussed at the time, Title VII proved to be a major policy decision that would significantly impact ATF. As a result of subsequent
court interpretation, this law prohibited the possession of almost all
firearms by convicted felons, although it did not prohibit the possession of firearms that had never crossed a state line. [57]

During the entire hearing process little attention was given to
details of policy implementation. Although both the Departments of
Justice and the Treasury testified, witnesses had little specific
knowledge of the impact of policy. In fact, virtually no one had any
such experience. Testimony and discussion seldom dealt with issues
of how the law would be enforced or the impact of changing any
part of the bill on its other provisions. Treasury was routinely represented by the commissioner of Internal Revenue, since the ATTD
was a division of that agency. Thus what little experience existed in
the ATTD was not available to the committee.

The resulting laws are commonly referred to collectively as the
Gun Control Act of 1968. In fact, there are three distinct pieces of
legislation consisting of: the GCA, Title VII of the Omnibus crime
bill, and changes to the NFA. Together, they established the following as federal gun control policy:

- Convicted felons, illegal aliens, adjudicated mental incompe-
  tents, drug addicts, and certain others could not lawfully
  possess a firearm that had ever moved in commerce.
- Explosive, incendiary, and poison gas bombs and missiles; ar-
  tillery; land mines; and certain other destructive devices were
  required to be registered under the NFA, and their transfer
  was taxed and controlled.
- All persons engaged in the business of dealing in firearms
  were required to be licensed and to maintain records of
  firearms sales. License fees were set at $10 per year. Sales by
  dealers to prohibited persons, out-of-state residents, or un-
  derage persons were prohibited.
- Any person not prohibited from possessing firearms, and
  who declared the intent to engage in the firearms business,
  was entitled to a dealer's license.

- Transfers of firearms to residents of other states, other than by licensed dealers, were prohibited with some exceptions.
- Importing surplus military firearms and firearms not suitable for sporting use was prohibited.

The results were clearly a compromise and did not constitute a significant change in public policy. Felons had long been prohibited from receiving guns "in commerce" under the FFA. Dealers had been licensed and required to keep records. The new law contained a preamble that stated it was not the intent of the law to deny firearms to citizens for lawful purposes. The secretary of the treasury was authorized to promulgate regulations to implement the law, but this authority had existed under the FFA, though it was little used. And the law remained split between Title 26, the tax code, and Title 18, the criminal code.

In spite of the limited change in policy, if viewed from a cross-cultural perspective, there were significant changes for those charged with implementation of the law. The new law required extensive new regulations to be developed. It also apparently extended federal authority over possession of firearms by individual felons. It created criminal penalties for those engaging in the firearms business without licenses and for dealers who falsified their records or knowingly transferred firearms to prohibited persons. In addition, the political climate had changed and the priority of firearms regulation and enforcement had clearly ascended over liquor. Most important for ATF, the law was a political compromise with almost no input from anyone who was concerned with the mechanics of implementation.

The Federal Alcohol Administration Act

Although collection of the excise tax on alcohol and tobacco has always been the most critical function of ATF and its predecessors, tax collection is what James Thompson called a routinized and well-buffered core technology. Taxes are primarily collected from large producers who have built the calculation and payment into their own highly automated operations. Although government officers were present at distilleries for many years after the end of Prohibition, this proved to be unnecessary. The majority of the taxpayers are corporations, which are highly profitable enterprises with little to gain and a great deal to lose by attempting fraud.

For this reason, the focus of federal regulatory function became the Federal Alcohol Administration Act. Passed in 1935 under the interstate commerce authority, this bill specified trade practices in the liquor industry. It impacted labeling; distribution; relations among manufactures, wholesalers, and retailers; and a variety of business practices. Its intent was to assure an open market and free competition. The Federal Alcohol Administration Act grants more discretion than the tax laws. The law was originally administered by a separate organization, the Federal Alcohol Administration, but the duties were transferred to the ATU in 1940. Over the years the ATU and its successors became very entwined with the alcoholic beverage industry. Regulatory personnel usually began their careers working at a distillery. Most of their daily contact was with employees and management of the distillery, who had every reason to cooperate with the government agent, known as a "storekeeper-gauger," or "on-premises inspector." Numerous functions had to be carried out under government supervision. A cooperative ATU official could facilitate daily operations by being prompt, available, and willing to enforce the spirit of the law and regulations rather than holding to the letter of the law.[58]

Notes

1. James Q. Wilson, *Bureaucracy: What Government Agencies Do and Why They Do It* (New York: Basic Books, 1989) 33.

2. Martha Derthick, *Agency Under Stress: The Social Security Administration* (Washington, D.C.: Brookings Institution, 1990) 4.

3. Curt Gentry, *J. Edgar Hoover: The Man and the Secrets* (New York: W. W. Norton, 1991) 169.

4. For an extensive discussion of the early evolution of federal enforcement agencies see Arthur Millspaugh, *Crime Control by the Federal Government* (Washington, D.C.: Brookings Institution, 1937).

5. Not until 1995 in *U.S. v Lopez* did the Supreme Court impose a constraint on the use of the interstate commerce clause to extend criminal jurisdiction. In this case the Court nullified a prohibition on possession of firearms on school grounds for lack of adequate nexus to interstate commerce.

6. Robert Reich, ed., *The Power of Public Ideas* (Cambridge, Mass.: Ballinger Publishing, 1988) 1–13. In the introduction, Reich postulates that ideas about the nature of man, human behavior, and what is desirable for society are often more important in the development of public policy than the process of balancing and compromising competing interests.

7. See Philip J. Cook, "The Effect of Gun Availability on Crime Patterns," *Annals of the American Academy of Political and Social Science* (no. 455, May 1981) 63–69; George D. Newton and Franklin E. Zimring, *Firearms and Violence in American Life: A Staff Report Submitted to the National Commission on the Causes and Prevention of Violence* (Washington, D.C.: National Commission on the Causes and Prevention of Violence, 1969); Franklin Zimring and Gordon Hawkins, *The Citizen's Guide to Gun Control* (New York: MacMillan, 1987).

8. The Coalition Against Handgun Violence and Handgun Control Incorporated have focused their efforts almost entirely on handguns, although "assault weapons" have recently become part of their agenda.

9. See Don B. Kates, ed., *Firearms and Violence: Issues of Public Policy* (Cambridge, Mass.: Ballinger, 1984); Gary Kleck, *Point Blank: Guns and Violence in America* (New York: Aldine de Gruyter, 1991).

10. B. Bruce-Biggs, "The Great American Gun War," *The Public Interest* (fall 1976); Lee Kennett and James Anderson, *The Gun in America: Origins of an American Dilemma* (Westport, Conn.: Greenwood Press, 1975) 254–255.

11. William R. Tonso, "Social Problems and Sagecraft: Gun Control as a Case in Point," in Kates, ed., *Firearms and Violence.*

12. John Kaplan, "The Wisdom of Gun Prohibition," *Annals of the American Academy of Political and Social Science* (no. 455, May 1981) 11–21. Although Kaplan primarily characterizes the advocates of gun control as utilizing the issue to define the opponents as less worthy, a review of the rhetoric by both camps seems to produce similar results. The most extreme advocates characterize gun owners as violent, unsocialized dullards and ask rhetorical questions such as, "Why would anyone ever want a gun?" At the other extreme, opponents characterize control advocates as wimps, cowards, elitists, and occasionally traitors.

13. Zimring and Hawkins, 159–169.

14. Richard Hofstadter, "America as a Gun Culture," in *American Violence: A Documentary History*, Richard Hofstadter and Michael Wallace, eds. (New York: Alfred Knopf, 1970).

15. Robert Dahl, *Dilemmas of a Pluralist Democracy* (New Haven, Conn.: Yale University Press, 1982) 176–178.

16. Benjamin Barber, *Strong Democracy: Participatory Politics for a New Age* (Berkeley: University of California Press, 1984).

17. Ibid.

18. John C. McWilliams, *The Protectors: Henry Anslinger and the Federal Bureau of Narcotics, 1930–1962* (Newark: University of Delaware Press, 1990) 46–52.

19. Kleck, 38–41.

20. Neal Knox began his discussion with the author by stating that "gun control is about power." This same theme runs through the publications of such groups as the Gun Owners of America and the Second Amendment Foundation. It can be seen on bumper stickers available in most gun shops, declaring "the Czechs registered their guns" or associating the swastika and hammer and sickle with gun control.

21. Don B. Kates, "Toward a History of Handgun Prohibition in the United States," in *Restricting Handguns: The Liberal Skeptics Speak Out*, Don Kates, ed. (Croton-on-Hudson, N.Y.: North River Press, 1979) 7–30.

22. See Alexander Hamilton, James Madison, and John Jay, *The Federalist Papers*, ed. and foreword by Clinton Rossiter (New York: New American Library, 1961), numbers 29 and 46.

23. John A. Rohr, "Ethical Issues in French Public Administration: A Comparative Study," *Public Administration Review* (51:4, July-August 1991) 283–298.

24. In over twenty-five years of enforcing firearms laws in the United States, the author has had many opportunities to observe the behavior and attitudes of prosecutors at both the state and federal levels, as well as jurors and judges. The pattern of reluctance to prosecute for violations that are not

related to other "evil" behavior is common. This pattern is often most pronounced among those characterized as liberal and likely to support gun control.

25. See James G. Haughton, "Doctors Should Be Fighting to Ban Guns," *Medical Economics* (66:16, August 21, 1989) 24–27; Jaurie Jones, "MD Groups Support Semiautomatic Gun Ban," *American Medical News* (33:8, February 23, 1990) 11; Daniel Webster, et al., "Reducing Firearms Injuries," *Issues in Science and Technology* (7:3, spring 1991) 73–80; Bijou Yang and David Lester, "The Effects of Gun Availability on Suicide Rates," *Atlantic Economic Journal* (19:2, June 1991) 74; James Price, Sharon Desmond, and Daisy Smith, "A Preliminary Investigation of Inner City Adolescents' Perceptions of Guns," *Journal of School Health* (61:6, August 1991) 255–260; Colin Loftin, et al., "Effects of Restrictive Licensing of Handguns on Homicide and Suicide in the District of Columbia," *The New England Journal of Medicine* (325:23, December 5, 1991) 1615–1621; John Sloan, et al., "Handgun Regulations, Crime, Assaults and Homicide: A Tale of Two Cities," *The New England Journal of Medicine* (319:19, November 10, 1988) 1256–1263; Arthur Kellermann and Donald Reay, "Protection or Peril: An Analysis of Firearm-Related Deaths in the Home," *The New England Journal of Medicine* (314:24, June 12, 1986) 1557–1560; Garen Wintemute, Stephen Teret, and Jess Kraus, "The Epidemiology of Firearms Deaths Among Residents of California," *Western Journal of Medicine* (146:3, March 1987) 374–377.

26. Don B. Kates has examined combined suicide and homicide rates for a variety of nations and demonstrated that the combined rates are higher in a number of nations other than the United States, due to higher suicide rates and firearms accident rates. See "Guns, Murder, and the Constitution: A Realistic Assessment of Gun Control" (San Francisco: Pacific Research Institute for Public Policy, 1990).

27. A number of persons interviewed by the author viewed this paradigm as having the potential for largely shifting the entire policy argument. Legislative staff at the California State Legislature noted that health care professionals were particularly effective in pushing for new legislation in that state in 1979.

28. William J. Vizzard, "Practical Implications of Crafting for Compromise: The Case of Assault Weapons," paper presented to the Academy of Criminal Justice Sciences, Boston, 1995.

29. William J. Vizzard, "The Evolution of Gun Control Policy in the United States: Accessing the Public Agenda," DPA dissertation, University of Southern California, 1993.

30. Lee Kennett and James Anderson, *The Gun in America: Origins of an American Dilemma* (Westport, Conn.: Greenwood Press, 1975) 199–200.

31. Carol S. Leff and Mark H. Leff, "The Politics of Ineffectiveness: Federal Gun Legislation 1919–1938," *Annals of the American Academy of Political and Social Science* (no. 455, May 1981) 48–62.

32. Ibid.

33. Kennett and Anderson, 204.

34. Leff and Leff.

35. Kennett and Anderson, 207–208.

36. U.S. Congress, Senate, *National Firearms Act*, hearings, 1934, and House of Representatives, *To Regulate Commerce in Firearms*, hearings, 1937, testimony of Brig. Gen. Milton Rockford, president of the NRA, 11.

37. House hearings, 1937, 205–206; Josh Sugarmann, *National Rifle Association: Money, Power, and Fear* (Washington, D.C.: National Press Books, 1992) 30.

38. Kennett and Anderson, 210; Leff and Leff.

39. Sugarmann, 33.

40. Senate hearings, 1934.

41. House hearings, 1934, 124–125.

42. Sugarmann, 33.

43. Sugarmann, 34; Kennett and Anderson, 211. Also see House hearings, 1937; an examination of the questions and testimony of NRA president Rockford reveals that he explained the proposed legislation to the subcommittee members more as an author than an interested advocate.

44. For an in-depth evaluation of the failings of the FFA, see U.S. Congress, the Senate, *Federal Firearms Act*, hearings, 1965, 65–185, 274–290, 343–373, and 421–459.

45. House hearings, 1937.

46. Kennett and Anderson, 192–193; Sugarmann, 30.

47. Sugarmann, 30.

48. U.S. Department of Justice, *Violent Crime in the United States* (Washington, D.C.: Bureau of Justice Statistics, 1991).

49. Franklin E. Zimring, "Firearms and Federal Law: The Gun Control Act of 1968," *Journal of Legal Studies* (475, 1975) 133–198.

50. Neal Knox, "The Thirty Year War for Gun Ownership," *Guns and Ammo* (August 1988).

51. A reading of magazines such as *Guns* and *Guns and Ammo* during the period reveals repeated articles on the evils of gun control. Also see the testimony of Thomas J. Siatos, publisher and editorial director of *Guns and Ammo*, Committee on the Judiciary, Subcommittee to Investigate Juvenile Delinquency, *Federal Firearms Act*, hearings, 89th Congress.

52. Senate hearings, 1965, 213.

53. U.S. Congress, Senate, *Federal Firearms Act*, hearings, 1967, 124–127.

54. Zimring, "Firearms and Federal Law."

55. Ibid.

56. Interview with Pete Velde, minority counsel for the Subcommittee to Investigate Juvenile Delinquency of the Senate Judiciary Committee.

57. U.S. Congress, Senate, *Federal Firearms Legislation*, hearings, 1968, testimony of Attorney General Ramsey Clark, 69. Interview with Pete Velde, who confirmed that changes were to be made in committee, but the bill passed on a voice vote before this could be done. The meaning of "possession in commerce" remained unclear until the Supreme Court stated in a footnote to *Bass v U.S.* that any prior movement of the firearm across a state line was adequate nexus to fulfill the requirement for "in commerce." Thus, the shipment of a new firearm from the manufacturer in one state to a dealer in another placed the firearm in commerce for all time.

58. The author has interviewed, informally and formally, well over a hundred former and current inspectors. Their descriptions of relationships with the industry proved remarkably consistent. For many years inspectors (formerly gaugers) worked almost exclusively at a single distillery and identified far more with the distillery than with ATF. They attended company functions and often were given employee discounts. At a management level, industry officials maintained close relations with the regulators.

CHAPTER 3

A Radical Change in Mission

Passage of the Gun Control Act ushered in an era of radical change for the ATTD. In the years between 1968 and 1972 the agency doubled its law enforcement force, while refocusing its mission from alcohol to firearms. It also assumed additional jurisdiction in explosives, which along with the new firearms jurisdiction required retraining of its entire enforcement staff. Concurrently, routines for licensing of firearms and explosives dealers were developed and the licensing and regulatory mission of the agency was greatly expanded. These external forces greatly impacted the agency's tasks, culture, and political environment. By 1972 external forces precipitated the removal of the agency from the IRS and its establishment as an independent bureau. Among all the forces that would shape the future ATF, the Gun Control Act was, distinctly, the most important. From the moment it was passed, things were never the same.

Not surprisingly, the implementation of the new law was erratic. The law enforcement branch of the ATTD exercised control over all aspects of the firearms laws. What expertise ATF had in regulation was concentrated in the regulatory side of the agency and not applied to firearms. Although the IRS was one of the most experienced agencies in the government in the computerization of information, the quasi-independent nature of the ATTD and the failure to integrate its operations with the rest of the IRS denied the vast expertise and computer support of the IRS. Unlike the regulation of the alcohol industry, the ATTD was responsible for firearms commerce down to the retail level. This required licensing and controlling not just a few very profitable and visible enterprises, but thousands of small entrepreneurs. Many were not in the business full-time or were not in business at all but had obtained licenses to order firearms wholesale for their own use. Raising the yearly license fee to $10 did little to deter the continuation of this process.[1]

The entire culture of the ATTD's law enforcement branch mediated against developing an effective licensing operation. Prior to passage of the GCA, firearms dealers licenses had been mailed out by the IRS to every applicant without any screening or investigation. The ATTD now had to develop procedures and routines to check backgrounds for criminal records, inform dealers regarding their record-keeping obligations, and assure that the applicant intended to legitimately engage in the firearms business from a business premises. Most law enforcement personnel disdained such work, and the positions responsible for these tasks in the regional offices were not coveted. The culture and values of law enforcement personnel were not conducive to developing the types of routine administrative procedures required by licensing. The responsible positions in the regional offices, therefore, did not attract the most motivated and able agents. Agents had been attracted to their positions because they involved law enforcement duties. In addition, liquor enforcement was largely outdoor work that had been appealing to persons from rural backgrounds. A more inappropriate pool of talent from which to select effective organizers of a licensing function would have been difficult to find within the federal bureaucracy.

In addition to the licensing functions and the formulation of regulations, another task demanded immediate attention. Shortly before the GCA passed, the Supreme Court had ruled that the registration requirements of the NFA were self-incriminatory.[2] To overcome this problem, the GCA allowed for an amnesty period in which anyone could register an NFA firearm without question. Registration information also was restricted from use in prosecuting other crimes. ATF had to implement the amnesty in January 1969. This required providing forms to potential registrants, assisting with the execution of the forms, and processing the registrations. The necessity of performing these administrative tasks, coupled with such limited administrative experience and capacity, clearly overtaxed the agency. Attention and resources that should have been directed at policy, planning, and training were consumed in responding to the immediate demands created by amnesty and licensing. In addition, the regional fragmentation, organizational structure and culture, and historic lack of experience with policy formulation all mediated against an effective plan of implementation by ATF.

In spite of the obstacles, field agents generally developed good relations with dealers and did a credible job of dealer education. Often this was not difficult. Many dealers operated small hardware and sporting goods stores and were not highly dependent on their firearms trade. They were eager to comply, and the majority of special investigators were familiar with firearms and not particularly officious. They had not hired on to be regulators and viewed the task as a temporary diversion.[3] The contacts also provided most of the investigators with positive experiences with dealers, whom they came to know as individuals.[4] Although the inspection and education of dealers was largely successful, the establishment of licensing sections at the regional offices was less so. Those responsible for licensing had virtually no experience with regulatory or licensing systems. The vast expertise of the IRS was unavailable, because of ATF's semi-autonomous status and the low priority of the ATF mission in the IRS.[5] Even the limited experience within ATF's own regulatory function was not utilized effectively, because firearms licensing was assigned to law enforcement.

Although the ATTD, later ATF, grew substantially between 1968 and 1972, little changed in its structure. Jurisdiction over the Explosives Control Act was jointly assigned to ATF and the FBI in 1970, and some personnel resources were shifted to more urban areas. The rural roots of the agency were largely intact, however. Well into the 1970s, the Southeast Region retained a disproportionate share of the law enforcement resources and remained the center of power, at least for law enforcement. Although the ATTD had been assigned responsibility for the firearms laws prior to 1968, not a single manager or executive of the agency actually had any working experience that was applicable to the new law.[6]

After ATF became an independent bureau, the licensing function was transferred to its regulatory arm, then called the Office of Regulatory Enforcement. The relationship between the "special agents," as they were now known, and the dealers soon became more remote. Over the next several years ATF concentrated most of its resources on the prosecution of felons who acquired firearms in violation of the law, bombers, and possessors and makers of NFA-restricted firearms. This allowed law enforcement to continue its culture and core technology with little change from alcohol enforcement. These cases created very little controversy as the defendants were mostly criminals with no organization or access to power. Some cases, however, were, directed at unlicensed firearms traffickers and licensed dealers. After 1977, these cases increased, due to Justice Department prosecutive guidelines changes that emphasized federal interest (see Chapter 5). Although these cases never, in fact, were a majority of those prosecuted by ATF, they proved to have the greatest impact on interest groups and thus on ATF's political environment.

A review of the initial implementation of the GCA clearly reveals that ATF was ill-prepared for the task. The agency's position as a division of the IRS had limited its independence, isolated it from the policymakers, and inhibited the development of strong leadership. The change of administration in 1969 and the sharp divisions in Congress on the issue of gun control precluded creation of an entrepreneurial agency with a mandate to aggressively interpret the law. These factors also ended any possibility that the GCA would be the first act in an incremental move toward strict national gun control. In 1968 the government was not prepared structurally or politically to administer a more sweeping law than the GCA.

In addition to the lack of a clear political mandate, ATF lacked the experience and resource base, both human and structural, to administer and enforce a universal registration and licensing law.[7] Few models existed at the federal level to emulate. Collection of income taxes and administration of social security did face similar massive numbers, but these functions were administered by two of the largest agencies in the federal government. The IRS employed approximately 80 percent of all Department of the Treasury employees. Both of these programs were provided with extensive information from employers and experienced their greatest noncompliance among small businesses and self-employed persons, the very type of business that accounted for most gun sales. The IRS has also been largely unable to detect and tax transactions between individuals. Such private transactions, not sales by dealers, accounted for the majority of firearms transfers. Another example of the federal government's inability to control numerous dispersed individual behaviors was visible in its failure to effectively control illegal immigration. Unlike most European states, the United States had no experience with the administration of national identification systems. ATF was faced with administering a law that had potential for generating widespread resistance and noncompliance, under the mandate of weak legislation, with little experience and no precedents. The situation was further complicated by a shortage of resources and trained personnel.

From Guns to Bombs

The task of implementing new gun laws was complicated by the passage of the Explosives Control Act in 1970. Beginning in the late 1960s, political bombings began to occur in the United States. Viewed in perspective to terrorist bombings outside the United States or the bombings of the World Trade Center and the Oklahoma City Federal Building, the bombings that occurred between 1969 and 1975 do not appear particularly monumental. To a nation with no experience in such events, however, these bombings, coupled with urban riots and antiwar protests, seemed a grave new threat. It quickly became apparent that there was no general federal bombing statute and little control on the purchase or sale of explosives. The FBI attempted to assume jurisdiction in all cases involving known or suspected political dissidents but lacked statutory authority, unless the target was federally owned property. Quite incidentally, the 1968 revisions of the NFA had added destructive devices to the definition of firearms. Thus, possession of an unregistered explosive device became the legal equivalent of possession of an unregistered machine gun, giving ATF jurisdiction over the manufacture and possession of explosive or incendiary bombs.

This jurisdictional twist of fate set ATF and the FBI on a collision course over turf. Neither agency was particularly well prepared to assume jurisdiction. Neither had agents trained in bombing investigation. ATF resources were still primarily in the rural South and the organization lacked experience in investigating groups motivated by politics. ATF did, however, have some advantages. Primary among them was a high level of innovation among its agents. More through accident than intention, many of these agents enjoyed substantial discretion. They also were used to functioning with little specialized training or central direction. Many did not wait to be told to investigate bombings nor to be provided with training and equipment. They just went ahead on their own and improvised.

The FBI had far greater resources and their personnel were better trained, better equipped, and more uniformly dispersed. On the other hand, their experience in investigating the Communist Party and other radical activity was of limited value. The typical bombing during this era was the work of a small cell and not part of a national conspiracy. The FBI lacked informants in the university settings that were a hotbed of radical activity, and their agents enjoyed far less freedom to improvise. The tradition in the FBI was to wait for direction from the center and proceed cautiously after receiving training and establishing procedures. This difference in organizational culture allowed ATF to successfully compete with an agency that was far larger, better known, more prestigious, and infinitely better funded.

Working relations between the FBI and other federal agencies were not close. During the J. Edgar Hoover regime, agents from other federal enforcement agencies were routinely treated as less-than-trustworthy outsiders. It was common for the FBI reports to list information coming from other federal agents as originating from a "confidential source" rather than identifying another agency.[8] The result was open competition between ATF and the FBI for jurisdiction over bombing investigation. In spite of subsequent changes in the law, memoranda of understanding, and a much changed FBI management, the competition continues.[9] FBI agents often appear to perceive their ATF counterparts as coming from the "second team." In return, ATF agents tend to characterize the FBI as being composed of arrogant dilettantes.

In 1970, Congress acted to create federal jurisdiction over bombings of federally financed, as well as federally owned, facilities and businesses in interstate commerce. The law also prohibited bomb threats over the telephone or through the mail, established storage requirements for explosives, required all explosives dealers to obtain licenses and maintain records of purchasers and inventory, restricted interstate explosives sales, and prohibited possession of stolen explosives. Although the Justice Department initiated the bill, and the FBI was the intended recipient of authority over criminal violations, the need for a regulatory agency complicated the problem. The FBI had never exercised a regulatory role and has viewed such a role as incompatible with their organizational culture and their public image. There was no other Justice bureau that could assume the regulatory role while relinquishing enforcement to the FBI. The Bureau of Narcotics and Dangerous Drugs did have regulatory experience but that agency was overwhelmed with the drug mission. The BNDD also viewed itself primarily as a law enforcement agency and would not have willingly accepted a regulatory mission to support the FBI's law enforcement jurisdiction. Initially, regulatory jurisdiction was proposed for the Bureau of Mines. ATF, however, pursued the jurisdiction and was far better prepared to exercise it.[10] Jurisdiction was, therefore, jointly granted to both the attorney general and the secretary of the treasury and the departments were left to sort out the details of jurisdiction.

Although the subsequent memorandum of understanding between the FBI and ATF divided the criminal jurisdiction, the entire licensing and regulatory responsibility was assumed by ATF.[11] This added jurisdiction mandated the writing of new regulations, dealer inspections and education, and new training procedures. Although this further complicated the tasks of ATF, the new jurisdiction proved far less troublesome than firearms. There were far fewer explosives dealers than firearms dealers and many were small hardware stores that made little profit from explosives and were happy to have an excuse to cease selling them. The number of dealers, therefore, quickly declined once storage and records-keeping requirements were imposed. There were no organizations opposed to explosives control. The only interest group represented manufacturers, and the interest environment resembled alcohol far more than firearms. Although the strict storage requirements were a far greater financial burden than anything imposed by the GCA, they were widely accepted with no debate. From the beginning, ATF personnel noted that the dynamics of enforcing and administering laws and regulations relating to explosives were far different from those relating to firearms.

Notes

1. The $10 yearly fee for dealers' licenses proved one of the most fateful decisions made in the writing of the GCA. It encouraged numerous noncommercial applicants, thus straining ATF's ability to monitor dealers. At the same time, the law required that licenses only be issued to those with intent to engage in the business, thus forcing the agency to make decisions based on apparent intent. Ironically, the original $100 proposal was lowered in response to complaints that it would be a hardship to small retailers who sold guns as a service to their customers. Subsequent inflation drastically altered the actual fee, and the expansion of national chains, such as Walmart, wiped out most of the small retailers.

2. *Haynes v U.S.*, 390 U.S. 85, 1968. Although the decision did not invalidate the NFA, it rendered it temporarily unenforceable by allowing self-incrimination as a defense. The ruling might never have occurred, except that Haynes's appeal was linked with appeals of two cases involving the wagering-tax laws, which were conspicuously designed to force illegal gamblers to incriminate themselves by registering and paying a tax. The firearms laws differed, in that most persons possessing NFA firearms were not prohibited from firearms ownership. Prior to 1968, the ATTD routinely registered NFA firearms if the applicant was not a felon. Even felons who voluntarily surrendered their firearms were not charged. Thus the registration requirement did not, in fact, function as a mechanism for self-incrimination.

3. The author spent months contacting as many as fifteen dealers per day in Alaska and Washington State during the final months of 1968 and the early months of 1969. He continued to perform this function intermittently for several years in the Northwest and later in California.

4. At its best, the dealer compliance program resembled community policing with an emphasis on prevention and positive personal contacts.

5. The IRS placed the administration of the income tax and the collection of revenues as their primary mission. ATF's licensing mission was well down the priority scale.

6. This is based upon the author's observations and interviews with numerous persons who were in the ATTD at the time.

7. See the testimony of ATF director Rex Davis before the Subcommittee on Crime of the Judiciary Committee, House of Representatives, March 20, 1975. This is also confirmed by the author's own observations and interviews with numerous other ATF employees.

8. The author has personally read a number of FBI reports in which information provided by ATF agents was described as coming from "confidential sources." In several of these cases, entire FBI reports consisted primarily of information received from ATF. These reports were then provided to ATF with the notation that they were the property of the FBI and any redistribution of the contents was prohibited. Another galling practice was

meeting with agents from other agencies in interrogation rooms, superficially disguised as offices, to avoid allowing other agents within the actual FBI working area. In spite of policy, working relationships did develop between individual agents, especially in outlying resident agencies.

9. In many bombing investigations the issue of jurisdiction has taken on as much importance as solving the crime. During the early 1970s, two agencies often raced each other to the crime scenes. Although this no longer occurs, they still attempt to gain initial control over physical evidence to preclude the other from exercising jurisdiction.

10. Interview with former ATF director Rex Davis.

11. Memoranda of understanding are common practice among agencies sharing jurisdiction. They are essentially contractual agreements, signed by each agency, to assume specific tasks or funding. In this case the primary purpose was to spell out the limits of each agency's jurisdiction.

CHAPTER 4

The Quiet Years

Although the period between 1972 and the election of Jimmy Carter as president appeared relatively calm for the new bureau, political currents were evolving that would threaten its existence. The Nixon administration displayed no interest in additional firearms legislation after the passage of the GCA, and executive attention did not again focus on the issue until the appointment of Edward Levi as attorney general. Congress also displayed little interest until 1972, when a series of bills relating to handguns were introduced. Most of the legislation centered around the so-called Saturday Night Specials. Although no precise definition exists for these firearms, Saturday Night Special refers to a small, inexpensive handgun.[1] This issue grew naturally from one of the many inconsistencies of the GCA. Under the law, firearms not suitable for sporting purposes could not be imported. No such restrictions existed for domestically manufactured firearms.

Charged with operationalizing the phrase "not suitable for sporting purposes," ATF proceeded with predictable caution. In an effort to minimize conflict, ATF crafted the definition very narrowly. Although the law applied to all firearms, ATF's definition only applied to handguns, effectively eliminating all long guns from possible exclusion. A point system was devised that gave points for such characteristics as target sights, safety devices, and barrel length. The resulting criteria prohibited primarily small, inexpensive handguns of poor quality, or Saturday Night Specials.[2]

Importers soon adapted to the ban by importing the parts and assembling the firearms in the United States. Advocates of gun control advanced the proposition that the standards for domestic manufacture of firearms should be changed to match the standards for imported firearms. In 1972 a bill restricting the manufacture of certain such handguns passed the Senate but not the House.[3] The concept of establishing firearms quality standards had once received rather extensive backing in the gun community.[4] The majority of firearms enthusiasts did not buy these inexpensive firearms and

45

tended to look upon them and their buyers with disdain. Some form of the Saturday Night Special legislation very likely would have passed, along with other minor modifications in the act, but for two developments. First, the NRA began to feel pressure from its more libertarian wing, which viewed firearms control primarily as a sovereignty issue.[5] This faction of the NRA was convinced that all gun control was a step in the eventual prohibition of private ownership. The second development was the progressively public advocacy of an incremental approach to handgun prohibition by some control advocates.[6] This latter trend greatly reinforced the legitimacy and influence of the libertarian forces within the NRA, making any acceptance of compromise on legislation impossible for the NRA leadership.

The Saturday Night Special legislation was the first in a series of strategies utilized by control advocates to advance their agenda by reformulating the issue.[7] As the strategy evolved, definitions for Saturday Night Specials became more inclusive, and the proposed controls evolved from restrictions on manufacture of new firearms to possession and transfer of existing firearms. The high-water mark of this effort was reached in 1975 with introduction of S. 1447 by Senator Edward Kennedy of Massachusetts. As proposed, the bill would have, in the senator's words, "banned the manufacture and possession of over 99.9 percent of all handguns."[8] There was clearly some basis for the fears of gun control opponents.

Attorney General Edward Levi was the primary advocate for gun control in the Ford administration. Shortly after taking office, he proposed legislation that would invoke federal restrictions on the sale and possession of handguns in specific metropolitan areas. The federal restrictions would be invoked automatically if the violent-crime rate reached a predetermined level.[9] Levi envisioned this approach as a means of compromising the rural opposition to firearms controls with the urban demand for such controls.[10] By the time an administration bill, S. 1880, reached Congress, the regional prohibition approach, which was very likely unconstitutional and achieved no reduction in opposition, had been abandoned.[11] The administration bill would have increased controls on firearms dealers, raised licensing fees, mandated a waiting period for handgun deliveries by dealers, and prohibited the manufacture of small handguns. Again, the term "Saturday Night Special" was used but with a less inclusive definition than in Senator Kennedy's bill.[12]

The administration crafted its proposal around the pursuit of compromise, even at the cost of internal consistency and rationality. Although the bill mandated a waiting period, it included no provisions for checking purchasers for criminal records during the wait.

Apparently, the drafters hoped that the states would take advantage of the period and mandate a check, although numerous states had shown no interest in waiting periods or records checks of buyers. Even the prohibition on small handguns begged the issue. It allowed a minimum barrel length of four inches, which eliminated very small handguns that are easily carried in the pocket but allowed handguns that can be concealed under a jacket. The proposed restriction would likely have had some impact on a few individuals who habitually carried handguns but would not have significantly restricted concealable firearms. This pattern of drafting proposals primarily in search of compromise rather than impact or structural consistency has continued.[13] Most recently, the pattern is apparent in the Brady Bill's mandate to report gun sales to local police, who are prohibited from retaining information from those reports, and in the application of the assault weapons ban to only a few unpopular semi-automatic firearms.[14]

Two proposals of the era did not follow the pattern of seeking compromise. Senate Bill 750, proposed by Democrat Philip Hart of Michigan, would have prohibited the manufacture, importation, sale, and ownership of firearms except for a few categories of people such as police and organized competitive shooters.[15] At the opposite extreme, Idaho Republican James McClure proposed Senate Bill 141, which would have revoked the Gun Control Act of 1968 in its entirety.[16] Although neither of these bills came close to passing, they clearly staked out the intellectual parameters of the issue during the mid-1970s. Senator Hart was an unabashed advocate of very strict gun control, and his bill was clearly grounded in a crime control paradigm.[17] Senator McClure, conversely, was opposed to all firearms legislation, and his bill was rooted in the sovereignty paradigm.[18]

None of the firearms legislation proposed during the mid-1970s passed Congress. Even relatively innocuous provisions increasing control of licensed dealers and differentiating fees between handgun dealers, long-gun dealers, ammunition dealers, and gunsmiths failed. Although the stiffening resistance of the gun lobby and its key supporters in Congress was a factor in this phenomenon, the weak leadership of House subcommittee chair John Conyers may have been equally important.[19] Conyers was in a key position to move legislation, and his failure to do so was likely critical. Rather than passing legislation, Conyers succeeded only in creating substantial publicity through extensive hearings held across the country. The result appears to be an increase in the paranoia and fear among gun control opponents but little advancement of a control agenda.

A Brief Diversion

In 1974 Congress passed a revision to the wagering-tax statutes. Although technically tax statutes, the wagering laws originally were drafted as a mechanism of enforcement against illegal gambling. The pre-1974 law had imposed a 10 percent tax on gross wagers and had required all those engaged in the business to register and make their records available to all law enforcement authorities. The Supreme Court ruled in 1968 in the Grosso and Marcheti cases that a defendant could invoke a defense of self-incrimination against charges of failure to register.[20] Although a similar problem with the NFA was remedied with the passage of the GCA in 1968, no corrective action was taken for the wagering statutes until 1974. In the interim, the law imposed a 10 percent tax on the gross wagers of legal bookmakers in Nevada that could not be enforced against their illegal competitors. Since 10 percent was the normal commission for booking a wager, the law was essentially confiscatory for legal bookmakers, who lobbied Congress for a change. The new law lowered the tax to 2 percent and removed the provisions for law enforcement access to the wagering-tax records.

The assistant secretary of the treasury assigned enforcement jurisdiction over the new law to ATF rather than the IRS. An unsophisticated ATF did not realize that the primary reason for the change in the law was to benefit legal bookmakers, and therefore proceeded to develop a law enforcement strategy directed at illegal bookmaking. If the origins of the change in the law were not an adequate hint at the priority of gambling enforcement, the lack of supplemental budget for the purpose should have been. ATF also should have noted the relatively low priority given by the FBI to gambling investigations and the limited prosecutive appeal of those cases that the FBI did pursue.[21] ATF management, however, was inclined to take a mandate at face value, and the agency was hungry for a more diverse jurisdiction. Although ATF had emerged from the political isolation of the IRS, its management was not yet sophisticated in the intricacies of the political process.

For approximately one year, ATF agents pursued wagering investigations. Although ATF provided training to all agents and was successful in a number of arrests, the lack of funding soon communicated that there was no congressional or administrative support for the activity. Within a year, jurisdiction over wagering was reassigned to the IRS by the Department of the Treasury, a decision that Rex Davis attributes to Deputy Assistant Secretary James Featherstone.[22] Although some in ATF perceived this as a significant loss in jurisdiction, wagering cases have proven of little import to the IRS and would likely have had little impact on ATF.

Shortly after losing jurisdiction over wagering violations, ATF gained jurisdiction over new federal laws prohibiting the interstate transportation of cigarettes to avoid state tax.[23] Although some in the agency again believed that the added jurisdiction would result in a major transformation of the agency, it did not come to pass. Contraband cigarette cases consistently have constituted less than 1 percent of the agency's investigative activities. Although diversification of jurisdiction most likely would have benefited the law enforcement component of ATF by enhancing its image as a general law enforcement agency, firearms and explosives laws were to remain the agency's only significant jurisdiction. Of the two, firearms clearly dominated the agenda. For ATF, this was both a strength and a weakness. Although firearms laws were increasingly controversial, they also provided the federal government with one of the few jurisdictional areas that related to violent crime. Because violent crime had become a major political issue by the 1970s, firearms jurisdiction raised the visibility and importance of the bureau, particularly when Congress or the president wished to display resolve in fighting street crime.

Focus on Firearms Enforcement

Prospects for quick passage of Attorney General Levi's proposed gun control legislation did not appear good, and the president faced a difficult reelection fight in 1976. Therefore, in 1976 the administration shifted its emphasis from the pursuit of new legislation to implementation of existing law. The resulting proposal included a significant expansion of ATF and raised the visibility of both ATF and firearms enforcement.[24] President Ford proposed adding five hundred additional ATF agents to eleven major metropolitan areas in an effort to reduce violent crime by reducing the availability of firearms to criminals. The proposal was formulated with almost no ATF input, apparently based on policy options drafted in the Department of Justice and the White House.[25] The tactic of expanding resources to enforce existing law was not a surprising turn of events. With the president facing a difficult campaign in 1976 and violent crime at its highest level in decades, gun laws provided one of the few available strategies for taking federal action against violent crime.

Although pursuing new legislation is the most common means for a president to demonstrate commitment to an issue, past experience

had demonstrated that new firearms legislation was not easily
moved through Congress. Even such longtime opponents of expanded federal jurisdiction as Senator Roman Hruska of Nebraska,
however, were willing to back increased enforcement of the existing
statutes, and liberal Democrats primarily favored gun control, making their support likely.[26] If consensus on firearms policy could not
be found for new legislation, then it might be obtained by shifting
the focus to allocating resources for the implementation of existing
law. This strategy was more comfortable for ATF than one which pursued significant policy change through legislation. ATF's culture was
comfortable with the familiar functions of enforcement and regulation but not with the less familiar and more controversial task of policy formulation.

Once the announcement had been made, the agency began a
flurry of planning to capitalize on the proposed expansion.[27] Almost
all of ATF's attention was directed toward the details of personnel
actions and space acquisition, rather than toward developing a
workable strategy for utilization of the additional resources. The
only familiar precedent for ATF was Operation Dry-Up, which had
concentrated additional investigative resources on specific areas of
the Southeast to suppress moonshine.[28] Given the magnitude of the
proposed expansion—almost a one-third increase in the total number of agents and a massive shift in existing personnel—the logistics
alone were at the margins of ATF's ability to manage. The concurrent development of an entirely different enforcement strategy exceeded the agency's capacity.[29] Even the reduced level of expansion
that ultimately did occur was more than the agency could comfort-
ably handle.

The proposal for eleven cities and five hundred agents was reduced by the White House and Congress before it was ever implemented. Only three cities—Washington, Chicago, and Boston—were
selected as test sites. ATF designated the effort as Project CUE, for
Consolidated Urban Enforcement. Approximately 180 additional
agents were recruited and hired, but these were not the majority of
the agents used in the three designated test cities.[30] In both Washington and Chicago, the majority of additional agents were transferred from the Southeastern Region, where liquor work had declined and districts were overstaffed.[31] Of the three cities, Chicago
received the greatest increase in manpower, 300 percent. Not surprisingly, the Chicago District experienced the highest levels of employee
dissatisfaction.[32] The net impact of this initiative on violent crime was
not particularly significant. The three field divisions were ill-prepared for this level of growth and lacked the necessary logistical resources in all areas, from investigative funds to clerical support.[33]

More important, the agency lacked any comprehensive strategy for impacting violent crime through use of the gun laws.[34] Agents continued to do what they knew how to do; they investigated individual criminals and referred cases to the United States Attorney's Office. The United States attorney lacked the resources to prosecute these additional cases, and the penalties for those cases that were prosecuted were light.[35] Ultimately, the entire federal justice system lacked the capacity to process large numbers of additional cases against street criminals. If viewed in perspective, it is not surprising that ATF lacked the capacity to produce noticeable impact on street crime by pursuing individual street criminals. The 300 percent increase in ATF agents in Chicago constituted less than a 1 percent increase in the overall law enforcement staffing in the city, and the federal system was far less adept than the state and local systems at handling high volumes of cases.[36]

The greatest impact of Project CUE was on the structure, culture, and organization of ATF. The predominance of the Southeastern Region came to an end seven years after the agency had shifted from liquor to firearms enforcement.[37] The organizational culture was impacted by a shift from rural to urban focus, even more so by the involuntary transfers. Many ATF agents had sought out the agency because of its regional character. They believed that there was an implied contract that they would not be moved from their region against their will. This, in fact, had been true until 1975. Reaction to the change in procedure had its most dramatic impact on agents from the Southeastern Region. In return for a guarantee of remaining in the region and receiving salaries that substantially exceeded those of local and state law enforcement, they had accepted very authoritarian management and a lower grade structure than other federal enforcement agencies with little complaint.[38] After the CUE transfers and concurrent closures of small enforcement offices in the Southeast, these agents began to display a significant change in attitude.[39]

Organizationally, Project CUE forced ATF to begin weaning itself from an entirely regional structure and to conduct some central planning and analysis. A new management information system was implemented in an effort to track the results of resource application. Headquarters began an effort to utilize information from gun tracing to profile the sources, type, and age of firearms seized by the police. Compliance inspectors were used in the target cities in a concerted effort to support law enforcement. Most important, the agency had crossed the Rubicon with regard to perceiving itself as a national organization. The requirements to engage in national planning, shift resources between regions, and move away from its rural southern roots had changed the agency permanently. Within two years of the initiation of CUE, the regional structure for enforcement was dismantled and all enforcement operations were directed from headquarters. Also, ATF enforcement of firearms laws had been raised to a new level of visibility and tied to national criminal justice policy. The organizational culture forged within the IRS, which had been regional and discouraged involvement in policy formulation or the pursuit of public attention, was changing. Although these cultural values remained an influence on many in ATF for years to come, the new imperatives were higher visibility as a national organization and more active participation in national criminal justice policy. Inevitably, this new organizational identity was destined to place the agency on a path toward conflict with those opposed to gun control.

The Advocacy Groups Dig In

Although the administration was pursuing consensus by shifting away from a legislative strategy, other forces were moving in very different directions. The first organizations to focus on advocating gun control legislation, the National Coalition to Ban the Handgun and Handgun Control Incorporated, had come into existence by 1974 and were committed to advancing a national gun control policy. Both advocates and opponents of gun control viewed the creation of these lobby groups as a major step toward passage of stricter national gun control laws.[40] Concurrently, a strong contingent in the NRA was advancing the argument that all guns would be prohibited if gun legislation were not stopped immediately. These events were occurring in the context of a national political trend in opposition to expansion of federal regulation that had begun with the Nixon election and has continued through the 1990s.[41] Ironically, the compromise that expanded enforcement resources and shifted focus to reducing the availability of firearms to criminals in urban areas provided a key step in shaping the coming confrontation between interest groups.

The existence of special interest groups in support of eliminating handguns, combined with legislation such as Kennedy's sweeping Saturday Night Special bill and Hart's bill to prohibit private ownership of handguns, greatly energized the opponents of gun control. NRA membership, which had increased greatly during the Dodd hearings, again climbed.[42] The NRA formed an official lobbying arm, the Institute for Legislative Action, and ceased all discussion of compromise. In 1977, control of the NRA was finally seized in a well-planned coup by its militant, libertarian faction led by Neal Knox and Harlan Carter.[43] A core of board members led by Representative John Dingell of Michigan and Harlan Carter, a retired United States Border Patrol manager, had been pushing the NRA to increase its opposition to existing laws as well as to new legislation.[44] Although the past leadership of the NRA had long expressed reservations about gun control, they were not thoroughly libertarian in outlook. Most had served as civil servants or military officers for many years before coming to the NRA and were uncomfortable with directly attacking those in high office. The new leadership that took control in 1977 was both libertarian and confrontational.[45] The change in leadership was not incremental but radical; events at the 1977 convention are referred to almost universally as a coup or revolution.

For the libertarian purists in the NRA, sovereignty of individuals over government constituted the dominant paradigm for analysis of gun control. In the words of Neal Knox, "Gun control is about power, and the person with the guns has the power."[46] This paradigm interlocked closely with a world view or cultural paradigm that had long dominated the NRA. In its more benign form, this view extolled the values of outdoor life, shooting, and hunting. It took on a harder edge as it merged with radical libertarianism in an environment fueled by paranoia.[47] The result paralleled events when the balance of power becomes unsettled in nations with multiple cultural enclaves. In this sort of an environment, every action by one's opponent takes on sinister meaning, and voices of moderation are drowned out. Leadership must harness the fear and cultural hostility or lose control. In the case of the NRA, the leadership lost control and was replaced. As the NRA shifted to a more confrontational view, ATF and the gun control lobbies fueled the fires of paranoia. ATF reinforced existing paranoia by raising the profile of firearms enforcement and by adopting an official strategy of impacting firearms markets. Gun control advocacy groups did so by espousing incremental increases in firearms restrictions. In a setting in which Watergate had undermined the credibility of government and popularized conspiracy theories, the opponents of gun control saw the actions of the government and control advocates as well-orchestrated steps toward firearms prohibition.

ATF sought widespread publicity in an effort to utilize Project CUE as a base for future expansion of its resources and jurisdiction. At the NRA this barrage of publicity was interpreted as part of a coordinated effort to pass restrictive legislation and prohibit private ownership of firearms.[48] Concurrently, the pro-control advocacy groups were attracting far more attention than their numbers would

justify. Even experienced politicians mistakenly read the development of these groups as a major shift in the political dynamics of
gun control.[49] It is very likely that both the opponents and advocates had misread the impact of the "Watergate Congress."[50] In light
of future events, the political impact of Watergate could better be
characterized as generating suspicion of government than as the beginning of a new wave of liberalism.[51] Thus, instead of a flurry of
new social legislation after 1974, Congress began to focus more and
more on its oversight function.[52] The suspicion generated by Watergate proved more conducive to attacks on alleged excesses by government agencies than to expanded authority for those agencies.

The election of Jimmy Carter in 1976 was as much a signal of
distrust of Washington as a mandate for a Democratic Party agenda
of social action. Carter clearly ran his campaign as a Washington
outsider. Viewed in this perspective, a political cycle that had begun
with the 1968 election was moving ahead at full speed. Unfortunately for ATF and the advocates of gun control, they had misread
the signs. Although the NRA also had done so, the impact differed
significantly. As the pronouncements of Harlan Carter and Neil
Knox made clear, the NRA was motivated toward conflict without
compromise. Thus it was able to utilize the actions of the control advocates and ATF to energize its membership and consolidate its
leadership.[53] The more attention that the activities of ATF and proposals for additional gun control received, the stronger and more
intransigent the NRA became.[54]

Neither ATF nor the Ford or Carter political appointees appreciated the intensity of the opposition developing within the NRA.
ATF followed a classic bureaucratic model of seeking greater resources and wider public approval and attention. Relations between
ATF and the NRA had already begun to change after the passage of
the GCA, as was evident with the increased criticism of ATF in the
American Rifleman after the Kenyon Bellew incident (see Chapter 1),
and the increasing power of the NRA's libertarian faction made negotiation virtually impossible. ATF leadership, however, did not understand this evolution and still pursued a strategy of negotiation
with the NRA.[55] ATF's long history of accommodation with the
liquor industry had served it well and established a pattern of seeking accommodation with interest groups. Although the agency had
not achieved an equally harmonious relationship with the NRA, it
had avoided conflict prior to 1968.[56] The Department of Justice,
which displayed far less inclination to seek accommodation with
the opponents of gun control than did Treasury or ATF, attracted far
more attention than the ATTD or the IRS.[57]

End Run with Regulation

The election of Jimmy Carter did nothing to assuage the fears of the NRA and its supporters. As a Democratic president, Carter was expected by both supporters and opponents to pursue gun control. Faced with demands for action from the gun control lobby and the fact that Saturday Night Special bills had twice passed the Senate and failed in the House, the administration faced a politically difficult situation. The White House decided to bypass the political pitfalls of new legislation and pursue quick results by using the regulations already authorized under the GCA.[58] Under the existing law, the Department of the Treasury had broad authority to control licensed firearms dealers through changes in the regulations. Treasury's authority was broad enough to allow establishment of a waiting period and mandatory reporting for all gun sales by dealers.[59] Although the impetus to take action came from the White House, Treasury crafted the details of the proposal with heavy input from ATF.[60] Given the historic caution of both entities toward gun control proposals, this delegation precluded any chance that the proposals would contain anything as radical as requiring the reporting of gun purchasers.

The proposals were, in fact, deliberately conservative. Treasury, with ATF encouragement, crafted them so as to generate minimal resistance and concern. Manufacturers would be required to identify all new firearms with a unique serial number indicating the manufacturer and model of the gun. Licensed dealers would be required to report all gun thefts to ATF within twenty-four hours of discovery and make quarterly reports of all firearms sold to other dealers. Military personnel importing firearms into the United States upon returning from foreign tours would need advance approval. No one in the administration or ATF was prepared for the reaction to these proposals. During the required period for public comment, ATF received 350,000 letters, which ran 38 to 1 against the regulations. An examination of the letters revealed that most of the writers did not even know the content of the proposals. They primarily expressed opposition to confiscation, registration, and violation of the Second Amendment.[61] Clearly, the significance of the regulations derived more from symbolism than content or potential impact.

The proposal that aroused the greatest interest was the required reporting of transactions by dealers. Originally, the GCA had required licensees to maintain such records and to make such reports as the secretary of the treasury prescribed by regulation.[62] Regulatory discretion had been one of the major concerns of opponents during the Dodd hearings.[63] Although this section had allowed a report-of-sale system and waiting period to be invoked by regulation through regulatory action by ATF, no consideration had ever been given to this option. While the proposed regulations did not require the reporting of retail transactions or of retail buyers' names, they did set a precedent for requiring reports from dealers. To opponents of the law this precedent was the first step toward reporting purchasers, which they considered tantamount to registration.

ATF planned to computerize the information on transfers between dealers for two distinct uses. First, ATF would facilitate gun tracing by avoiding the need to contact manufacturers and multiple intermediary dealers to locate the ultimate seller. These traces were the only practical means of linking a firearm to its owner, a service that has proven valuable to numerous law enforcement agencies in a wide variety of investigations.[64] By computerizing the dealer-to-dealer transfers, ATF could bypass much of the tracing process and immediately access the identity of the last dealer in the chain. First, the trace could start with the retail seller, saving time and guarding against gaps caused by dealers who had gone out of business.[65] Second, ATF would be provided with an automated record of a dealer's acquisitions to facilitate audits of the dealer's books.[66]

Notes

1. A lengthy discussion of the issues of the period are provided in Robert Sherrill, *The Saturday Night Special* (New York: Charterhouse, 1973).

2. Although opponents to gun control have characterized ATF as pursuing an aggressive regulatory agenda to restrict firearms, the agency has displayed a strong aversion to aggressive use of regulatory authority. Other examples of this pattern include the unwillingness to require reporting of firearms sales by dealers and the interpretation of the law relating to restoration of rights to possess firearms for persons convicted of felonies. In the latter example, the agency even interpreted persons convicted of assault while armed with knives as potentially eligible for consideration if the knife was not specifically designed as a weapon.

3. U.S. Congress, Senate, *Handgun Crime Control—1975–1976*, 1976, 45.

4. See the testimony of Franklin Orth, executive vice president of the NRA, Senate hearings, May 21, 1965.

5. Interviews with Neal Knox and John Acquilino, former NRA staff members.

6. Statement of Representative Conyers, *Congressional Record*, December 17, 1975, H. 12896.

7. As it became apparent that broad-based gun control legislation could not be moved onto the active agenda of Congress, advocates began efforts to recast the issue in narrower terms. In addition to the Saturday Night

Special approach, the "cop-killer bullet" issue and assault weapons are later examples of this tactic. See William J. Vizzard, "The Evolution of Gun Control Policy in the United States: Accessing the Public Agenda," DPA dissertation, University of Southern California, 1993.

8. See the statement of Senator Edward Kennedy before Senate hearings, April 23, 1975. The proposal would have prohibited handguns with barrels of six inches or less in length.

9. See text of address delivered by Attorney General Edward Levi before the Law Enforcement Executives Narcotics Conference on April 6, 1975, at Washington, D.C. Possession of handguns inside one's home would not have been affected, but all other possession would have been banned.

10. In the above address, Levi specifically cited the demand of such groups as the International Association of Chiefs of Police and the United States Conference of Mayors for stricter federal controls. He also cited the concerns of those opposed, who resided in areas in which crime rates are of far less concern.

11. See testimony of Attorney General Levi, Senate hearings, July 22, 1975. Attorney General Levi acknowledged that the Department of Justice concluded that the earlier proposal was not practical, although he did not acknowledge any political considerations in its abandonment.

12. Ibid.

13. Vizzard, 1993.

14. William J. Vizzard, "The Impact of Agenda Conflict on Policy Formulation and Implementation: The Case of Gun Control," *Public Administration Review* (July-August 1995) 341–348.

15. U.S. Congress, Senate, *A Bill to Prohibit the Importation, Manufacture, Sale, Purchase, or Transportation of Handguns, Except for or by Members of the Armed Forces, Law Enforcement Officials and, as Authorized by the Secretary of the Treasury, Licensed Importers, Manufacturers, Dealers, Antique Collectors and Pistol Clubs*, S. 750, February 10, 1975.

16. U.S. Congress, Senate, *A Bill to Repeal the Gun Control Act of 1968*, S. 141, January 15, 1975.

17. S. 750. The preamble clearly establishes the logic of the bill and its intended purpose.

18. *Congressional Record*, January 15, 1975; Senator McClure delineated the rationality of his bill focusing on two issues. The predominant issue was individual sovereignty and constitutional rights, and the secondary issue was the utility of gun control in impacting crime.

19. Interview with Eric Sterling, a former House Judiciary Committee staff member who was very involved in this issue. He cited the poor quality of Conyers's subcommittee staff as a key to the failure to pass a Saturday Night Special bill. From the opposing ranks, Neal Knox stated to the author that "a Saturday Night Special bill would have passed except that Conyers was more interested in holding hearings than passing legislation."

20. The Court issued this opinion in conjunction with *Haynes v U.S.*, 390 U.S. 85, 1968; see Chapter 3, note 2.

21. Gambling statutes, enforced by the FBI, were not impacted by the Grosso and Marcheti rulings. These laws were enacted under the interstate commerce authority.

22. Perceived in ATF as hostile to federal controls, Featherstone later became director of legal affairs for the NRA.

23. Jurisdiction over the wagering-tax and tobacco-smuggling laws was not strongly contested among federal law enforcement agencies. Both were

linked to taxation, long accepted as in Treasury's sphere of influence. Within Treasury, ATF was the only agency both structured to and interested in enforcing the tobacco-smuggling laws.

24. The importance of perception over reality was highlighted in March of 1976, when a group identifying itself as the Red Guerrilla Family bombed the regional ATF office in San Francisco. Communiqués attributed the bombing to alleged repression of the people by the greatly expanded ATF operation in San Francisco. Ironically the local special agent in charge had announced the build-up based on White House proposals, but no such build-up ever took place. ATF's San Francisco operation remained small and rather ineffectual.

25. This is confirmed by former ATF director Rex Davis, who remembers inquiries as to ATF's potential contribution but no participation in the planning process prior to the announcement. The author was involved in the planning at the regional level. ATF did not begin any work until after the president's proposal was made public.

26. U.S. Congress, Senate hearings, S. 524 and S. 543, 1975.

27. ATF planners drafted detailed plans for the project at a staffing level of five hundred, including the identity and future location of every agent to be moved, before any funding was available.

28. Tanna Pesso, "Gun Control (B): The Bureau of Alcohol, Tobacco and Firearms," unpublished case study prepared for the John F. Kennedy School of Government, Harvard University, Boston, 1981. The circumstances were far different from the moonshine situation, where ATF had occupied a dominant and direct enforcement role. ATF would now have to indirectly impact a large crime-prone population by enforcing the firearms laws against a small number of firearms violators.

29. In fairness to ATF, it is unlikely that any strategy existed for quickly lowering crime rates by utilizing the GCA. If it had, the lack of information regarding the firearms market and the lack of analytical experience among ATF personnel would have made its discovery unlikely.

30. The development cycle for an agent to reach full journeyman status took at least two years, with the first year devoted almost exclusively to training. Thus, experienced agents had to be transferred to the test cities if their impact was to occur within the first two years.

31. Pesso. The Comptroller General of the United States, Handgun Control: Effectiveness and Costs (Washington, D.C.: General Accounting Office, February 6, 1978) 43.

32. Dissatisfaction was generally high among those transferred and agents soon coined the verb, "cued," to describe the involuntary transfers of this period. The term had distinctly pejorative connotations. Chicago received, by far, the greatest number of cued agents.

33. Pesso. The author is acquainted with numerous agents and supervisors who participated in this operation. He was also assigned to the Firearms Enforcement Branch at the time internal analysis of this operation was being conducted. Although ATF employed a consulting firm to do an analysis of the project, which found positive impact, the results appear to be questionable. Many of the agents transferred to Chicago and Washington against their will were very hostile and applied themselves minimally.

34. The dilemma was not new. Existing law did not allow ATF to close off the supply of firearms, and there were inadequate resources and commitment to arrest and prosecute all armed criminals.

35. The maximum penalty for possession of a firearm by a felon was two years imprisonment, with two-thirds of this sentence being parole. Most persons convicted of firearms violations received probation and virtually none served more than three years.

36. Historically, the federal system has not been structured to handle high volumes of street crimes, as this has been the responsibility of local police and state courts.

37. Even after the passage of the GCA, the Southeastern Region of ATF retained more personnel than any of the other six, with more agents in Georgia than any other state. Each state in the Southeastern Region remained a separate district until 1981, while districts in other regions contained as many as six states. Although CUE ended the concentration of personnel in the Southeast, managers from that region dominated the law enforcement operation in ATF for ten more years.

38. The typical ATF agent was a GS-11 at this time, while most other Treasury agents were GS-12s and most FBI agents were GS-13s.

39. Before Project CUE, agents in the Southeastern Region did not even raise a protest when ordered to get a haircut or shave a mustache. After CUE, the National Association of Treasury Agents, founded by retired Mississippi special agent William Pace and populated primarily by agents from the Southeast, became the focal point of employee criticism and opposition toward ATF management.

40. Interviews with Neal Knox and Charles Beard, founder and director of the National Coalition to Ban the Handgun, respectively. Also see Vizzard, 1993, for an in-depth discussion.

41. The importance of this move to the right was not well understood in the 1970s, but became far clearer with the election of Ronald Reagan.

42. After the passage of the GCA, NRA membership expanded to over one million; see Lee Kennett and James Anderson, *The Gun in America: Origins of an American Dilemma* (Westpost, Conn.: Greenwood Press, 1975) 238.

43. John Sugarmann, *National Rifle Association: Money, Power and Fear* (Washington, D.C.: National Press Books, 1992) 45–52; Roger Davidson, *The Postreform Congress* (College Park: University of Maryland Press, 1992) 34–35.

44. Interviews with John Acquilino and Neal Knox.

45. Ibid.

46. Interview with Neal Knox.

47. The emergence of interest groups solely committed to gun control combined with pronouncements by control advocates and the rising suspicion of government to greatly enhance the fear of even moderate gun owners. While many dealers and gun enthusiasts had shown little concern about the GCA in 1968, by 1975 they routinely expressed the belief that "they" want to take all "our" guns.

48. Interview with John Acquilino.

49. See exchange between Senators Hart and Kennedy on April 23, 1975, Committee on Judiciary, Subcommittee to Investigate Juvenile Delinquent Handgun Control, 1975–1976, 94th Congress, 1st session, 30–31.

50. According to Neal Knox the election of the 1974 "Watergate" class in Congress significantly affected many in the NRA and generated real fear that legislation would now be passed. In contrast, Michael Beard remembers this as a time of real optimism that legislation would pass Congress to significantly restrict the uncontrolled possession and transfer of handguns.

51. The popular media seem to have been more perceptive of the changing national mood. Significant numbers of government conspiracy films and books, such as *Three Days of the Condor,* began to emerge in the mid-1970s.

52. Davidson, 14.

53. The NRA possessed a tactical advantage in opposing rather than advocating legislative action. The NRA did not need to craft compromise or fear alienating those in the middle. Their message could be crafted solely to activate that portion of the population that already opposed gun control.

54. John Acquilino cites ATF arrests of unlicensed dealers and seizures of their inventories and ATF press releases about these same actions as being the key elements in a developing consensus among the NRA leadership that there was a well-organized plan to "take our guns." Neal Knox stated that ATF and Treasury were part of a plan to pursue registration and the eventual licensing, if not prohibition, of firearms.

55. Interview with Rex Davis.

56. The prevailing policy of cooperation with the liquor industry is documented elsewhere in this book. In his 1965 testimony before the Senate hearings, NRA executive vice president Franklin Orth spoke in glowing terms of the NRA's many friends in the ATTD and the admirable job done by the agency. Committee on Judiciary, Subcommittee to Investigate Juvenile Delinquency, Federal Firearms Hearings, 89th Congress, 1st session, 1965, 200.

57. A comparison of the testimony by the two departments reveals Treasury making far more modest proposals than Justice during the mid-1970s. Treasury focused on mild "clean-up" legislation that would not alter policy in any significant way, while Justice advocated prohibiting a substantial number of handguns through a bill similar to Senator Kennedy's but slightly less comprehensive. More important, the attorney general openly stated that the Second Amendment did not apply to individual possession of firearms and that guns in the home were more of a danger to the owner than to criminals. The symbolism of these statements was very likely more important than any proposal for legislation because they attacked the critical underpinnings of the sovereignty and world view paradigms.

58. There is no indication that either the Justice or Treasury departments played a significant role in formulating the policy decision to pursue action through regulation. Both former assistant secretary of the treasury Rich Davis and former ATF director Rex Davis have stated that the idea originated with the White House staff.

59. The law authorized the secretary of the treasury to establish the records and reporting requirements for dealers. By requiring a report of all purchasers and by restricting delivery until a fixed period after the report, a waiting period with potential for a records check would have been created.

60. Interviews with Richard Davis and Rex Davis.

61. Author's conversations with ATF personnel who reviewed the letters.

62. 18 USC, Sec. 223 (g), October 22, 1968.

63. Testimony of Franklin Orth, executive vice president of the NRA, Senate hearings, July 19, 1967.

64. Established in 1972, ATF's National Tracing Center, which now traces over 77,000 firearms per year, provides the only means to link a

recovered firearm to its owner. A unique ATF function, tracing engenders significant support from law enforcement for the agency. Unfortunately, the process is slow and laborious. Tracing requires ATF to contact the manufacturer or importer and each dealer who received the firearm by telephone until the retail seller is located. At this point, an agent or local police officer must continue the trace by using the dealer's records to contact the first buyer and often several subsequent owners. Although high-priority traces, such as that on the revolver used by John Hinkley to shoot President Reagan, can be completed in hours, routine traces often take weeks. A significant portion prove unsuccessful due to missing dealer records or the failure of buyers to be able or willing to identify the later disposition of the gun.

65. Dealers have been required to submit their records to ATF upon going out of business since 1968, but not all comply. No effective mechanism exists to assure compliance.

66. Because no central records exist to determine what firearms have been shipped to a dealer, effective audits of a dealer's records have always been difficult. Unscrupulous dealers can enter only a portion of their acquisitions in their log book and sell the guns not recorded with documentation. This has been a fairly common means of circumventing the law and can involve hundreds of firearms without the dealer being detected. Eventually, the dealer's inability to locate recovered firearms traced to them may raise suspicion. At this point inspectors must attempt to determine likely wholesale sources and audit their records for shipments to the suspect dealer, a process known as "forward tracing."

CHAPTER 5

Centralization

The Carter administration's policy on law enforcement was, ironically, far more conservative than preceding or succeeding Republican administrations.[1] Prior to the 1976 election, the Justice Department had begun to question the use of FBI resources on cases that did not appear to warrant federal attention, particularly investigations of the Dyer Act, which prohibited the interstate transportation of stolen cars. J. Edgar Hoover had utilized these cases to inflate FBI arrest figures.[2] After Hoover's death, the practice was openly questioned in the FBI and in Justice. The Carter administration expanded on this trend, and the Department of Justice issued instructions to all United States attorneys to shift their prosecutions to what were defined as federal interest cases.[3]

ATF's law enforcement activities had predominantly consisted of investigations of individuals with criminal records or reputations who possessed firearms unlawfully. The majority of these involved convicted felons, who possessed conventional firearms, although others concerned possessors or sellers of sawed-off shotguns or machine guns. Although the cases varied in quality between offices, the emphasis was on active criminals and those with serious criminal records. Several forces reinforced this trend. Primarily composed of former police officers, the agent cadre was professionally socialized to focus their attention on this type of suspect. The close relations between local police and ATF and preferences of United States Attorney's Offices also reinforced the ATF's investigative priorities. The police primarily directed information to ATF on individuals they viewed as problems, and ATF agents had a vested interest in good relations with local police, who could provide informants and information. Assistant United States attorneys were both professionally and personally motivated to prosecute individuals who could be easily classified as criminals.[4] The administration's priorities directly challenged ATF's enforcement operations and required innovative action by

ATF to survive as a law enforcement agency. ATF responded by using the explosives laws to encompass arson fraud, a crime that met the white-collar criteria.

Arson

The expansion of ATF's jurisdiction into arson is a classic example of bureaucratic entrepreneurship that highlights the agency's greatest strength. The National Firearms Act provided ATF with jurisdiction over a limited number of arsons in which an incendiary device was used. These included chemical, mechanical, or electronic delays as well as the more primitive Molotov cocktail. In 1975, ATF agents conducted an investigation of a firebombing in Philadelphia that had resulted in multiple deaths. The investigation was initiated at the request of the United States attorney after the local police were accused of beating a confession from a suspect to the murders. ATF eventually established that two subjects with local political ties were responsible for the crime and that the original suspect was innocent. Subsequently, the United States attorney requested that ATF conduct the investigation of a large restaurant fire believed to be an arson fraud. In this case no device had been used and it appeared that ATF lacked jurisdiction. The agents responded with an innovative theory. Since ATF had jurisdiction over the destruction by explosives of any business engaged in interstate commerce, classification of the accelerant as an explosive would give ATF and the federal courts jurisdiction. They utilized a chemist to prove that gasoline, once distributed in a room, became an explosive under the definition in the Explosives Control Act.

As is often the case, the timing of events proved critical. The United States attorney in Philadelphia was a Republican who was fighting to retain his position in a Democratic administration. When he became aware of the potential for federal pursuit of arson, which recently had become the focus of some attention as a growing white-collar crime in inner cities, he called a press conference to announce a campaign against arson fraud. Subsequently, Wally Hay, the Philadelphia special agent in charge, seized upon the opportunity when the chief of the Organized Crime Section of the Department of Justice visited the city. Hay was able to sell the idea of using ATF jurisdiction to attack arson fraud, and the Organized Crime Section to encourage Organized Crime Strike Forces across the country to pursue these cases.[5] Other ATF offices began to emulate Philadelphia and two of the Philadelphia agents were sent to headquarters to develop agency guidelines. Although they met with some resistance from within the agency, they managed to provide information to the Department of Justice, which in turn placed pressure on ATF.[6] The arson effort proved to be such a success that the explosives laws were eventually modified to include arson with explosives under Section 844(i) of Title 18 USC (see Chapter 7).

Although arson has never rivaled firearms in the number of cases investigated, it combined with ATF's explosives jurisdiction to provide the agency with a much broader base than would have been possible with firearms alone. Arson and explosives investigation also generated unique expertise that has provided the agency with added legitimacy (see chapter 7). Equally as important, arson has also provided constituencies in the form of the insurance industry and fire departments, while not creating any organized opposition.

Focus on Policy

As often happens, the prior administration had initiated changes that would impact adaptation to the policies of the incoming administration. ATF regional directors were eliminated in 1976, and all the regional law enforcement personnel were moved to headquarters. Subsequently, additional staff was drafted into headquarters to create a centrally directed organization that emulated the FBI and the Secret Service.[7] A regional compliance function was continued, as was some administrative support. Thus the division between the bureau's two operational functions was further widened. The elimination of the regional law enforcement structure laid the foundation for a centrally directed response to the administration's directives. Although Project CUE had been less than successful in impacting crime, it had disrupted the complacent isolation of the regions and provided some experience with central planning. ATF's strategy in response to the administration's mandate focused on firearms trafficking and commercial arson. The firearms policy was directed at interdicting the flow of firearms to criminals.

For the first time in its short history, ATF had begun to address policy and planning with the inception of Project CUE. With the elimination of regional directors, decisionmaking was forced on headquarters, which now had a much larger law enforcement staff. Although regulatory procedure had always required some centralization and standardization, the law enforcement component of the agency had little experience with centralized policymaking, and the vocabulary and trappings of a rational bureaucracy were introduced. Because ATF had been a highly decentralized organization for years, the change did not come easily. In the minds of many agents, interdiction and Project CUE merged into one continuous process designed to destroy the old way of life. During CUE, small offices in the Southeastern Region and adjacent states were closed, and agents were involuntarily transferred. The new policy of interdiction demanded that agents shift from work on individual criminal violators and focus on trafficking operations. In many areas, the transition from liquor to firearms and explosives enforcement had not been difficult. Good relations with local police and United States Attorney's Offices had allowed the agents to shift their efforts to street-level criminals with relative ease. Interdiction disrupted the status quo in a way that Project CUE had not. More small offices were closed and agents moved to larger metropolitan areas. Relations with local and state police suffered when agents, complying with the new policy, refused to present cases involving felons with firearms or sawed-off shotguns for federal prosecution. Local police in firearms source states had little interest in attacking a problem that impacted areas hundreds of miles away. ATF focused its efforts on gun shops in Ohio, Virginia, Florida, the Carolinas, and along the Mexican border. Often the owners of these shops had good relations with local police officers, to whom they gave discounts on firearms and shooting supplies. In some areas, local authorities openly protested the shift in ATF resources.[8]

In spite of some opposition, ATF did change its way of doing business, particularly in relation to firearms enforcement. Resources were targeted at licensed dealers suspected of illegal transactions, unlicensed dealers, sting operations, and firearms exportation. Those cases that did target felons in possession, or possession of illegal firearms, were primarily directed at persons associated with other illegal enterprises such as drug trafficking organizations, organized crime, or criminal gangs. The storefront sting operations and concentration on gangs and organized crime created very little controversy. The investigations directed against licensed and unlicensed dealers, many of them operating out of gun shows, played directly into the strategy of the NRA and associated groups.

The targets of these dealer cases were generally white, middle-aged, and without prior criminal record. They all belonged to the NRA, and most also belonged to more strident organizations such as the Second Amendment Foundation. The two areas of greatest conflict were the definition of "engaging in the business" and a practice known as the "straw purchase."[9] The issue of engaging in the business created problems because the law did not precisely define the term. The courts historically had defined "engaging in the business" as devoting time and attention for profit. ATF and state liquor agencies had interpreted any sale of alcoholic beverage for profit in this manner with very little controversy. Unfortunately for ATF, guns and alcohol were symbolically very different commodities.

In many parts of the country, people had bought and sold guns freely, just as they did antiques and other collectibles. Some of these guns were collector's items, but most were ordinary firearms. Gun shows, which had begun as a way for collectors to display and trade their collections, evolved into swap meets for guns and associated items as the gun market expanded and evolved during the late 1960s and early 1970s. Individuals who regularly trafficked in firearms often sold at these gun shows or at swap meets and flea markets. Although sales were made routinely for profit, many of these persons pursued their activities on a part-time basis and did not consider themselves to be engaged in the business.

Although regulation of the firearms business would appear to be similar to regulation of the liquor business, significant differences existed. Licenses to sell alcoholic beverages are usually expensive and restrictive, with special exceptions for one-day events. They also require no record keeping or other obligations from sellers, other than not selling to minors and intoxicated persons. The sole purpose for dealing in alcoholic beverage is profit, and the authority of the state to regulate the activity is seldom questioned. As a result, licensing authorities have been granted discretion in issuing licenses. License costs serve to discourage applications by persons not committed to regular business activity. The GCA made firearms dealer's licenses very inexpensive and granted no discretion to ATF on issuance. The only basis for denying a license, other than the applicant being a felon or other prohibited person, was the applicant's lack of intent to engage in business from a premises. ATF, therefore, routinely refused to renew licenses for persons who did not carry on a regular volume of sales or did not have business premises.

The majority of casual and part-time sellers did not want licenses because they did not want to keep records nor operate from a fixed premises. In some cases, ATF refused to renew licenses because a dealer had made only two or three sales, usually to friends or relatives. This put ATF in the awkward position of denying licenses to those having only two or three sales but also defining engaging in the business as having even two or three sales for profit. The contradiction was not nearly so great in practice as it appeared, but it set ATF up for severe criticism.[10] Under existing law, all firearms offered by an unlicensed dealer for sale were subject to seizure and forfeiture. Seizures often involved thousands of dollars worth of guns and generated accusations that ATF was seizing whole gun collections. The crux of the problem was the lack of a clear definition of engaging in the business. This could have been easily solved with a definition that utilized the number of sales or offers to sell per year as the criteria for establishing the need for a license. For instance, any person selling or offering more than six firearms for sale in a single year could be presumed a dealer. Such presumptions existed in the definition of retail and wholesale liquor dealers. Curiously, neither side in the gun control debate pushed for such a solution, nor did ATF.[11]

The "straw purchase" issue could also be traced to gaps in the law. Dealers were prohibited from selling to certain categories of people, such as felons and minors. Nothing, however, prevented gun buyers from giving or selling the gun to a prohibited person. The dealer could not be held liable for the actions of the purchaser, and the law's authority did not extend to the purchaser. The issue was addressed in hearings, but no solution was crafted, primarily because it would have required a massive extension of the law into private transactions.[12] If the dealer were a party to the agreement, however, there was a criminal conspiracy and the dealer was criminally liable. In the most aggravated cases, out-of-state purchasers contacted a dealer to purchase multiple handguns and the dealer would provide someone to execute the forms, thus effecting a straw purchase. In these cases, the dealer knew the buyer of record was not a party to the transaction and therefore was making a prohibited sale. More often, the buyer brought his or her own straw purchaser to the dealer.[13]

Focus on Management

Although the Carter administration efforts at rationalization of federal law enforcement through reorganization failed (see Chapter 6), this policy theme did impact ATF in other ways. Rex Davis was eased out as director and replaced by a career administrator from the Customs Service, G. R. Dickerson, who was a lifetime member of the NRA and had spent his entire professional career in Washington. His experience had convinced him that problems had managerial solutions and that interest groups could be accommodated if a good-faith effort was made.[14] Although Customs operates in an active interest environment, it is one dominated by commercial entities. By their very nature, such entities are motivated to minimize public controversy and reach compromises that will maximize their economic interests. Typically these would be importers of a class of product who wished to receive favorable interpretation of the rules. Unfortunately for Dickerson, the firearms lobby had far different motives and character than most commercial lobbies. The NRA lobby was motivated to maximize conflict and public attention. Unlike commercial interests that sought friendly relations with administrative bureaucracies, the NRA had no need to pursue an amicable working relationship.

Dickerson attempted to reach accommodation with the leadership of the NRA and to separate the dealers and manufacturers from the ideological component of the lobby. Although he had numerous cordial meetings with NRA executive secretary Harlan Carter, he made little headway. Carter candidly explained that NRA interest was not served by compromise or accommodation.[15] The tactic of dividing the lobby failed because the commercial component was simply too weak. Although NRA membership stood at about two million, only about 10 percent of that number were licensed dealers or manufacturers. Of this number, only a small minority actually engaged in the business as a primary livelihood. Most were part-time dealers or individuals who had required the license to obtain wholesale guns through interstate shipment. Even among full-time commercial retail dealers, personal distaste for firearms control and the need to pacify their customer base precluded many from openly supporting initiatives that would financially benefit them.[16]

Dickerson experienced another frustration with political origins. Although he created the new position of assistant director for strategic planning and tasked that office with developing a comprehensive firearms policy, rational management could never overcome the lack of consistency in the firearms laws. Nor could it resolve the internal conflicts in Congress and public opinion that created these contradictions and inconsistencies. In an effort to merge political symbolism and rational planning, the new policy called for a focus on "crime guns." Unfortunately, there is no such rational category. Guns become crime guns when they are used in crimes. Research has revealed that such firearms came from a variety of sources, including theft, licensed dealers, unlicensed dealers, casual transactions, and associates.[17] Other than theft, these sources differ little from the sources of firearms for lawful purposes. In fact, because many crimes of violence are spontaneous, firearms could be converted from one category to another in an instant. The technology for interdicting firearms to criminals, while leaving all others unaffected, did not exist. There was no means for identifying either the firearms or the streams of commerce that should be controlled. The agency, therefore, experienced as much frustration in applying rational management solutions as in simply following the law. The lack of an acceptable solution precluded rationality in both writing law and designing administrative policy. Ultimately, any effective control would impact individuals who were not criminals and firearms that would never be used in crimes.

ATF was far more successful in applying management innovation to regulation of the alcohol industry. The long-established practice of placing inspectors on bonded premises was extensively examined. Test projects were run to verify that revenues were not impacted. All studies indicated that removal of the inspectors involved little risk and eventually would save four hundred employee years that could be redirected toward other duties. Surprisingly, resistance came not only from the union but also from the industry.[18] The presence of a government inspector had long been viewed as a deterrent to employee theft by distillers.[19] They emphasized that liquor in bond was protected by the government and its theft could result in federal prosecution.[20] In addition, the on-premises inspectors were well known to the distillers and trusted. There was fear that an audit system might result in more sanctions and fewer on-sight corrections. In spite of industry reservations, ATF was able to gradually proceed with the removal of inspectors from the premises over a three-year period, completing the project in 1979.[21]

Agency Under Attack

Martha Derthick has characterized congressional oversight as either blame casting or remedy seeking.[22] Congressional attention to ATF during the late 1970s was primarily the former. Although Congress later shifted to a more balanced approach, for a core of congressional opponents to gun control all oversight was part of a well-scripted production aimed at discrediting gun control laws by discrediting those who enforced them. The goal was to demonstrate that the laws, by their nature, were a threat to all citizens, and gun owners in particular. To this end, oversight functioned primarily as theater.

ATF's interdiction strategy was the last in a series of events that laid the groundwork for a concerted attack on the GCA. As with most political movements, this one involved well-scripted drama. Watergate and the Vietnam War had undermined trust in the federal government. Congress had shifted its focus from legislation to oversight, the gun lobby had energized its broad-based public support through fear, the 1978 elections had shown a continuing conservative shift in the voting public, and ATF had provided visible "victims" of gun control by prosecuting unlicensed dealers. Key opponents of gun control in Congress, such as Representatives Ashbrook and Dingell and Senator McClure, had advocated the repeal of the GCA for several years. The stage was set for the first key battle in the campaign against the GCA.

In the drama that was to unfold, the gun lobby and many in Congress assigned ATF the important role of villain. The new director, G. R. "Bob" Dickerson, had walked into an ambush, of which he would be the most visible casualty. The drama was to be played out in oversight hearings. The Carter administration lacked any ability to control even the Democrats in Congress by 1979, and it was every man or woman for themselves. Ironically, it would be Senator Dennis DeConcini of Arizona who chaired the first of the hearings, which was an oversight hearing for the 1980 budget. DeConcini was a former state attorney general and county prosecutor, who later became ATF's greatest advocate and protector in Congress.[23]

The NRA and other control opponents prepared meticulously for their assault on the GCA. The NRA had hired former assistant commissioner of customs Mike Acree and his investigative staff to review ATF cases in several eastern states and render an opinion on the propriety of ATF operation.[24] They also had retained Phoenix attorney David Hardy, who produced a monograph entitled *The BATF's War on Civil Liberties: The Assault on Gun Owners*.[25] These researchers had solicited information on cases in which the defendants felt wronged. They also concentrated on cases in which the government had failed to convict, particularly those in which the judge had dismissed actions or expressed displeasure with the government's case or tactics. Cases cited covered a nine-year period.

By merging fact, innuendo, opinion, and falsehood, the investigation produced several instances in which the defendants were alleged to be law-abiding citizens who were the victims of government abuse.[26] Their analysis was that although ATF had universally violated the rights of gun owners, the ultimate villain was an evil and ambiguous law that made such events inevitable.[27] Although ATF and the Department of the Treasury made some response, the tactics of Director Dickerson were largely to promise that such problems would not occur in the future. Although this tactic might have pacified an interest group pursuing compromise, with the NRA it served only to legitimate the accusations and encourage future attacks.

Notes

1. In this context, "conservative" relates to the willingness to expand federal authority and jurisdiction. Although Republican administrations

have generally advocated narrowing federal involvement in social issues, they have been supportive of increased involvement in drug enforcement, street crime, and sentencing.

2. James Q. Wilson, *The Investigators* (New York: Basic Books, 1978) 129.

3. Rooted in the assumption that the primary responsibility for law enforcement rests with the states and that the federal government should defer to state action unless the government is the victim or the states are unable or unwilling to act, the operational definition of "federal interest" has changed with the administrations and the political climate. The Carter administration defined large-scale drug cases, public corruption, and white-collar crime as the primary federal priorities.

4. The attitude and support of assistant United States attorneys differed significantly from district to district, but universally they viewed criminal record and reputation for current criminal activity as factors favoring prosecution.

5. Strike Forces were semi-autonomous federal prosecutive offices tasked to prosecute organized crime in major cities. They were largely independent of the United States Attorney's Office.

6. Interview with William Albright, one of the ATF special agents involved in the development of arson prosecutions in the Philadelphia Division.

7. The impetus for the merger apparently came primarily from the office of the assistant secretary and not from ATF management. A key participant in the effort to centralize ATF was Robert Sanders, who would later rise to the position of assistant director before leaving ATF and becoming closely identified with the NRA.

8. The most notable was Kentucky, where federal judges, prosecutors, and local and state police all directed protests to the director of ATF and members of Congress. Local and state officers began to take gun cases directly to the U.S. Attorney's Office for prosecution. This reaction was the result of several factors. In general, these states had weak firearms laws and poorly funded justice systems. ATF historically had provided substantial law enforcement support and the federal courts and prosecutors had been willing to litigate the cases. The federal courts and prosecutors had devoted substantial time to the prosecution of illicit liquor cases and made the transition to firearms when moonshine began to decline. Local and state officers came to depend on ATF resources to assist them in their efforts. Thus there was widespread vested interest among ATF agents, police, federal prosecutors, and judges in perpetuating the system. Prosecutions generally fell on common street criminals, who had few sympathizers and no organized interest group.

9. The testimony before the various oversight committees in 1980 and 1981 is replete with these two issues, as are numerous articles in every firearms journal. For an in-depth presentation of the argument, see David T. Hardy's monograph *The BATF's War on Civil Liberties: The Assault on Gun Owners* (Bellevue, Wash.: Second Amendment Foundation, 1979).

10. In fact, unlicensed dealers did not sell only two or three firearms but regularly offered dozens for sale. Common investigative practice was to make several purchases over a period of time. Because investigative funds and undercover agents were in limited supply, the number of buys was normally limited to three or four to show a pattern. Opponents regularly pointed to these cases and accused ATF of making someone a dealer for

three sales. This seldom created problems in court, where the offers of more sales could be introduced. But opponents did not have to present this aspect of the investigation and defendants seldom admitted to sales not documented by the government. Undoubtedly, some overzealous agents pursued cases against individuals who were not significant dealers and in some cases may have come close to the practice of entrapment. This was not, however, either policy or the prevalent practice. In addition to management controls, the United States attorneys acted as a very effective level of review, refusing to prosecute cases that did not appear to have jury appeal. Agents knew that "burning" an assistant U.S. attorney with a bad case would result in future rejections of cases.

11. Presumably, control advocates saw no political advantage in solving this dilemma and opponents would be unlikely to accept any limit that would be meaningful. ATF's failure to pursue a solution likely results from its lack of access to the policy process and the lack of input from the field, where perception of the problem was the greatest. The author personally attempted to develop interest in pursuing a legislative remedy, particularly in the Office of Chief Counsel, but had little success.

12. Committee on Judiciary, Subcommittee to Investigate Juvenile Delinquent Handgun Control, 1975–1976, 94th Congress, 1st session.

13. Successful prosecution depended upon being able to demonstrate that the dealer clearly understood and acknowledged that the purchaser of record was only an intermediary to conceal the identity of the true purchaser. Such falsification of records was a felony, even if the seller did not know the actual purchaser was a prohibited person. As with unlicensed-dealer cases, some agents very likely exercised poor judgment in pursuit of cases that might better have been terminated, but the review by the United States Attorney's Office was the greatest deterrent to poor cases. Because of the publicity given to such cases by the NRA and other organizations, most dealers were sure that they had been contacted by undercover agents seeking to test them. In reality, very few were. Several dealers told the author, proudly, that they had been approached by undercover agents but had refused to make such sales. None of these dealers was the subject of an ATF undercover investigation. It is likely that the NRA allegations accomplished a higher level of compliance with the law than ATF ever could have done.

14. Interviews with former directors G. R. Dickerson and Steve Higgins and with former associate director William Drake.

15. Interview with G. R. Dickerson.

16. Licensed dealers constantly complained to agents and inspectors that unlicensed dealers and licensed "kitchen table" dealers were not complying with the law. Although some joined the Stocking Gun Dealers and advocated higher dealer fees and stricter controls, most refused to make any public complaint, fearing that they would be associated with advocates of gun control.

17. Mark Moore, "An Analysis of the Potential and Current Importance of Alternate Sources of Handguns to Criminal Offenders," an unpublished paper, undated. Numerous ATF studies and agent experience are supportive of Moore's findings.

18. Interview with Steve Higgins, former ATF director.

19. Inspectors were only present where there was significant potential for revenue loss. Thus wineries and breweries usually did not have on-premises inspectors because their rate of taxation was much lower.

20. In fact, such prosecution was not common, although agents were occasionally requested to investigate losses.

21. Interview with Steve Higgins.

22. Martha Derthick, *Agency Under Stress: The Social Security Administration* (Washington, D.C.: Brookings Institution, 1990) 154.

23. DeConcini regularly defended ATF's budget and was the most visible defender of the agency after the incident at Waco, Texas, in which ATF agents and members of the Branch Davidians were killed in a shoot-out.

24. U.S. Congress, Senate, *Oversight Hearings on Bureau of Alcohol, Tobacco and Firearms*, July 11, 1979, 16–20.

25. Hardy.

26. The truthfulness and significance of the various charges are in great dispute. One version of events reflected the defendants' interpretation and the other the government's. Both sides cited court outcomes as proof of their position and ignored such outcomes when they were not favorable. The NRA investigators made no effort to compare the number or type of complaints generated by ATF action with those generated by like-sized agencies. The author conducted an extensive review of the official files on these cases in 1981 and was personally present at one of the incidents in question, the San Jose Gun Show. Based on this information, it is the author's conclusion that some of the information presented was less than truthful in specific fact and more so in overall impression. As an example, investigators alleged that only a small percentage of ATF investigations were directed toward deliveries of firearms to felons. The low proportion of cases in this category resulted from the nature of ATF's reporting system. These cases were classified as "felons receiving firearms" or "dealers falsifying records" and constituted the largest category of cases investigated by ATF. The investigators could have determined this by asking a few simple questions. Likewise, Acree's conclusions about the typical defendant in firearms cases (1979 Senate hearings, 17) do not conform with the observations of the author, who observed countless such cases first-hand and reviewed the files of many more.

27. See Hardy and conclusions and testimony of Neal Knox before the Subcommittee on the Constitution, U.S. Congress, *Gun Control and Constitutional Rights*, hearings, September 15, 1980.

CHAPTER 6

Mergers and Reorganizations

Throughout ATF's short history, reorganization and merger have been recurring themes. These initiatives derived almost exclusively from concern with the agency's law enforcement functions and largely ignored the regulatory component. Although collection of revenue is the most vital function performed by ATF, it has generated very little interest among politicians or the public, even though loss of the revenues produced by liquor and tobacco taxes would plunge the federal government into an immediate financial crisis. As with such vital municipal services as water and sewer, however, the revenue function has been routinized so successfully that it is taken for granted as inevitable.[1] Only if this function were disrupted would it attract attention. Ironically, the law enforcement function, which serves a far less vital function, has become the target of political entrepreneurs.

Certain structural and political dynamics have generated the recurrent attention directed at ATF's law enforcement function. Much of the attention grows from the peculiar structure of federal law enforcement, which derives from a series of historical accidents. The random division of the law enforcement function between departments, particularly Treasury and Justice, and the subdivision into several bureaus and agencies directly affronts the values and culture of modern public administration. Public administration has long favored orderliness and consistency not present in federal law enforcement structure. There are two potential models for structuring the government's law enforcement function. A generalist design would focus on criminal investigation as the core technology and assign all criminal investigation responsibilities to a single agency. If the technology of criminal investigation requires subdivision by specialty, then agencies would be organized around those specialties. For example, all investigation of organized crime or all investigation of financial crimes might be assigned to a single agency. The existing federal system mixes these two models randomly and without any apparent concern for consistency, efficiency, or clear lines of authority.

The FBI exists as a generalist agency, while the Drug Enforcement Administration (DEA), ATF, the IRS, Customs, the Secret Service, and the Immigration and Naturalization Service (INS) exercise jurisdiction over specialty areas. The logic of this system has been undercut by multiple agencies exercising jurisdiction over the same criminal acts, and tasks requiring the same technology being assigned to different agencies. As an example, the DEA has primary responsibility for drug law enforcement, but the FBI, Customs, the IRS, the INS, and ATF have all pursued major narcotics enforcement initiatives. In the case of bombing investigations, ATF is generally recognized as the agency with the greatest specialization. Yet the most sensitive cases are likely to be pursued by the FBI on the grounds that they constitute domestic terrorism. The existing structure assures competition and conflict over turf, duplication of effort and expertise, and substantial confusion regarding jurisdiction. The most common justification for fragmentation or decentralization—preventing excessive concentration of power—does not provide much support for the existing system. The existence of other agencies has not served to effectively limit either the size or authority of the FBI, always the prime suspect in any concern over excessive federal authority. The exclusive jurisdiction over national security concentrates the most potentially dangerous authority entirely within the FBI.

Concern with reorganizing the rather fragmented and irrational structure of federal law enforcement has surfaced periodically for over half a century.[2] Although other areas of government have similarly fragmented structure, such as the division of public land management responsibility between the Departments of Agriculture and the Interior and the further division within Interior between the Park Service and the Bureau of Land Management, they have commanded less attention. The underlying political reasons for this disparity in interest help to explain the second element that has driven efforts to reorganize ATF's law enforcement function. Federal law enforcement activities have received far more attention than can be explained by the relative magnitude of the federal role.[3] An examination of political campaign rhetoric since 1968 provides a probable explanation. Despite the federal government's relatively small role in providing law enforcement services in the United States, law enforcement and crime have been a recurrent theme of every national election campaign since 1968. This was particularly true of the presidential elections of 1968, 1972, 1980, and 1988. In each instance the Republicans successfully utilized crime issues as a key component in their successful campaigns. Because law enforcement and crime have proven important symbolic political issues, the structure and operation of the federal law enforcement bureaucracy has been an appealing target for political entrepreneurs.

ATF, in particular, is an appealing target for reorganization because of its unique structural situation and the lack of potential political and functional consequences that would result from a reorganization. Although it is situated in the Treasury Department, its law enforcement jurisdiction has little to do with Treasury functions. Other Treasury enforcement agencies have much stronger ties to historically Treasury functions. The Criminal Investigation Division of the IRS and the Customs Office of Investigation are deeply imbedded in far larger functions, with long histories in Treasury. ATF's revenue and compliance functions share a similar history, and alcohol enforcement was highly compatible with revenue protection, while firearms and explosives are not. The United States Secret Service has long been the Treasury Department's primary enforcement arm. Although the core technology and skills necessary for counterfeiting investigation are not unique, protection of the currency has long been a Treasury function. The Secret Service might have been a target for consolidation with the FBI except for its close association with the currency and its jurisdiction over presidential protection. Although no compelling reason exists for presidential protection to be assigned to Treasury, there may be a number of reasons that presidents do not wish the role assigned to the FBI.[4] Secret Service agents have access to extensive knowledge of the personal affairs of presidents and their immediate families. This confers immense potential power to damage the president and it is likely that few presidents desire this power to be merged with that already conferred on the director of the FBI. The Secret Service's long history of discretion has, no doubt, endeared it to presidents and assured the agency's continued independence.

The federal enforcement function most often the focus of reorganization has been narcotics control.[5] This is likely because narcotics have been politically sensitive and resistant to enforcement solutions. ATF, on the other hand, has been a target for consolidation and reorganization not because of the interest in its jurisdiction but because of its apparent vulnerability and its lack of a well-defined, specialized enforcement mission. On first inspection, merger or reorganization appears to present few problems technically or politically. However, numerous efforts have failed.

The Carter Reorganization

Jimmy Carter made government reorganization a central theme of his presidential campaign.[6] He promised to consolidate and rationalize the federal bureaucracy as he had the state government in Georgia. A large reorganization task force was assembled, utilizing personnel detailed from existing agencies. Teams were assigned to specific areas, one of which was law enforcement. Early in the evaluation process, the enforcement team was informed that the FBI was not subject to any reorganization. Subsequently, this mandate was also extended to the Secret Service.[7] The primary focus became border operations, where Customs and the INS frequently overlapped and duplicated functions. A proposal for creation of a Border Management Agency that would control all primary border operations was developed. Originally, the agency was proposed as a Justice function, but the Reorganization Committee reversed this proposal and recommended Treasury as the parent department. The resulting plan would have required the transfer of numerous personnel from the INS to Customs.[8]

At this point events become somewhat less clear. Attorney General Griffin Bell gave at least one speech in which he proposed the merger of the FBI, the DEA, and ATF. He subsequently pursued the FBI-DEA merger but did not address ATF. The understanding in ATF was that its law enforcement functions would be moved to the Justice Department as a means of balancing the loss of INS personnel and jurisdiction.[9] The proposal for the first phase was presented to Congress, where it met opposition from House Judiciary Chairman Peter Rodino.[10] Opposition had developed from the union representing INS employees and from Mexican-American political organizations.[11] More important, the transfer of personnel to Treasury would remove the Judiciary Committee's control over their activities.[12] Chairman Rodino managed to convince the administration to withdraw the proposal, allegedly for resubmission the next year. There was no resubmission, and Rodino inserted language precluding the use of funds for movement of uniformed personnel from the INS to Customs in the 1979 budget. The border management reorganization was stopped dead and with it the entire Carter reorganization initiative.[13] Although ATF was not to be directly included in the border management initiative, its fate very likely turned on the success of that effort.

As Derthick has noted, Congress has often contested the president for control of an administration.[14] She also has characterized Congress as both imperious and indifferent to agency operations. In this case, Congress displayed all of these characteristics. Congress also became more assertive in its relations with the executive branch, a pattern that has continued since. The precedent of inserting language blocking executive reorganization into budget bills would again play a part in ATF's history. Although the Carter administration's reorganization proposals initially appeared important for ATF's future, they ultimately had less impact on ATF than administration efforts at directing federal law enforcement resources at federal interest cases and the emerging militancy of the firearms lobby. With the exception of a few top-level executives, ATF personnel largely ignored the entire event. Such would not be the case in the next reorganization effort.

From Abolition to Merger

The election in 1980 of Ronald Reagan brought an administration with strong conservative credentials to power and shifted control of the Senate to the Republicans. The Reagan-Bush campaign had expressed concern for what it described as the entrapment of legitimate gun owners by ATF, and the gun lobby had backed the ticket.[15] Conventional wisdom in Washington was that ATF would soon be abolished as an agency.[16] Initially, the administration considered transferring ATF's functions to the IRS or the Customs Service.[17] In the fall of 1981, a plan was hatched among outgoing Assistant Secretary of the Treasury Richard Davis, incoming Assistant Secretary John Walker, Deputy Assistant Secretary Robert Powis, and Secret Service Director John Simpson to attempt a merger of ATF's law enforcement personnel and functions into the Secret Service. Powis was a former assistant director of the Secret Service and close friend of Simpson's. He had a strong motivation to both protect the agents in ATF and expand the Secret Service. Davis was seeking a means of protecting the agents and the firearms enforcement function, and Walker likely viewed the merger as a means of reducing political conflict and serving the administration. The plan was approved by the White House, no doubt with the expectation that it would please everyone.[18] In conjunction with moving the law enforcement function to the Secret Service, the administration initially considered moving the regulatory and compliance functions to the IRS but eventually decided to move these functions to the Customs Service.[19]

The Secret Service and ATF had a long association. New agents for both agencies attended the same initial training and many continued to socialize. Other Treasury enforcement agencies had long been mandated to assist the Secret Service with protective duties, but the demand greatly accelerated in June of 1968, when Robert Kennedy was assassinated and the Secret Service assumed responsibility for candidates. Subsequently, the protection of visiting foreign heads of state was transferred from the Department of State to the Secret Service, further increasing the need for periodic support. Among the Treasury agencies, ATF usually provided the greatest support and was the first called upon. At the same time, the Secret

Service found itself with ever-increasing protective responsibilities but little increase in its basic law enforcement mission. This had two effects. There often were not adequate agents to fill short-term protective assignments, particularly during campaigns, and the opportunity to work criminal investigations rather than protection was decreasing. Although some agents pursued the higher-profile protective assignments, which offered lucrative paid overtime and a dashing image, others soon tired of the work. Protection is not law enforcement. Security personnel are usually second-class citizens at the beck and call of others, and although the work appears glamorous to outsiders, it is often deadly dull. Secret Service morale had therefore suffered from the limited law enforcement jurisdiction.

Although some have assumed that the Secret Service was the primary opponent to the merger with ATF, it would more appropriately be described as a principal advocate. Even the majority of ATF employees accepted the merger as both inevitable and the best available option.[20] Many within ATF's law enforcement staff welcomed the proposal as a means of ending their perceived vulnerability to political attack from the firearms lobby. Initially, even the compliance component of ATF did not actively oppose the merger.[21] This ended, however, after Assistant Secretary Powis addressed senior ATF law enforcement managers and advised them that protection was assured for all law enforcement personnel but not essentially for other ATF employees.[22]

Concern among regulatory employees increased, and in December 1981 Deputy Assistant Director for Compliance William Drake met with Chuck Chamberlain, a former congressman and partner in Webster, Chamberlain, and Bean, and Burkett Van Kirk, from the staff of the Senate Appropriations Committee, to discuss opposition to the merger.[23] Webster, Chamberlain, and Bean were lobbyists for Miller Brewing Co. Both Chamberlain and Van Kirk had close ties with the NRA.[24] The purpose of the meeting was to initiate an effort by the liquor industry to stop the merger. The alcohol industry had a vital interest in preserving ATF's role in regulation of the industry.[25] Their concern for the impact of the merger on this role was heightened after representatives of the alcohol beverage industry met with Commissioner of Customs William Von Raab, as well as ATF and Treasury officials, to discuss the transition of the revenue and compliance function to Customs. Von Raab, who had a reputation for lacking prudence and tact, took a very adversarial position and alienated the industry representatives.[26]

Initially, the firearms lobby seemed confused and unable to decide on a response to the merger.[27] They had called for ATF's elimination for several years and the administration had responded to their demands. Within a few weeks, however, their opposition to the proposal began to solidify. Ostensibly, the opposition reflected concern that the Secret Service would constitute an equal threat to citizens' rights in enforcing gun laws. In reality, the opposition was more likely reflective of the potential loss of a symbolic issue. As long as ATF existed, the firearms lobby could utilize it as a symbolic opponent. Without an ATF, the firearms lobby lost a key actor in the ritual drama—the villain. This would have undermined recruiting and organizing, as well as shifting focus away from abolishing gun laws. Although their opposition made sense politically, it appeared irrational on the surface and discouraged taking a high-profile position. This did not prevent behind-the-scenes opposition.

The Senate Appropriations Committee conducted hearings during February and March of 1982, ostensibly as a function of budget oversight. Although the merger had been announced late in 1981, it was to take effect incrementally over a period of several months. The Senate hearings were chaired by Senator James Abnor of South Dakota, a recipient of substantial NRA financial support. A key Abnor staff member, Van Kirk, had been present, along with Chamberlain, at the initial meeting to plan opposition to the merger.[28] The hearings were dominated by witnesses from the alcoholic beverage industry, state liquor control agencies, and the insurance industry, all of whom were opposed to the merger.[29] As a result of the hearings, Congress included language in the fiscal 1982 budget that prohibited the use of funds to merge ATF and the Secret Service. Without this action the merger would have moved ahead automatically, since ATF was not created by legislation but by administrative order. Congress thus blocked what had appeared an inevitable administrative action primarily in response to interest group pressure.

Although the Secret Service was supportive of the merger and on the surface made every effort to communicate that it was a joining of equals, no one in ATF or the Secret Service believed this. The agencies were roughly comparable in size, and although ATF had broader law enforcement jurisdiction, Secret Service was far more politically powerful. It had over twice as many field divisions as ATF and thus far more special agents in charge. In general, their managers were one grade higher than comparable ATF managers. This would have assured that most key positions in the new organization would have gone to Secret Service people. Secret Service also had the advantage of a better public image and close association with the president. Most of all, the protective mission positioned the Secret Service for structural domination. This mission would have remained the top priority and justified placing managers with protective experience in almost every key position. Although Secret Service personnel were very careful never to say so, ATF agents knew they would always be second-class citizens.[30] ATF agents accepted the merger idea only because they saw no other escape from their politically vulnerable position.

Postmortem of a Failure

The merger plan had appeared to be a natural solution for the administration. The campaign promises to do something about ATF would have been fulfilled, while providing needed resources to the Secret Service. The natural opponents of merger, the effected agencies, were largely co-opted. Any Secret Service opposition was muted by an interest in expansion of its mission, while for ATF the alternatives had been framed as abolition or merger. Although no one actually knew the long-term impact on budget, this type of merger can always be portrayed as a cost-cutting measure that eliminates duplication. Neither agency was responsible for dispersing government benefits and no congressional committee had displayed a proprietary interest in ATF, thus Congress was not expected to take much interest. Equally as important, full legal authority rested with the secretary of the treasury, thus not requiring legislation.

Given the favorable conditions, why did the merger fail? The primary reason was the lack of institutional knowledge within the Department of the Treasury. Success required avoiding opposition from the interest groups. The relationship between the alcoholic beverage industry and ATF had a long history, well understood within ATF. ATF management, however, had no part in the planning process. The firearms lobby presented even more complex problems than the liquor interests. Most lobbies are motivated by the economic interests of their members. They have a vested interest in working quietly behind the scenes and in seeking compromise. The gun lobby is quite the opposite. They have every motivation to maximize conflict and make every issue public.[31] The gun lobby does not depend upon a few powerful commercial clients. It is a grass-roots lobby in the truest sense. It shares this characteristic with certain other interest groups, such as retired persons, abortion opponents, and the Christian Right.

The merger plan also overlooked the historic reservations in Congress toward the administrative presidency.[32] Congress does not recognize an absolute executive prerogative in issues of administration. In a repeat of the pattern that had blocked Secretary Morgenthau's 1936 effort at consolidation of Treasury enforcement into a single organization and the Carter administration's plan to shift border functions, narrow lobby interests had been able to mobilize a key committee chairman and block the reorganization. Unlike a parliamentary system, American political culture and structure allow the legislature to directly intervene in the daily operation of the bureaucracy. There are always key legislators who presume any initiative generated solely by the executive is suspect and a challenge to the authority of the Congress. In this, as in most cases, the administration likely could have pushed the action through, if it were willing to pay the political price. Issues of organization and administration seldom have enough political value to justify the cost, however. They have few external constituencies and seem always to have some opposition.

In the case of Treasury, law enforcement is peripheral to the primary focuses of the department: tax and monetary policy. Even the secretary is therefore unwilling to waste any credits with Congress to facilitate law enforcement operations. This leaves the bureaus largely to fend for themselves.[33] In the case of the merger, both the opponents and supporters of ATF found common ground in opposition to the plan. The Secret Service, which is largely buffered from direct congressional intervention because of its protective role, had never had the need nor opportunity to develop effective external interest support. Because the Secret Service has a relatively small and noncontroversial law enforcement jurisdiction, the agency has little experience with hostile congressional oversight. A merger with ATF and the assumption of the firearms laws very likely would have been a new and disturbing experience for an agency used to little controversy and an environment of benign neglect.

Notes

1. The concept of routinizing and buffering critical technologies and functions was developed by James Thompson in his classic study *Organizations in Action* (New York: McGraw Hill, 1967).

2. Arthur Millspaugh, *Crime Control by the Federal Government* (Washington, D.C.: Brookings Institution, 1937).

3. Because the federal government was not granted police power by the Constitution, law enforcement has always been predominantly a state and local function.

4. Congress mandated protection of the president after the assassination of President McKinley. The federal government had only one law enforcement agency at the time, the Secret Service.

5. William Lee Colwell, "An Examination of the 1982 Decision to Reorganize the FBI and the DEA," DPA dissertation, University of Southern California, 1985.

6. Lawrence Lynn, *Managing the Public's Business* (New York: Basic Books, 1981) 88.

7. At the time of the study, team members advised the author that this was the prevailing understanding.

8. Interviews with Mike Lane and Michael Wink. Both served on the reorganization task force and were primarily concerned with the border initiative.

9. The exact agenda is not clear. Very little of this plan was committed to paper and memories have become hazy. Mike Wink told the author that he remembered discussion but not specific plans. The person appointed liaison to Justice from ATF is no longer available and the agency was essentially between directors. Many of the details are reconstructed from the author's conversations with participants and observations at the time.

10. Interviews with Mike Lane and Michael Wink.

11. The union opposition apparently derived from two concerns. INS employees believed that their Customs counterparts would dominate the consolidated agency, and union officials feared loss of membership because Treasury prohibited bargaining-unit representation of law enforcement employees. The Mexican-American opposition is more difficult to explain. The border management effort was apparently seen as an attempt to stop illegal immigration and thus hostile. In addition, the commissioner of the INS, who was a Mexican-American, would lose direct control of his staff and jurisdiction. The reduction in the authority of one of the few high-level Hispanic officials may have been seen as symbolically hostile by Hispanic political organizations.

12. Rodino's committee had obtained a significant increase in power over Justice Department operations in the 1976 Law Enforcement Assistance Authorization Bill, which required the department to submit a consolidated budget to the Judiciary Committee for approval. Although the committee would have retained control over immigration law, it would have lost direct control of the staffing and operations relating to border functions. Control over these functions would have moved to committees overseeing the Treasury Department budget.

13. The Carter administration did not accomplish a single agency merger but did reorganize the Civil Service Commission.

14. Martha Derthick, *Agency Under Stress: The Social Security Administration* (Washington, D.C.: Brookings Institution, 1990) 17.

15. Undated press release from the Reagan-Bush Committee entitled "Gun Control."

16. Rodger Davidson, *The Postreform Congress* (College Park: University of Maryland Press, 1992) 51. The author, who was assigned to ATF headquarters in 1981, can also confirm this.

17. U.S. Congress, Senate hearings, *Proposed Dissolution of the Bureau of Alcohol, Tobacco and Firearms*, 1982, 374.

18. Interviews with former deputy assistant secretary of the treasury Robert Powis and former assistant secretrary of the treasury Richard Davis.

19. Testimony of Assistant Secretary John Walker, Senate hearings, February 23 and March 8, 1982.

20. Testimony of Joseph Price, Federal Criminal Investigators Association, Senate hearings, 1982, 131.

21. Interview with William Drake, ATF deputy assistant director for compliance.

22. Ibid. Treasury officials continued to assume the regulatory function would be transferred to either the IRS or Customs. Eventually the Customs option was favored. Either option would have significantly reduced the status and autonomy of the regulatory function and eliminated regulatory and administrative positions.

23. Interview with William Drake.

24. Ibid.

25. ATF served as a stabilizing force in the liquor market, and thus filled a vital role. Its regulatory management was highly accessible to industry representatives and sympathetic to their needs.

26. Interview with Robert Powis. Powis, G. R. Dickerson, and Steve Higgins all report that Van Raab was confrontational and condescending in his approach. Van Raab's lack of prudence gained significant attention when he restricted all passage across the Mexican border without notifying the State Department or White House.

27. Senate hearings, 1982, 223–224.

28. The hearings were clearly orchestrated by the liquor lobby. Although the NRA was supportive of the effort, it was not the principal actor. Any knowledgeable observer could see that there was only one possible outcome to the hearing well before it concluded.

29. A review of the hearing record reveals that the witnesses were stacked against the merger proposal and that the tone of questioning by subcommittee members, particularly Senators Abnor and DeConcini, was distinctly hostile to the proposal.

30. This would likely have been far less pronounced among field agents than managers. A number of ATF agents did transfer directly to the Secret Service in the period immediately following the blocking of the merger. Based on periodic contacts with these agents and reports from individuals in the Secret Service, the author has determined that these agents quickly integrated into the Secret Service and became indistinguishable. They were, however, almost universally young agents with fewer than ten years service with ATF.

31. For a general discussion of the gun lobby, particularly the National Rifle Association, see Davidson; Josh Sugarmann, *National Rifle Association: Money, Power and Fear* (Washington, D.C.: National Press Books, 1992); William J. Vizzard, "The Evolution of Gun Control Policy in the United States: Accessing the Public Agenda," DPA dissertation, University of Southern California, 1993.

32. James Q. Wilson, *Bureaucracy: What Government Agencies Do and Why They Do It* (New York: Basic Books, 1989) 235–256; Derthick, 82–92.

33. Interview with Charles Sorentino, former Treasury Department law enforcement staff member.

CHAPTER 7

Recovery

Although ATF's budget and staffing were reduced in the period immediately following the merger effort, the agency's fate took a sudden and unexpected turn within a year. The confluence of several forces began to generate a recovery in the agency that would result in its most successful era. The first of these was the commitment of Senator Abnor to rebuilding ATF. Abnor, who had been the pivotal member of Congress in blocking the merger with the Secret Service and had presided over the subcommittee hearings that assured congressional action on the merger, began to shepherd increases in ATF's budget through Congress.[1] Beginning with the 1984 budget, ATF was able to begin a rebuilding of staff and resources that later received support from the Reagan and Bush administrations as a component of their crime and drug initiatives. Between 1984 and 1992 ATF's law enforcement staffing nearly doubled.

In addition to the emergence of support in Congress and the administration, internal changes within ATF proved critical to the resurgence of the agency. The most important of these was the appointment of Steve Higgins as director. Higgins had spent his entire career in the regulatory functions of ATF, and his selection was very likely influenced by the preferences of the alcohol beverage lobby.[2] He had risen rapidly after beginning as an inspector in Omaha in 1961, becoming the only regional director with a regulatory background in 1973. By 1979, he was the deputy director and became acting director with the departure of G. R. Dickerson. Although he had a regulatory background, Higgins was well regarded by most law enforcement personnel who knew him. Higgins's appointment assured both close relations with the alcoholic beverage industry and management support for continuation of ATF as an independent bureau with both regulatory and enforcement functions.

Higgins proved an able manager, and worked well with Congress and the department. The bureau was soon restructured by eliminating the position of deputy director and elevating the two primary assistant director positions to associate director. Although assistant directors remained for such functions as administration and internal affairs, the two associate directors, who headed law enforcement and regulation, became the director's deputies. Higgins delegated operation of the Office of Law Enforcement almost totally to the new associate director, Phillip McGuire. The Office of Compliance was headed by longtime Higgins associate William Drake. This team of managers proved to be highly successful in maneuvering the constantly shifting waters of official Washington. Although it was never apparent in television interviews, Higgins's disarmingly open and egalitarian style won over large and small audiences. Drake, who had been the principal actor in engineering industry opposition to the merger, was a bright and able manager who was held in high regard by both Higgins and the alcoholic beverage industry. McGuire, a charming North Carolinian, proved even more adept than Higgins at winning over almost everyone he met. Although McGuire's roots were distinctly southern, he proved far less provincial and more adaptive than his predecessors and provided a bridge between the law enforcement culture of the past and future.

With the new management team in place, two themes clearly predominated. ATF would be one bureau, not two, and it would focus on developing political and public support. The new senior managers had internalized the lessons of the past decade. ATF was no longer an obscure agency of little concern to politicians or interest groups. Constituencies, in the form of organized interest groups, were necessary to protect an agency from its opponents and to support its requests for resources. The critical role played by constituent groups during the merger hearings had dramatically demonstrated this. The new management team's efforts at rebuilding agency image and support were aided in the latter by the Reagan administration's initiatives on law enforcement and drug control.

Shortly after taking office, members of the administration began seeking initiatives that could be quickly and cheaply implemented and that would demonstrate an interest in maintaining law and order and suppressing drugs. One of the first was a joint effort by the Departments of Justice and the Treasury to provide specialized training to local and state officers at the Federal Law Enforcement Training Center (FLETC) at Glynco, Georgia.[3] ATF became a major supporter and participant in the program. The program's advisory board, composed of the presidents of every major law enforcement association in the country as well as representatives from all participating federal agencies, proved a critical springboard for McGuire and Higgins to begin cultivating personal relationships with law enforcement leaders. Both proved highly proficient at the task.

ATF managers also became very active in the International Association of Chiefs of Police. At a time when police organizations were being driven away from the firearms lobby over the issues of armor-piercing ammunition and the Gun Owners Protection Act, ATF moved to capture their support.[4] ATF had long experienced excellent relations with most local police officers, but these relations were primarily at the operational and not management levels. The reasons for the history of close cooperation and amicable relations were multiple. More than any other federal enforcement personnel, ATF agents were likely to be former police officers. In addition, they concentrated their efforts on those involved in traditional street crime and not on investigation of corrupt public officials or white-collar criminals, actions that local police viewed as both helpful and nonthreatening. Most important, agents actively pursued cooperation and displayed an attitude that did not communicate condescension or assumptions of superiority. Their behavior was born of a reality formed by ATF's lack of exclusive jurisdiction, limited resources, and weak political support. ATF agents could ill afford to antagonize or alienate local police. They therefore willingly offered assistance and cooperation to assure that the same would be forthcoming when they required it. These conditions had cultivated a reservoir of support and friendship with police at the working level; however, senior ATF managers played little part in the process. By the 1980s, police had become an important, organized interest group, and the new management team pursued police support as a conscious agency policy.[5]

South Florida Task Force

Another administration law enforcement initiative proved even more fateful in shaping ATF's future. During the late 1970s and early 1980s the Miami, Florida, area was overrun with drug activity as a result of the rapid expansion in cocaine trafficking. Violent crime greatly increased and local authorities were saying that they were on the verge of losing control of the streets. The administration responded in 1982 with the South Florida Task Force, under the direction of Vice President George Bush. Additional federal agents, prosecutors, and judges were added, in the most concentrated federal enforcement effort in the nation's history, and ATF responded with enthusiasm. The South Florida area had long been a center for firearms trafficking as well as drug trafficking, and the Colombian drug gangs that dominated Miami's criminal underworld had a penchant for both violence and firearms.

These conditions would have provided ATF with at least a peripheral role in the task force, but ATF artfully interpreted its jurisdiction as going beyond the investigation of simple firearms violations and began to pursue drug traffickers directly. Federal firearms laws contained a section that made it a separate crime to be armed while trafficking in drugs.[6] Originally, both ATF and the Justice Department interpreted this section as a sentencing enhancement, which was likely the congressional intent. The law's wording, however, created a separate crime for possessing or carrying a firearm while trafficking in drugs. This provided ATF jurisdiction over the act of selling drugs if the seller was armed, and allowed much more extensive ATF participation than would have been possible pursuing only firearms violations.[7]

While participation raised ATF's profile with the administration, it did so at the cost of the first shooting deaths of ATF agents in almost twenty years. The first case occurred in December 1982, when a group of suspects shot Ariel Rios and Alex D'Atri in a Miami motel room. As the agents attempted to purchase cocaine from several suspects inside the motel room, the suspects produced guns and demanded the purchase money. Assuming the suspects intended to kill them, the agents preempted the suspects by initiating their own move. The agents simultaneously swept the suspects' guns away, while attempting to retrieve their own concealed firearms. D'Atri was successful, but Rios was shot in the head and died at the scene. D'Atri was shot numerous times as he engaged in a face-to-face gun battle with several suspects while a team of covering agents frantically labored to pry open a security door. Although ATF lost a second agent, Eddie Benitez, to gunfire before the project ended, it was this first event that most impacted the organization.[8]

The shooting significantly raised ATF's profile as a participant in the Miami task force and sent shock waves through ATF.[9] D'Atri's heroic fight against overwhelming odds was the stuff of law enforcement legend and, along with the deaths of Rios and Benitez, pulled all of ATF law enforcement together. Over time, the shootings and the task force operations became blurred into a single symbolic event that altered ATF's image both internally and externally. In addition to the change in ATF's self-image and its public profile, the events in Miami had another long-term effect on the agency. Management was convinced that law enforcement operations had changed drastically and had become far more dangerous.[10] As much as the shootings themselves, the inability of the cover team to intervene quickly enough to protect the agents shook ATF's managers. Historically, the details of tactical operations had been delegated to individual agents and supervisors, a process that had served ATF well. The events in Miami invoked a classic bureaucratic response to crisis by convincing management that circumstances had drastically changed. ATF began to move progressively toward standardization and centralization of tactical planning. Problems of tactics, tactical training, and tactical equipment began to take on a level of importance that they had never before enjoyed.[11] The natural tendency for centralization in response to perceived risk was aggravated by the desire of ATF's headquarters staff to participate in the details of field operations.[12]

Federal Street Cops

Although ATF was reemerging as a law enforcement organization, its law enforcement priorities were being reshaped by the prevailing political environment. The enthusiasm demonstrated in the Miami operation did not extend to certain categories of firearms investigations. In a 1979 effort to blunt congressional criticism, G. R. Dickerson had instituted a requirement to obtain prior headquarters approval for all investigations of licensed firearms dealers or any investigative activity at gun shows.[13] The requirement continued under the new management team. Before conducting these investigations, agents were required to submit requests in writing. The request was then reviewed by the agent's immediate supervisor, the field division staff, the special agent in charge, and at least three staff levels in headquarters before being presented to the associate director for approval.[14] Effectively, any reviewer could deny approval. Once approved, the investigation was subject to time constraints, headquarters monitoring, and special reporting requirements. This process clearly communicated a preference for avoiding these investigations if possible and effectively discouraged most agents and supervisors from pursuing these investigations.[15] As ATF had previously shifted from a focus on individual violations to trafficking in response to the policy mandates from the Carter administration, it now shifted virtually all its enforcement resources to street-level drug traffickers and criminals in response to the priorities of the Reagan administration. If the administration's focus on street crime and drugs were not enough to communicate a shift in the focus of ATF's enforcement resources, congressional action would have done so.

Firearms Owners Protection Act

Congressional priorities were communicated through special funding for specific antidrug, violent crime, and arson initiatives and

through support of the McClure-Volkmer Bill. The McClure-Volkmer Bill, or Firearms Owners Protection Act, was first introduced in
1981. It was the direct outgrowth of the NRA campaign to characterize the Gun Control Act and its enforcement as a threat to every
law-abiding American gun owner. As originally introduced, the bill
would have rendered the GCA virtually unenforceable. Although
the administration would not allow ATF to openly oppose the bill, a
considerable amount of back-channel lobbying took place to moderate the bill.[16] The final version, enacted in 1986, proved a public
embarrassment for ATF. It established unique procedural standards
for property forfeiture, proof of guilt, and classification as a felon,
applicable only to firearms cases. It also restricted inspections of licensed dealers and prohibited ATF from issuing regulations requiring the reporting of firearms purchasers.

Three specific changes in the law had the greatest operational
impact on ATF. First, the falsification of records by firearms dealers
was reclassified from a felony to a misdemeanor, essentially precluding prosecution in most jurisdictions. United States Attorney's Offices have long been hesitant to file misdemeanor charges. This often
precluded prosecution of firearms dealers who were delivering
firearms to prohibited persons or were failing to keep records on
firearms transactions.[17] Second, engaging in the firearms business
without a license remained a felony; however, changes made it very
difficult to establish that a person was, in fact, engaged in the business.[18] The final change was to mandate minimum sentences and
prohibit probation or parole for certain firearms violators. The minimum sentence for any person with three or more prior robbery or
burglary convictions, who was convicted of possessing a firearm,
was set at fifteen years.[19] For any person convicted of possessing a
firearm during a drug-trafficking offense or violent crime, the minimum sentence was set at five years.[20] Although most violent crimes
were not prosecutable in federal court, virtually all drug-trafficking
offenses were.

The cumulative impact of these changes in law, combined with
the previous congressional oversight hearings, was to communicate
a clear preference for the use of firearms laws against street criminals and drug traffickers, rather than to control firearms commerce.
This fit well with the priorities of the administration, which had
made the "war on drugs" and violent street crime central issues in
the campaign. Not surprisingly, ATF responded by focusing its enforcement resources on these areas. Special emphasis was placed on
suspects subject to mandatory sentencing under Sections 924(e) and
924(c) of Title 18 USC, which were designated as Project Achilles.[21]
Although the arson and explosives programs continued to receive

strong support, they only constituted about 40 percent of the law enforcement work.[22]

The prevailing political climate not only affected the law enforcement operations but also regulation. In fiscal year 1983, only twenty-nine positions were allocated to the inspection of firearms dealers. This was a deliberate effort by the Department of Compliance to protect staff years if a renewed attempt was made to separate firearms from alcohol and tobacco.[23] ATF made every effort to disassociate itself from the concept of gun control. This was not as difficult as it might seem. The compliance function had consistently emphasized its relationship to alcohol regulation. The majority of ATF special agents, who perceived themselves as law enforcement officers, viewed the firearms laws as a tool for controlling criminals rather than guns. This process was reinforced by the history of hostility from many in Congress toward firearms enforcement and the obvious lack of enthusiasm in the administration.[24]

Experience revealed that aggressive pursuit of licensed and unlicensed firearms dealers generated substantial opposition and very little support. Curiously, liberals, who historically supported more restrictive firearms policies, could not be counted on to support the enforcement of these laws. This likely results from the strong civil-libertarian, anti-statist character of American liberalism. Although liberals often support firearms laws in the abstract, they are not at ease with supporting the state against individual defendants, who often characterize themselves as victims of an officious police apparatus. Thus the agency was potentially vulnerable to political attack from conservatives, who opposed gun laws, with little support from liberals, who sympathized with the defendants.

Explosives and Arson

One means of avoiding the pitfalls of firearms enforcement was to place maximum emphasis on other areas of jurisdiction. Although ATF had been given jurisdiction over interstate smuggling of cigarettes to avoid state tax, activity in this area proved less than initially expected. Far more successful initiatives were developed in the arson and explosives areas. ATF had exercised jurisdiction in arson cases on the tenuous legal argument that an accelerant was an explosive (see Chapter 5); specific jurisdiction was needed to secure the program. Senator John Glenn of Ohio had long pursued a federal arson law, but had been unsuccessful at accomplishing its passage. Although it initially was assumed that the FBI would assume jurisdiction of any such law, ATF had established a substantial track record of arson investigation and had developed close relationships with numerous local arson units. ATF proposed a solution to Senator Glenn that would achieve his goal, while protecting ATF turf. The existing law, prohibiting destruction of property involved in interstate commerce by use of explosives, could be modified by adding "or arson." Thus, with two words, the federal explosives laws would be expanded to encompass all commercial arsons. Because jurisdiction over the section to be modified, 844(i) of Title 18 USC, had been granted exclusively to ATF in the existing memorandum of agreement with the FBI, ATF would be granted exclusive federal jurisdiction over commercial arson. Senator Glenn successfully ushered the change in the explosives law through Congress and ATF's position was solidified.

A concurrent development with the successful expansion of jurisdiction into arson was the development of National Response Teams (NRTs) to investigate arsons and explosions. From the very beginning, agents realized that there were two unique skills required in bombing investigation. One was the ability to handle and disarm explosive devices. ATF resisted providing this resource, although some of its personnel were trained and qualified to do so.[25] The other skill was processing bomb scenes. This required special equipment, trained forensic chemists, and knowledgeable explosives technicians. ATF personnel have consistently cultivated these skills, more so than personnel in any other agency. The skills necessary for investigating explosives scenes are also directly applicable to arson scenes. It is in this area that ATF has reached its highest level of technical expertise.

Although the scene response by individual division offices was successful from an investigative perspective, it had several disadvantages. All other operations in the division were disrupted if a large scene response was necessary. Procedures for shifting resources from one division to another were not well established, nor were experience, equipment, and resources consistent from one division to another. Equally important, the responses lacked the symbolic impact necessary to impress all involved that the experts were on the scene and should be given deference. ATF's solution was a series of NRTs. Actually regional teams, each was operationally commanded by an assistant special agent in charge and included volunteer agents with special training, a forensic chemist, and an explosives technician.[26] Standard operating procedures for team call-outs and responses were developed, allowing rapid assembly of a team at a scene. Once on the scene, the teams work with local agents and police, providing both crime scene investigation and general investigation for the immediate follow-up of leads. The advanced preparation and working familiarity among team members greatly shortened the time necessary to deploy agents to a bombing or arson and increased the appearance of professionalism and competence. The actual and apparent effectiveness of the teams was also enhanced by extensively equipping them and providing funds and authority to on-site commanders to rent heavy equipment.[27]

Whether the teams have had a significant impact on the solution of crimes might be open to some debate, though their expertise is not often challenged.[28] Little question exists, however, regarding the public relations value of the NRTs. In the era of television, a team of investigators, wearing uniforms with ATF in large gold letters, provides an excellent opportunity for visual news. When combined with a bomb or arson scene, the teams created an irresistible focus for television news teams. Local fire and police authorities, often protective of their turf, welcomed the assistance at these scenes, which they find intimidating. Within the management of ATF, the NRTs have been perceived as an unmitigated success, a perception based primarily on their symbolic value.[29]

ATF's status as the federal agency with expertise in bombing was significantly enhanced in 1985 by investigations of abortion clinic bombings. Although bombings occurred in several parts of the country, the most visible were a series in the Washington, D.C., metropolitan area.[30] Abortion choice supporters called for a national investigation by the FBI of what they characterized as a terrorist campaign.[31] Contending that they lacked jurisdiction, the FBI deferred to ATF.[32] ATF mounted a massive effort to solve the Washington area bombings, bringing in agents from throughout the East. Three suspects were apprehended and subsequently convicted.[33] As a result, the press, which had earlier criticized the administration for passing the investigation off to a second-rate agency, was effusive in their praise of ATF.[34] For ATF, the politics of abortion were unimportant. The investigations provided the agency with what it most sought: clear jurisdiction, a defined mission, visibility, and prosecutive support. As ATF continued to pursue abortion clinic bombings and arsons with substantial success, the victims ceased viewing ATF's involvement as a sign of benign neglect. ATF's enthusiasm and technical expertise won out over political symbolism, enhancing agency confidence, pride, and image.

Public visibility, success, and jurisdiction did not always come together in explosives cases. In many joint investigations, ATF's participation tended to disappear, particularly in national news coverage. One such example was a series of letter bombs mailed to attorneys, civil rights organizations, and federal judges in 1989 by Walter Leroy Moody. Although the FBI assumed primary jurisdiction of the case, a task force incorporating ATF, postal inspectors, and the FBI was formed to work the investigation. Only days after the bombings, Lloyd Erwin, an ATF forensic chemist assigned to the Atlanta forensic laboratory, recognized the devices as similar to one he had examined several years before. In that case, Walter Leroy Moody was convicted of building the device and sentenced to prison. ATF agents quickly focused on Moody, who had since been released from prison, as the primary suspect; meanwhile, FBI agents directed their interest toward another suspect and showed little interest in ATF's views. As details began to eliminate the primary FBI suspect, attention shifted to Moody, who was subsequently arrested and convicted of bombing and murder. Although ATF's experience and expertise in bombing investigation proved critical in this case and the lead ATF agent, Brian Hoback, received a presidential commendation, the national news focused primarily on the FBI.[35]

Conversely, the FBI's capacity to overshadow ATF in joint investigations sometimes served to shield ATF from embarrassment. The FBI assumed early jurisdiction of the so-called Unabomber investigation, based on the bomber's attempt to bomb an aircraft in 1979. Although the aircraft bombing was within FBI jurisdiction, subsequent bombings clearly fell within ATF and Postal Inspection Service jurisdiction.[36] Although all three agencies and local police investigated the cases, the FBI dominated both the investigation and the competition for publicity. The Unabomber remained at large for many years and became a public embarrassment for the FBI, while the ATF and Postal Inspection Service roles were largely ignored by the media.[37] The dynamics of this case shifted again when Theodore Kaczynski was identified as a suspect by his brother. With Kaczynski's arrest at a remote Montana cabin, the FBI again became the sole recipient of favorable press attention to the case.

Sources of Future Problems

On the surface, the 1980s were highly successful for ATF. Although the decade had begun with ATF under attack in Congress, followed by administration proposals for its elimination, fortunes had reversed. By the early 1990s ATF's law enforcement staffing, which had begun to decline under the Carter administration and reached a low in the early days of the Reagan administration, had been rebuilt to 1972 levels.[38] Firearms prosecutions were receiving higher prosecutive priorities from United States attorneys than at any time in the past, and the arson and explosives programs were generating public support and favorable press attention. The firearms lobby, which had redirected its attention to the pending Brady Bill, was largely ignoring ATF. Congress generally displayed support for ATF's law enforcement initiatives, while all remained well with the compliance and revenue functions. The alcoholic beverage and insurance industries and law enforcement actively supported the agency, and the firearms industry had few complaints. ATF's fortunes were running counter to the general trend of declining budgets for federal agencies. ATF's status at Treasury had greatly increased for several reasons. First, Customs had replaced ATF as the problem child of Treasury enforcement.[39] For the first time since its inception as a bureau, ATF had a distinct advantage over its sister agency, the Secret Service. ATF could participate in the administration's attack on violent crime and drug trafficking, while the Secret Service did not have applicable jurisdiction. Director Steve Higgins had succeeded in assembling a management team that could effectively deal with Congress and Treasury and the results were showing. The agency's successes were not, however, universal. Peace with Congress and the gun lobby had been purchased at the price of largely ignoring certain classes of firearms violations. No progress had been made toward developing a national policy on gun control, and the strategy of using the firearms law to pursue low-level street criminals and drug dealers ignored the traditional federal role in law enforcement and was leading the agency toward a risky future. Finally, the successes in external relations were not mirrored in internal management.

Notes

1. Although the reasons for Abnor's support were not entirely clear, the probable reasons were the interests of the liquor industry and a real interest in the agency. The latter may have resulted from testimony by numerous ATF supporters during the hearings.

2. Although well positioned for elevation to the director's position and highly regarded within ATF, Higgins would not have been the likely selection of the assistant secretary, according to Charles Sorentino. Since ATF was perceived as a law enforcement agency, an outside selection with a law enforcement background would have been the likely choice. Sorentino, who was the law enforcement adviser to several assistant secretaries, stated that Assistant Secretary John Walker had to accept Higgins's appointment or provide substantial reason for not doing so. At least one well-placed official in Justice informally pursued the position and was advised that Higgins had already been selected. The likely source of the intervention was Senator Abnor acting at the behest of the alcohol beverage industry, which was committed to preserving ATF as a unified agency and preventing future efforts to transfer authority over regulation to Customs or the IRS.

3. The original proposal assumed that declining federal hiring would result in the underutilization of FLETC. Residual funds from the recently disbanded Law Enforcement Assistance Administration (LEAA) were used as seed money and Treasury and Justice provided staff from existing positions. Various Justice and Treasury enforcement agencies provided the staff

to develop and teach the courses, which were modeled after arson and explosives courses developed by ATF and offered to local agencies through LEAA. The program's full-time staff was composed entirely of former LEAA employees and ATF personnel.

4. Roger Davidson, *The Postreform Congress* (College Park: University of Maryland Press, 1992) 111; William J. Vizzard, "The Evolution of Gun Control Policy in the United States: Accessing the Public Agenda," DPA dissertation, University of Southern California, 1993.

5. ATF was not alone in recognizing the importance of police as a major constituency. National politicians universally sought police endorsements from the early 1980s on. Even presidential candidates routinely sought opportunities to pose with police officials.

6. Title 18 USC 924(c).

7. The act of selling drugs became an element of the crime of being unlawfully armed during a drug transaction. ATF could thus justify gathering drug evidence through such means as making undercover purchases or serving search warrants, because the drug evidence was a necessary element in proving the gun violation.

8. ATF's headquarters building was subsequently renamed the Ariel Rios Building and the vice president praised D'Atri's courage in a subsequent speech on drug enforcement, although he misidentified him as a narcotics agent. Within ATF, the inability to protect or rescue the agents produced frustration and a demand for more-advanced tactical organization, equipment, and training.

9. The author was duty agent in headquarters on the night the event occurred and the impact then and later on ATF managers in particular was very apparent.

10. Interview with former associate director Phillip McGuire.

11. The process of change was gradual. Phillip McGuire was opposed to the development of any special tactical units, but did support additional training and equipment. In addition, management was expected to be far more involved in the details of all arrests and raids. The natural outcomes of added attention from all levels of management were reduced discretion for field agents and efforts at standardization.

12. Involvement in such special projects served to both raise the profile and promotion potential of the participants and to allow desk-bound agents a chance to feel more a part of the field operations that were their primary interest. Regardless of the duration of their tenure in staff or management positions, agents always perceived themselves as agents first.

13. U.S. Congress, Senate hearing, *Oversight Hearings on Bureau of Alcohol, Tobacco and Firearms,* 1979; statement of G. R. Dickerson.

14. Over a period of years the authority for approving dealer investigations was redelegated down the organization in incremental steps to the special agent in charge.

15. If a field office or division displayed a tendency to pursue this type of case, they would receive an inquiry from the chief of the Firearms Division, requesting an explanation. The message was clear, and only a few field managers chose to ignore the implications. The policy raised serious ethical questions by creating a class of potential violators for whom investigation and prosecution were less likely. Although such deference has often been informally extended to powerful groups by law enforcement agencies de facto, this order made it agency policy. Although ATF management alleged

that the order served simply to assure quality investigations, it clearly did more. In spite of this, no critic of ATF, in Congress or elsewhere, ever raised a single question or protest to the policy, a clear indication that, whatever its ethical shortcomings, it was politically prudent.

16. Interviews with Robert Powis and former chief of the Firearms Division, Richard Cook.

17. Although other potential charges often existed, falsification or failure to maintain records was often the only charge that could be proven. For a detailed discussion see Vizzard, 1993.

18. Rather than define "engaging in the business" by the number of firearms offered for sale in a specified time frame, as is the pattern with liquor and motor vehicle dealers, livelihood and profit must be shown. In addition, several exceptions were added to the law that provided excellent defenses for any defendant. These changes virtually stopped all prosecution for engaging in the business without a license, without revoking the law.

19. Title 18 USC 924(e).

20. Title 18 USC 924(c).

21. The law mandating sentencing radically changed the perception of firearms cases for many United States attorneys. Previously, felons convicted of possessing firearms faced a maximum sentence of two years. Until the introduction of federal sentencing guidelines in 1987, only one-third of the sentence was spent in custody. Thus a felon convicted of possessing a firearm served less than one year in prison, if judges imposed the maximum possible sentence. In practice, many defendants received lesser sentences, often probation. Although ATF had advocated the firearms laws as a tool for impacting violent offenders, many United States attorneys had not responded. The change in the law not only mandated minimum sentences but set no maximum. Judges were free to sentence "armed career criminals" to up to life in prison, and no parole was allowed. The law provided ATF with a very potent tool for impacting habitual violent offenders. In 1989, the Department of Justice formalized the prosecution of these offenses under Operation Triggerlock and directed United States attorneys to give them very high priority. Subsequent changes to the law expanded the predicate crimes from burglary and robbery to any violent crime. In addition, subsequent changes in sentencing guidelines generally increased sentences for felons in possession of firearms.

22. This volume is based on agent hours and not cases. Using the standard of cases investigated, the percentage would be even lower, as arson and explosives cases tend to consume far more time.

23. Interview with William Drake, former ATF associate director for compliance.

24. Between 1981 and 1992 any public discussion of firearms control was discouraged by the administration. All ATF personnel interviewed, as well as numerous others that were not formally interviewed, confirm that the topic was to be avoided. Although eager to discuss crime and crime control, ATF officials avoided linking crime control to gun control. Essentially, the concept of gun control did not officially exist.

25. Explosives handlers were certified, as this skill was necessary to conduct explosives training. Explosives ordnance disposal, or EOD, was never embraced by ATF management. Although some of the agents and all of the explosives enforcement officers or explosives technicians had this

skill, they were prohibited from exercising it. This prohibition has been frequently violated but seldom reported. ATF has experienced only one death from explosives mishap, which occurred during the destruction of illegal fireworks and killed a Seattle agent.

26. Although not agents, firearms and explosives technicians became a critical component of the enforcement operation. This was particularly true of the explosives technicians, several of whom have built national reputations as experts in reconstructing bombing and arson scenes. For an excellent account of one such technician, or explosives enforcement officer— Jerry Taylor—see Steven Naifeh and Gregory White Smith, *The Mormon Murders* (New York: Penguin, 1989).

27. Large-scale bombing and arson scenes often require extensive equipment and safety preparations to facilitate the crime scene investigation. Two extreme examples were the New York World Trade Center and the Oklahoma City Federal Building bombings. In the New York bombing, the ATF explosives enforcement officer, who discovered the serial number of the rented truck used to transport the bomb, was suspended from a rope in a crater that was several stories deep.

28. ATF teams have conducted several scene investigations at the request of the FBI where FBI jurisdiction over the bombing was clear.

29. ATF not only received substantial favorable publicity from the NRTs but also developed constituencies in local and state police and fire agencies and insurance companies. Although ATF management evaluation of the explosives and arson responses was largely tied to publicity and constituent support, the participants were far more focused on professional performance. ATF's success in both arson and explosives investigation matches and likely exceeds that of any other agency.

30. *Washington Post*, "No Conspiracy Seen in Bombings," January 6, 1985.

31. *Washington Post*, "Call for Fed Investigation," March 1, 1985; "Mayor Criticizes FBI for Not Leading Abortion Clinic Probe," March 3, 1985; "ATF Called Experts Despite Low Profile," January 4, 1986.

32. These cases clearly were within ATF jurisdiction under the memorandum of understanding between ATF and the FBI. See the *Washington Post*, "FBI Defends Decision Not to Investigate Abortion Bombings," January 13, 1986.

33. *Washington Post*, "Abortion Foe Convicted in 10 Bombings," May 22, 1986.

34. For an example, see the *Washington Post* editorial of January 22, 1986.

35. For details of this investigation see Mark Winnie, *Postmark Terror* (New York: Scribner, 1995).

36. The FBI routinely has pursued jurisdiction over high-profile bombings on the grounds that they constitute domestic terrorism. This approach has been used even when preliminary investigation points at the suspect being a single disgruntled individual.

37. "Who Is He?" *Newsweek* (May 8, 1995) 40–41.

38. Two thousand special agents by the 1991 fiscal year.

39. Charles Sorrentino, former adviser to the undersecretary for enforcement, attributed this both to ATF's successes and to problems created by Customs Commissioner William Von Raab.

CHAPTER 8

Managing the Good Times

The favorable state of ATF's external relationships under Steve Higgins's direction reflected both the deliberate attention accorded the cultivation and maintenance of such relations and fortuitous circumstance. The attention and effort directed at external relations, however, came at the expense of internal management issues. A full decade of a benign, if not favorable, political climate and increasing budgets was not utilized to address historic weaknesses in structure, staffing allocation, planning, and procedures. Management did devote significant effort to rebuilding staffing levels and diversifying the employee and managerial ranks.[1] Several alternate hypotheses would explain the lower priority accorded management issues by Higgins and his senior staff. Kaufman noted that high-level government managers seldom have the opportunity to focus on managerial issues because other demands consume their time and attention.[2]

A second possibility is a lack of incentive. Ultimately, Congress holds the keys to incentives for an agency; and as Derthick noted, Congress cares little about the details of administration and management.[3] Constituency groups that influence Congress display even less concern with such details. Therefore, the incentives favor pursuing external relations and satisfying constituent groups over devoting time and attention to the details of internal administration. Finally, there is simple bureaucratic inertia. As former director Higgins noted, every administrative change involves costs, and, ultimately, organizations function regardless of how they are structured.[4] ATF was operating with few complaints from Congress or the administration. With the environment supportive and no external pressure for change, it was easier to avoid the frustration and cost of attempting change.

Neglect of Administration

ATF's weakness in administration derived from both its structure and culture. The two primary operational functions, compliance and enforcement, had always vied for control of the organization. Although enforcement personnel were more numerous and visible, they lacked administrative experience, and their core culture was hostile to assuming administrative duties. In addition, their law enforcement retirement status was dependent on remaining in positions classified as law enforcement or enforcement management. The Office of Administration was managed by generalists, who did not closely identify with either regulation or law enforcement. They theoretically exercised responsibility for general administrative tasks such as personnel, training, budgeting, procurement, and data systems. The associate directors for both law enforcement and regulation distrusted these "outsiders" and developed their own shadow administrative staffs to monitor the Office of Administration and protect their interests.[5] In effect this created three administrative staffs, one in the Office of Administration and one in each of the operational staffs. This structure resulted in duplication of effort, muddled planning, and conflict over turf. In the end, no one knew where final accountability for a task resided.[6]

In addition to the obvious cost of triplicating all administrative operations, divided administrative staffs generated more serious problems. As an example, the bureau developed four separate, and incompatible, computer systems to serve administration, enforcement, compliance, and internal affairs. Computer functions as fundamental as checking to determine if a location or person were licensed to engage in the firearms business were not made available to agents. High-level managers, who could not spare a few hours to resolve problems of automation and systems coordination, routinely pursued every opportunity to enhance ATF's image, for instance by spending days at law enforcement Explorer Scout encampments.[7]

Although the computer system was a highly visible manifestation of the lack of interest in the details of administration, numerous less visible but equally important problems existed. In spite of widespread dissatisfaction with the awkward and antiquated system for reporting criminal investigations, no meaningful revisions were ever made. A field agent receiving information that a licensed dealer had offered to sell a firearm unlawfully would have to prepare separate reports to open the case, utilize the informant, obtain authority to record an undercover contact, obtain funds for a buy, and conduct the undercover contact.[8] No system of identifying and developing future leaders and managers was developed. Most importantly, issues of structure and staffing were not addressed, leaving the law enforcement and compliance divisions with incompatible structures. The distribution of law enforcement division offices continued to reflect the work loads of the liquor enforcement era. Thus, Colorado and Utah were supervised from San Francisco, while the Deep South had six division offices. Although the Office of Law Enforcement utilized a staffing model for the assignment of personnel, the model lacked internal and external validity.[9]

Because the culture of the regulatory operation was more amenable to administrative activities, the administrative issues that pertained exclusively to that function were noticeably better managed than those in enforcement.[10] Compliance assumed responsibility for collecting retail liquor dealer special occupational taxes for the IRS during this period and apparently decreased significantly the number of nonpayers.[11] A general policy of consolidating all regulatory functions relating to alcohol sales was pursued.[12] Although management of firearms licensing was difficult, three-year licenses were initiated to allow the bureau to keep up with demand.[13]

Some of the barriers to effective administration were common to both law enforcement and regulatory functions. Any change in procedure that required an order or form change was a laborious process. Proposed changes in almost any procedure first had to be drafted within the affected office and then circulated throughout the bureau for comment and coordination. In principle, this process prevented components from implementing changes that would impact the operations of other components. In fact, many changes did not require this process, as they impacted law enforcement or regulatory functions exclusively. Any new directive or form had to make its way through the Office of Administration and eventually to the printer. To accomplish this within one year was a significant feat. Thus, staff and managers attempted to avoid addressing administrative change when possible and to circumvent the official process when change was necessary. The result was usually an innovative use of implementing instructions imposed upon existing procedures: One set of instructions was piled upon another in efforts to solve immediate problems with temporary, short-term solutions. This process was a constant frustration for operational employees in the field, who regularly became confused in the maze of temporary procedures. The quality of administrative and staff functions was also plagued by an inability to preserve institutional memory, particularly in law enforcement. The need to constantly change incumbents of various positions in the service of career development resulted in a constant loss of institutional knowledge. Yet as in virtually all bureaucracies, position rather than expertise or experience dictated who would participate in the decisionmaking process.[14]

104 MANAGING THE GOOD TIMES

Management Style

Several factors influenced ATF's management style, although they were generally more applicable to enforcement than compliance. Although the regional history of the organization had attracted numerous employees resistant to moving, the dispersed structure of the agency resulted in most promotions being accompanied by transfers. As the agency moved away from a regional structure, it became far move likely that these moves would be to a new regional area. Thus, mobility became the most important trait necessary for promotion. The dispersed location of offices influenced the selection of managers in another significant way. Employees could not be exposed to a variety in job experience or supervisors without being moved, which generated cost for the agency and disruption for the employee. This increased the potential for parochialism in many managers by limiting the diversity of their experience and often meant that a single supervisor would evaluate an employee's promotional potential. Few options existed for providing either tests of capability or diversity in experience.

The constant attacks on the bureau from outside interests and the lack of exclusive jurisdiction created an atmosphere in which avoidance of problems usually overshadowed innovative management solutions. These forces reinforced the common bureaucratic traits of managers to avoid risk and resist change, increasing the likelihood of attack for error and decreasing the general sense of security within the agency. In enforcement, in particular, the tradition was distinctly anti-intellectual. Although this is common in law enforcement organizations, which value action over thought, rural southern roots and the recruitment of numerous former police officers without college educations exacerbated this tendency in ATF. Because education never served as a criteria for promotion, and management typically endeavored to replicate itself, no force existed to concentrate intellectual talent in management positions.[15] Thus law enforcement managers tended to be conservative and cautious with a distaste for abstraction, complexity, and ambiguity. The culture tended to ignore the political and policy aspects of administration and concentrate on controlling operations. For persons who favored action over ideas, the familiar activities of agents were far more inviting than the unfamiliar world of management in a dynamic political environment. Thus the majority of time not spent on external relations was spent reviewing the operations of the field. ATF's politically vulnerable position reinforced its management culture. It was difficult to justify the pursuit of abstract planning or policy formulation, especially if the future consisted primarily of adapting to outside political forces.

Unlike the FBI and the Secret Service, the organizational culture of ATF has never been fully homogenized. The history of regionalism, the lack of a unified organizational goal or technology, and the absence of strong central management have impeded development of a single culture. The development of an organizational culture through a strong sense of identity and mission has been well documented, even in geographically dispersed organizations such as the Forest Service and the FBI.[16] In both cases, strong directors have used initiative and discretion to deliberately mold the organization. This was the case for agents in the Southeastern Region until Project CUE transfers and the elimination of regional structures disrupted the process. ATF attempted to mold more uniformity by greater central control and by linking transfers to promotion. During the late 1970s and early 1980s, both the law enforcement and regulatory functions experimented with a variety of approaches. During the late 1970s, candidates for promotion were selected without their consent and arbitrarily transferred to new positions, a procedure known affectionately among field personnel as "rope-a-dope." Some of those selected challenged the authority of the bureau to promote them against their will, and management eventually stopped the process. The alternate approach was to require that persons either option in or out of a career program. Selection of the participation in the career program subjected the employee to transfer anywhere in the country for the purpose of promotion. This resulted in the majority of employees choosing to forgo participation. Ultimately, both operational branches returned to allowing persons to bid for specific promotions, but not before the legacy of regional cultures had been greatly reduced.

The management styles and cultures that had existed in ATF before 1977 were very much influenced by regional history. The Southeastern Region had been highly authoritarian, while other regions were far less so. Compliance managers and law enforcement managers from regions with stronger compliance functions were far more influenced by the IRS, which practiced a participative style of management. Rigid management control was not enhanced during the years of expansion, even though enforcement managers from the Southeastern Region were placed in key positions throughout the country and in headquarters. The rapid influx of new law enforcement employees facilitated a change in both organizational culture and a new and evolving core technology. Senior managers, isolated from the evolving field operations, lagged behind and had only their liquor enforcement experience as precedent. Over time, the first-line supervisors, many of whom were physically separated from their special agents in charge, became the recognized sources of authority.[17] With administrative and policy functions highly centralized and operational decisions made primarily at the agent or first-line supervisory level, SACs devoted most of their time to personnel actions, public relations, and review.[18] The resistance of senior law enforcement managers to delegation of authority actually served to isolate middle managers and, in many cases, reduce their roles.

That centralization of authority could result in the dilution of management control seems counterintuitive and requires some explanation. By requiring approval from SACs or headquarters for a wide variety of routine functions, ATF assured two results.[19] The first was that the field agents would seek to keep as many activities as possible out of official reports, thus avoiding burdensome reporting and loss of discretion. The second was that SACs would be so inundated with perfunctory decisions and routine processes that significant issues often blended into the background and did not receive adequate attention. This same pattern was replicated in ATF headquarters. Over time, headquarters had mandated special reporting for a wide variety of routine field activities in addition to the normal investigative reports. In addition, all investigative reports were forwarded to headquarters. This flood of incoming information overwhelmed the headquarters staff and rendered them largely incapable of focusing on important field activities. This pattern was far less pronounced in the regulatory operation, whose management culture was more amenable to delegation of authority.

In headquarters, the development of a single management style was inhibited by the presence of at least three distinct cultures emanating from the law enforcement, regulatory, and administration branches.[20] Law enforcement, the largest and most sensitive of the three, was fragmented and severely impacted by the rate of change in the field operation. Until the mid-1980s, none of the top management staff in headquarters, and few of the candidates for these positions, had working field experience with firearms or explosives investigations. In addition, the tendency for persons who received rapid initial promotion to ascend to top positions assured that future candidates often would have only limited first-hand experience. Higgins's personal style was one of participative management; however, the associate directors for law enforcement who served under him had opposite styles. Thus, the director granted great discretion to his associates, who, in turn, attempted to control every detail of field operations. A strong and cohesive cadre of senior field managers might have countered some of the impact of this if they had possessed the confidence, experience, and competency, but such was not the case.[21]

The headquarters staff included personnel with substantial pertinent field experience. First-line supervisors were required to cycle through headquarters as operations officers in the various divisions before they could advance to assistant special agent in charge. Although many of the most competent field agents refused promotion to avoid this duty, others did not. While some of the operations officers had only short tenure in the field, many had substantial experience, particularly by the early 1980s.[22] Potentially, these former field supervisors offered a wealth of experience. Unfortunately, the authoritarian culture of headquarters did not encourage consultation of the more junior members of the staff, who were greatly underutilized. They soon learned that getting promoted back to the field, an almost universal goal, could best be achieved by becoming associated with a highly visible program or project.[23] Rather than contributing to a cohesive, long-range policy, junior staff members pursued the short-term and highly visible objectives that promised rewards.

The agents and junior managers, assigned to headquarters, constantly vied for favorable attention from the associate director or his deputy, which they perceived as the most important component in selection for promotion and return to the field.[24] This pattern produced some notable successes, such as the NRTs, but had several distinct drawbacks. Since the goal was to obtain favorable attention over a relatively short period of time, programs or concepts were often initiated only to flounder when their advocates received promotions and transfers. There was also little or no impetus for cost analysis or realistic evaluation of implementation problems, since the initiator usually did not have responsibility for the eventual implementation. Issues requiring policy or legislative changes were usually avoided, because ATF lacked the political resources to initiate such change. Gun control policy was entirely off the table during the twelve years of Republican administrations.[25] ATF's narrow jurisdiction and placement in Treasury restricted input on general criminal justice policy, which traditionally has been the purview of the Justice Department. At the same time, such necessary but unrewarding tasks as updating operational orders, simplifying operational procedures, and examining resource allocation were assiduously avoided. One never became the center of attention for rewriting an order or researching and eliminating an unnecessary procedure. Thus the headquarters enforcement staff pursued the tasks that offered potential rewards. The compliance staff was far less inclined to avoid operational administrative details, because their management displayed more interest in this area.

To understand the organizational culture of the headquarters law enforcement staff, it is helpful to understand the nature of federal law enforcement. The federal government provides only a small portion of the law enforcement services in the United States. The vast majority of law enforcement is performed by state and local governments. Prior to 1968, law enforcement was not perceived as a function or issue worthy of much attention in political campaigns. It consumed only a minuscule portion of the federal budget and occupied the attention of only a small percentage of federal employees. After the successful use of the issue of law and order by both the Nixon and Wallace campaigns in 1968, the symbolic importance of law enforcement was elevated. Although the size and funding of enforcement agencies did increase after 1968, law enforcement remained but a small portion of the federal bureaucracy.

Although a visible and symbolically important function, federal law enforcement is not integral to the daily life of citizens. Neither does it constitute one of the most critical functions performed by the federal government. If the IRS or Social Security Administration ceased to function for even a brief period, the daily lives of millions would be impacted. Tampering with any function that has a direct constituency will bring immediate negative response. On the other hand, few people interact with federal law enforcement on a daily basis. Arguably, the currency would be undermined if counterfeiting were not suppressed, but most other enforcement functions would be conducted by state or local authorities. The federal government has assumed the primary role for suppressing drug importation, but has not been able to impact supply enough to discourage use. Although the federal government has sole responsibility for immigration laws, no means has been found to control illegal immigration, and millions of undocumented aliens reside illegally in the United States. Existing firearms laws lack the mechanisms to control firearms commerce, even if the political will to do so existed.

The failure of the federal government to assume a consistent, continuing role in the daily life of citizens through law enforcement does not translate into a lack of activity. Individual agents and bureaus engage in constant activities and often perform admirably. Yet the federal government has not assumed ongoing responsibility for specific tasks and jurisdictions, save those of espionage and counterfeiting. This can best be seen in the operation of United States Attorney's Offices, where jurisdiction is broadest. As administrations change, these offices shift prosecutive emphasis from one area to another. Thus, certain types of crimes may be prosecuted one year and not the next. The great majority of federal crimes, which are concurrently covered by state statute, are subject to declination by prosecutors in favor of state prosecution without reason or justification. This differs significantly from law enforcement and criminal justice at the local level, where police must routinely respond to reported crimes and calls for service from the public, and public expectation mandates prosecutorial action on most arrests.

Because federal law enforcement jurisdiction is fragmented among a number of agencies, the ability to shift emphasis, resources, and prosecutive priorities generates intense concerns over turf. Enforcement agencies compete for favor, resources, public attention, prosecutive priority, and, ultimately, legitimacy. Unlike the FBI, whose broad jurisdiction allows shifting among such diverse areas as economic crime, national security, terrorism, and street crime, ATF is vulnerable to any shift in priorities. Bombing and arson investigations are finite, while firearms violations, like drug or immigration violations, are virtually infinite. As with most drug and immigration violations, the majority of firearms violations involve individual acts and not large commercial enterprises. The default position of United States Attorney's Offices is that they do not prosecute most such crimes. ATF, therefore, must construct rationales to justify these investigations and prosecutions and enhance its legitimacy as a law enforcement entity.

The pursuit of individual prosecutions is necessary for several reasons. First, inadequate large-scale gun trafficking cases exist to justify ATF's law enforcement staffing, and these cases often have limited public appeal (see Chapter 4). In addition, without the less complex cases, agents could develop neither the skill nor the sources of information to pursue complex cases. For a law enforcement agency to function, it must receive information on illegal activity and maintain the skills of its personnel. Without routine cases, an agency would need a constant flow of information to be referred by other agencies or the public, and it would have to hire experienced investigators with skills well honed. Those conditions have never been present for ATF, nor most other federal enforcement agencies.

The need to constantly legitimate its law enforcement activities encouraged ATF to pursue special projects, joint task forces, or other high-visibility enforcement efforts in search of added legitimacy. The agency's law enforcement legitimacy was constantly subject to the dual threats of shifting federal law enforcement emphasis and criticism from the NRA and others opposed to firearms laws. When ATF pursued violations of the firearms laws against those selling firearms, its legitimacy was attacked as a means of attacking the law. Gun control opponents routinely accused ATF of pursuing tax-paying citizens instead of real criminals. It was analogous to demanding that the narcotics laws only be enforced against those who could be shown to be directly generating crime through their sales or vehicle laws only against those who had caused serious accidents. ATF responded by continually attempting to frame its enforcement activities as crime fighting and drug suppression in pursuit of prosecutive support and legitimacy. This strategy, however, left the agency vulnerable to attack for pursuing cases that did not meet the standard for federal interest.

This dilemma has dogged ATF since the passage of the GCA. On the one hand, ATF, interest groups, and often Congress demand that ATF apply the law only to criminals, meaning those with prior criminal records or persons actively engaged in other criminal activity. On the other, ATF operates in a policy environment that routinely rejects cases that do not meet the standard of federal interest.[26] These demands have proven to be something of a Gordian knot. If the firearms violation occurs incidental to some other crime, for instance robbery or murder, the state prosecution of that crime ordinarily takes precedence, leaving little federal role. The possession of firearms by felons or other prohibited persons has not been routinely viewed by United States attorneys and federal judges as being within federal interest, particularly in metropolitan areas. This leaves ATF with illegal trafficking cases involving either licensed or unlicensed gun dealers. These cases generate the greatest political reaction and usually involve persons who are not easily categorized as criminals. Dealing in guns, unlike drugs, does not automatically demonize the defendant. Investigations seldom reveal enough about the recipients of the illegally sold firearms to demonstrate the impact on crime. In some instances, this can be overcome by tracing recovered guns from crimes back to dealers, but only occasionally.[27]

ATF's primary strategy for escaping this dilemma has been to pursue defendants, such as drug dealers and organized crime members, whose associations or activities have already demonized them in the eyes of the public and prosecutors. Members of outlaw motorcycle gangs have been tailor-made to fit this strategy. The association of the gangs with violence and drug trafficking, as well as the overt behavior and appearance of members, have cast the gang members in the role of threat to the public safety. In addition, many gang members are felons and most have a propensity for possessing guns and explosives. ATF has repeatedly capitalized on this fortuitous combination of elements and has been at the forefront of numerous investigations and projects directed at these groups. To match this successful pattern elsewhere, ATF must focus on groups already perceived as criminal and whose members either have a proclivity for illegal firearms and explosives or are primarily armed felons or other prohibited persons. Mere occasional possession or use of guns is not adequate, because this does not provide the opportunity to detect and prosecute the crimes. It is for this reason that ATF has been less effective against highly organized crime groups.

A second ATF strategy involves participation in organized task forces that target specific criminal activity. ATF has been a primary participant in the original organized crime strike forces, the Nixon-era Office of Drug Abuse Law Enforcement (ODALE), the Miami drug task force, the current Organized Crime Drug Enforcement Task Force (OCDETF), Operation Alliance, and countless smaller and less visible operations. These task forces legitimate firearms prosecutions by linking them with an activity of more current federal interest, often drug trafficking.

Coming Up ACES

For the members of the law enforcement staff assigned to headquarters and seeking identification with a successful project, these operational realities defined the parameters of the options for innovation. Any new effort would remain within ATF's jurisdiction but not be limited simply to pursuing firearms violations. It could not extend into the operational turf of another agency. Success was also enhanced by visibility, favorable attention from some outside interest, and the need for headquarters coordination or direction to assure the advocate a role. In the mid-1980s, Jamaican gangs, known as "posses," suddenly burst on the U.S. crime scene. They displayed an extreme penchant for violence and were very active in drug trafficking. It is questionable if these groups significantly impacted the drug supply, but in a number of eastern and midwestern cities they attracted extensive attention by indiscriminately shooting competitors, bystanders, and witnesses. This was a classic opportunity for ATF, which became the lead federal agency in coordinating enforcement and intelligence efforts relating to the Jamaican posses. Although the groups primarily engaged in drug trafficking, they were not effective enough to divert the DEA from the more important Colombian cartels. The constant presence of firearms gave ATF numerous justifications for exercising jurisdiction, and the agency received substantial recognition and resources as a result.[28] The Jamaican project had been overseen in headquarters by the Special Operations Division. Although this division had responsibility for intelligence, automated systems, organized crime, and alcohol and tobacco enforcement, it had always been secondary in status to the Firearms and Explosives Divisions.[29] The Jamaican project put Special Operations in the business of overseeing active field operations, a status division members desired to retain.[30]

The Special Operations Division had an aggressive chief and a staff eager to make their mark. Automation and intelligence were potentially vital to the bureau's future, but they did not excite ATF management, Congress, or the administration. In the competitive environment of headquarters, success came most often to those associated with the implementation of law enforcement activities, preferably accompanied by positive press attention, congressional favor, or additional resources. The staff of the Special Operations Division had enjoyed favorable attention from their association with the Jamaican gang project, which was accompanied by favorable press attention, congressional favor, and additional funding. Thus, they began to search for additional projects.[31]

Washington, D.C., crime rates, which had declined during the early 1980s, had begun a steep rise with the crack epidemic beginning in the middle of the decade. The Washington press was again full of stories about violent crime. The staff of the Special Operations Division devised a proposal to conduct a demonstration project in the District of Columbia in which ATF would saturate the city with agents and prosecute massive numbers of firearms violations in an effort to lower the crime rate.[32] Although the majority of the resulting prosecutions would be for individual firearms violations, the creation of a project and the political need to attack the high crime rate in the nation's capital would elevate the federal interest in these violations. Senior ATF management quickly embraced the proposal but restricted it to two police districts.[33]

The selection of Washington was no accident. On at least two prior occasions ATF had mounted intensive enforcement efforts in the District of Columbia. The Kenyon Bellew shooting in 1971 (see Chapter 1) had resulted from one such effort, and Project CUE had targeted Washington as one of its three test cities. The reasons for this were both political and operational. Members of Congress and the administration read the *Washington Post* and were regularly exposed to local television news. Federal managers assume that success or disaster in Washington has far more impact on the future of a program than any other venue in the country. Operationally, the district's gun laws made possession of handguns virtually illegal, eliminating many problems normally present in proactive use of firearms laws. The mechanics of investigation become more akin to a drug investigation in which the mere presence of a handgun justifies arrest or search. In addition, Washington remains largely a federal city, where the United States attorney serves as the city's district attorney and the federal courts handle most serious crimes. This presented less complex jurisdictional and turf issues for federal law enforcement than other jurisdictions.

The project, entitled Armed Criminal Enforcement Study (ACES), operated for four months in the spring and summer of 1989 in two Washington police districts for the espoused purpose of evaluating the impact of concentrated firearms enforcement on violent crime. The importance of the research and evaluation aspects of the project became apparent with the failure of ATF to develop any research model or retain any qualified researcher to aid in designing the plan or to analyze the results. No one in ATF management even knew how measurement was to take place, nor did they show any understanding of the results after the project.[34] Originally, the intent was to emphasize the study aspect of the project only if it was successful.[35] Although no one really knows the impact of the effort, the ACES was perceived as an unrivaled success. Large numbers of agents were brought into Washington from all over the country. They developed a strong sense of esprit de corps and immediately set about pursuing street-level drug dealers and violent offenders. The agents primarily arrested suspects more active in drug than gun violations, but guns were usually present; and the arrests became the focus of local news cameras. Margie Moore, who would become ATF's first woman SAC, was placed in charge of the field operation, further enhancing media interest in it.

Although no serious effort was made to evaluate the impact of the project on crime, no question existed among ATF management regarding the success of the project.[36] It had provided ATF with an opportunity to demonstrate its law enforcement prowess against criminals in the most visible media venue in the nation. Footage of ATF agents serving warrants dominated the local news and found their way into news libraries. Congress and the administration responded with praise and funding for more such projects. ATF had become a key element of the administration's war on drugs, in both symbol and fact.

In an effort to duplicate the positive reaction to the ACES, ATF initiated the ACES II in Washington in 1991, followed by the ACES West the following year in Los Angeles. These projects emulated the ACES with strong congressional and administration support. All three of the projects reflected the multiple realities that were often present in ATF law enforcement operations. At the operational level, the ACES was an opportunity for agents to perform the work they most wanted to do, for instance proactive law enforcement with little attention to any long-term impact or political implications. At the headquarters division level and below, the ACES was an opportunity to remain involved with field operations and enhance the image of the division and its staff with the associate director. At top management levels it was a means of enhancing the image of ATF and competing for funds and favorable attention from the administration, Congress, and the press. Interest in and understanding of the working realities of implementation declined as the distance from the working agents increased.

The lack of headquarters focus on rational utility was highlighted at the termination of the ACES West. Each of the projects ended with a highly visible roundup of suspects. Although these roundups served little operational purpose and generated additional problems for the working agents, they provided excellent media events. At the termination of the ACES West, ATF was receiving inquiries from the military regarding opportunities to utilize military support. Congress had recently provided funds for drug enforcement support to the military, which was actively seeking to demonstrate compliance with the congressional mandate.[37] ATF headquarters developed a plan to fly agents and their vehicles from the East Coast to Los Angeles for the purpose of making the final arrests. In an operation that reflected poorly on the judgment of both ATF and the Air Force, agents from throughout the Middle Atlantic states drove to Dover Air Force Base and were flown to Los Angeles with their vehicles, while agents from the adjacent San Francisco Division were not utilized.

Tactical Operations

In addition to improving ATF's external image, the ACES produced a significant change in ATF's culture by enhancing the status of tactical operations. Historically, such operations had been viewed in ATF as ancillary to investigations. The nature of the ACES operations necessitated numerous arrests and the service of numerous search warrants on drug houses. Tactical operations became more routine and assumed a much larger role in daily operations. To a degree, this reflected a general trend in law enforcement. More heavily armed suspects, particularly in the drug trade, had increased the risks for law enforcement and justified the creation of Special Weapons and Tactics (SWAT) teams in most law enforcement agencies. In addition to the utility these teams offered, they became symbolic of a modern, state-of-the-art agency and a focus of the popular media.

Within ATF the forces favoring higher-profile tactical operations were more complex than the desire for more favorable media coverage.

The core technology of ATF's law enforcement component, investigation, primarily involved single agents or very small groups interviewing, checking records, or conducting surveillances, with little need for active management coordination or participation. Tactical operations involved more agents and resources. They also could be planned and their timing controlled. Thus, managers could intervene directly to coordinate and control these operations, giving managers a larger and more direct role. In the case of the ACES, headquarters personnel became directly involved in overseeing the operation.[38] Thus, strong motivation existed among managers and headquarters staff, who disliked being separated from field operations, to support increased tactical operations. In addition, many in ATF viewed dependence on other agencies' tactical teams as demeaning.[39]

As tactical operations increased, management became aware of the lack of equipment and training to perform these tasks.[40] Historically, ATF had resisted specialization among agents, preferring instead to view agents as generalists. The NRTs were an exception, but they were made up of agents who worked general assignments and came together only when necessary. Specialized arson groups began in the early 1980s in a few cities in response to funding and political support for arson investigation. However, ATF had resisted the trend toward development of special tactical teams.[41] In addition to an organizational culture that had favored generalists, ATF faced the practical problem of being a relatively small agency with a dispersed workforce. Although a police department of comparable size might have one or two tactical or SWAT teams, ATF would require many. Keeping the number of teams small would allow a high level of training and control costs, but the teams would seldom be available where they were needed. Training and equipping enough teams to serve most field offices required extensive resources and diversion of personnel.

One additional barrier to the creation of ATF tactical teams had long existed. Management had regarded anything that communicated a highly aggressive or confrontational approach to law enforcement as politically risky. ATF had been characterized as "jackbooted thugs" since the 1970s by the opponents of gun control (see Chapter 5). Unlike most other law enforcement agencies, however, ATF had never allowed any use of fully automatic weapons and prohibited agents from carrying any personal firearms.[42]

The agents assigned to the ACES were provided with uniforms, entry tools, ballistic shields, and additional weapons. They were trained as entry teams and spent a significant portion of their time making entries to serve search warrants. Because drugs were such a significant part of the enforcement effort, speed of entry was highly emphasized. In addition to the drug issue, the concept of dynamic entry began to dominate the conceptual thinking of the agents and ultimately those associated with the ACES project in headquarters. The principles of dynamic entry were well known to most field agents and occasionally utilized; however, it was not the underlying presumption of ATF training and planning. The dynamic entry concept is generally attributed to the development of hostage rescue teams, although the same concept has been utilized by narcotics officers for many years. Dynamic entry utilizes speed and surprise to overwhelm occupants of a building before they can effectively respond, thus protecting the raiders, the occupants, and any hostages. For narcotics officers, the preservation of evidence constituted the driving force for use of the tactic.

The creation of specialized tactical teams generated the imperative for agencies to utilize them, both as justification for expending the resources and to keep the teams in a high state of readiness. Hostage and armed-barricade situations were few; thus, the teams seldom worked together under actual field conditions. This reduced their level of readiness, but more importantly left them open to attack as a very expensive and seldom utilized luxury. Many law enforcement agencies addressed these problems by utilizing their teams during the service of search warrants, particularly if the premises was believed to be fortified or the occupants armed. The arrival of the crack epidemic corresponded with this trend and provided numerous targets. Crack houses were often fortified and guarded against robbery and presented significant difficulties for police. Thus the use of tactical teams to serve drug and other high-risk warrants reflected diverse influences, from the need to find work for the teams to practical problems presented by weapons and fortified structures.

Notes

1. "Staffing allocation" refers to the location and placement of personnel, while "staffing level" refers to the number of personnel authorized the agency in aggregate.

2. Herbert Kaufman, *The Administrative Behavior of Federal Bureau Chiefs* (Washington, D.C.: Brookings Institution, 1981).

3. Martha Derthick, *Agency Under Stress: The Social Security Administration* (Washington, D.C.: Brookings Institution, 1990) 82–83.

4. Neither Higgins nor McGuire is particularly receptive to the argument that management and administrative issues were neglected, although both acknowledge that external relations were accorded the highest priority.

The author's conclusions are based on personal observation and communication with numerous other members of the headquarters staff during this period.

5. Interviews with William Drake, former associate director for compliance, and Richard Cook, former chief of the Firearms Division. The author also served on the headquarters staff from 1980 to 1985.

6. The problem of duplicative and overlapping staff is almost universally acknowledged by all senior managers, including Higgins, McGuire, and Drake.

7. The author managed the law enforcement computer operation from 1983 through 1985.

8. Each of these would require separate authorization. Additional reports would be required under certain circumstances, for instance if the informant were an alien. Even the eventual automation of report preparation was not used as an opportunity to revise, integrate, and simplify the reporting. Instead of restructuring the process to capitalize on the use of automation, existing forms, complete with sections pertaining to programs long since terminated, were simply replicated on a screen and then printed out.

9. Although many officers incorporated multiple Standard Metropolitan Statistical Areas (SMSAs) as well as population outside any SMSA, calculations for population and crime rates were tied only to the core SMSA. Application of the model could result in wide disparity in staffing authorization for offices with comparable workloads. Although the structural inconsistencies of the model were brought to the attention of the Office of the Associate Director, no action resulted.

10. Interviews with William Drake and former headquarters regulatory staff member Richard Allen.

11. Interview with Richard Allen.

12. All federal functions relating to the regulation or taxation of alcohol, except those under control of Customs, were consolidated in ATF. Customs resisted relinquishing control over importing alcohol.

13. The number of licensees continued to grow during the period, reaching about 300,000 by the passage of the Brady Bill, which raised fees. These higher fees, combined with new application procedures requiring fingerprints and more extensive information, significantly reduced the number of new applicants. Although the three-year license was arguably a reduction in regulatory control, no alternative remedy allowed ATF to comply with the mandate to issue licenses within forty-five days of receiving the application.

14. Thus, the chief of the Firearms Division would serve as the principal adviser on a decision relating to firearms policy, even if that person had occupied the position only a short time and had only limited interest and knowledge in the area, while a far more experienced individual in the Explosives Division would have no input. Personnel were regularly assigned to positions in headquarters for which they had little preparation, either to round them out or simply because the position was vacant at the time they were promoted or transferred.

15. Officially, the position of special agent does not require a baccalaureate degree, although, unofficially, candidates without degrees have not been considered for employment since the early 1980s. Pursuit of graduate education after employment was not encouraged and seldom, if ever, a

consideration for promotion. The decision to cease hiring persons without degrees as agents reflected concern for status more than education. Concurrent with this change in hiring policy, Daniel Hartnett, who had not received a baccalaureate degree and thus would not have met the qualification for a new hire, was promoted to associate director for law enforcement, the highest ranking agent position in the bureau. For much of his tenure as associate director, Phillip McGuire's senior staff was composed entirely of individuals without college degrees, although the pool of potential candidates was composed predominantly of college graduates. This more than likely reflected a preference for loyal and compliant subordinates rather than a bias against education, but it does reflect the lack of importance law enforcement managers attached to education.

16. Herbert, Kaufman, *The Forest Ranger* (Baltimore: Johns Hopkins University Press, 1960); James Q. Wilson, *The Investigators* (New York: Basic Books, 1978).

17. ATF had fewer divisions than either the FBI or the Secret Service and thus had a larger proportion of remote resident officers. Cities such as Milwaukee, Denver, Jacksonville, Sacramento, and Pittsburgh were all resident offices reporting to distant divisions. In addition, ATF was unique in administratively classifying operational groups in cities with division offices, such as Los Angeles or Dallas, as independent offices or posts of duty. These groups therefore had separate records, evidence storage, and space allocation. As a result, they often were not co-located with the SACs. This was unique among federal law enforcement and encouraged greater isolation and independence.

18. In the San Francisco Division, as an example, special agents in charge have supervised between two and five judicial districts in up to four states. Outside the immediate San Francisco metropolitian area, even such tasks as coordinating policy with United States attorneys and chiefs of large police agencies is accomplished by the resident agents in charge.

19. The prior approval of firearms dealer or gun show investigations by headquarters has already been cited. ATF also resisted delegating authority to conduct consensual electronic monitoring. In addition, SACs had to approve all expenditure of funds, all informant use, and every investigative report. Even returning an item of property to the rightful owner required written approval from the SAC. After the Miami shootings (see Chapter 7), virtually every arrest or warrant service required management approval. This was comparable to requiring the chief of police to approve every nonexigent arrest made by a police department.

20. Technically, these were offices, subdivided into divisions and then branches. The author has simplified the official structure to avoid needless confusion and explanation.

21. Field SACs were not unified in their positions on management issues. Although this was largely attributable to diversity in attitude and background, geography also played a major role. These managers were physically separated and came together only twice a year at management conferences, where strict agendas did not encourage an active exchange of views or the building of strong alliances. Meetings between the SACs and all other field managers always followed these meetings and never preceded them. The message, though subtle, was clear. Information flowed down, not up. Management meetings were for the purpose of imparting policy and procedures, not for examining them.

22. Because there were few promotions during the Carter and the early Reagan years, a backlog of experienced supervisors available for promotion to headquarters developed. Rising housing prices made transfers less painful and increased the number of supervisors willing to transfer. As promotions depleted this backlog and pressure for the accelerated promotion of minority and female managers increased, less experienced personnel began to fill these positions.

23. The best projects generated favorable publicity or attention for the bureau and required the project manager to regularly brief the associate director. Positive, upbeat briefings proved more successful than those that focused on problems or costs. The process was much like the experience of lieutenant colonels assigned to the Pentagon.

24. There were always more agents seeking promotion out of headquarters than there were available positions. The autocratic style of management and lack of independent criteria for promotion made the opinion of the associate director the critical element in promotion. Experience demonstrated that details of administration and bad news were not means of currying favor with the incumbents of this position. Likewise, policy and legislative issues generally placed management in the embarrassing position of admitting their lack of political clout. On the other hand, projects that offered opportunities for favorable press attention or enhanced relations with constituencies or Congress were well received.

25. Interviews with Steve Higgins and Richard Cook.

26. As has been previously discussed in this book, federal interest is a somewhat amorphous concept and subject to constant reinterpretation. However, at its core, federal interest assumes functions that can or will not be performed at the state or local level.

27. ATF management has repeatedly tried to focus on "crime guns." Unfortunately, no such category exists. Guns become crime guns when they are used illegally. Although guns purchased illegally are more likely to be used in crime than those purchased legally, it does not follow that no legally purchased gun will be used in a crime or that all illegally purchased guns will be.

28. Interview with Richard Cook ATF division chief during ACES. As with many other ATF projects, much of the early work was done by field agents. The contribution of headquarters was most often to formalize and seek agency credit for work already under way but little recognized by the press or public.

29. When the elevation of division chiefs to senior executive status was first proposed, those in the Firearms and Explosives divisions were to be promoted but those in Planning and Analysis and Special Operations divisions were not, revealing the perception in law enforcement that operational questions were of primary importance and that administrative and managerial questions were secondary.

30. Interview with Richard Cook.

31. Ibid.

32. Ibid.

33. Interview with Daniel Hartnett, former associate director for law enforcement.

34. Cook is candid in admitting the research aspect of the project received little attention during planning or implementation. Daniel Hartnett seems convinced that the project was meant to measure the impact of the ATF action but has no recollection of details or methods.

35. Interview with Richard Cook.

36. The means and outcome of the analysis were not known to the key personnel interviewed. Richard Cook, the division chief responsible for initiation of the project, stated that little interest was focused on the study results and no professional analysis was done.

37. Although the military had substantial funds, its role was limited to support and not direct law enforcement activity. Liaison officers were appointed to each of the major federal law enforcement agencies and began to seek a role for military support.

38. Direct management participation became possible because the duration of these operations was far shorter and the timing more predictable than other investigations. It could be justified by the number of agents involved, the need for coordination of agents from different groups or field divisions, the potential for press attention, and the risk of danger.

39. Interview with Daniel Hartnett.

40. Ibid.

41. Phillip McGuire opposed the existence of specialized units, and formal tactical teams were implemented after his retirement.

42. This tradition had been inherited from the IRS. Under the IRS, agents were restricted to carrying only issued sidearms; auxiliary weapons, such as shotguns, were not issued. After separating from the IRS, ATF issued shotguns and carbines but retained restrictions against personal firearms of any type. Field agents have never been allowed any fully automatic firearms, but a small number of controlled-burst MP5, 9-mm submachine guns were purchased for the special response teams.

CHAPTER 9

Preludes to Waco

In addition to participation in the war on drugs, another type of case had highlighted ATF's lack of self-sufficiency in tactical operations and pushed the agency toward taking action to change this situation.[1] Because of its jurisdiction over firearms and explosives statutes, ATF inevitably came in direct confrontation with armed separatist groups, which derived from a variety of political and religious movements. ATF had periodically encountered violations of firearms or explosives laws by extremist-group members from at least the early 1960s, including both right-wing groups, such as the Minute Men and Ku Klux Klan, and left-wing groups, such as the Republic of New Africa and the Weather Underground. However, these groups had not usually created armed communes, and the leftist groups were primarily centered in areas of major population with large police agencies. ATF's investigative role normally involved violations by individual members and did not require major tactical operations. ATF did not endeavor to address the tactical aspects of dealing with these groups, presumably because other agencies were available to do so and because ATF was still dominated by an IRS tradition that resisted any association with the more coercive aspects of law enforcement.

By the 1980s the anarchist right had again emerged as the dominant form of militancy in the United States. In general, these groups all disdained gun control, taxes, and the authority of the federal government. Many, but not all, had strong religious overtones. Anti-Semitism and white racism were common, but not universal. The groups were based on several belief systems, although there was overlapping membership and some participants appeared to span several of these belief systems.[2] The Christian Identity movement evolved from Anglo-Israelism, a belief that Northern Europeans were the true descendants of Israel. As the movement evolved into Christian Identity it became militantly anti-Semitic and racist, predicting a coming world conflict between the Adamites, or descendants of Adam, and the descendants of Satan, the Jews and all other nonwhite peoples. Believers advocate a separate Aryan nation, usually in the Pacific Northwest. Other militant Christian fundamentalists share many of the same views as the Identity believers but separate themselves in their belief in the rapture. Separatist from other Christian denominations, such as Adventists and Mormons, also share a millenarian or apocryphal vision of history that is imminent.[3]

Apocryphal religious beliefs are common among separatist groups but not universal. Localists share a belief that the federal government, as currently constituted, lacks legitimacy. Many also challenge state and local governments. Their legal arguments vary, some harking back to common law, others to the Articles of Confederation, and still others to the Constitution. Localists encompass tax resisters and members of the Posse Comitatus, which refuses to recognize any authority but the county. The most militant localists recognize an almost unlimited right of individuals to resist government authority and define armed defiance of government process as self-defense.[4]

Groups representing all of these orientations have existed for some time in the United States. In some cases, they have established communities for an extended period of time with only limited conflicts with government.[5] The tendency of these groups to defy authority, while isolating themselves in armed compounds, however, has increased since the mid-1980s, and ATF has been drawn into several of the resulting conflicts.

During the 1980s Richard Butler, a former aeronautics engineer from southern California and Identity believer, founded the Church of Jesus Christ Christian and a corresponding political organization, the Aryan Nation, at Hayden Lake, Idaho.[6] The group was openly racist and advocated the establishment of a separate white homeland in the Northwest. They regularly displayed Nazi flags and symbols and engaged in military and firearms training. Butler held a yearly gathering for Aryan racist groups and worked to establish relations with other white racist organizations throughout the country. Although northern Idaho had long been a center for antigovernment feeling, the openly militant and armed character of the Aryan Nation raised the interest of law enforcement, particularly federal law enforcement.

Law enforcement interest increased significantly as a result of the activities of Robert Mathews and The Order. In 1983, Mathews recruited members and associates of the Aryan Nation into a secret organization he called Bruders Schweigen, or Silent Brotherhood.[7] More widely known as The Order, the group was dedicated to the violent overthrow of the government in preparation for the coming war between the races.[8] Mathews appears to have been deeply in-fluenced by *The Turner Diaries*, a novel by white supremacist and anti-Semite William Pierce, in which open warfare breaks out be-tween white patriots and ZOG (the Zionist Occupational Govern-ment).[9] Shortly after being formed, The Order began a crime spree which resulted in robberies netting over $4 million, counterfeiting, and multiple murders. In late 1984, Robert Mathews died in a fire during an armed confrontation with FBI SWAT teams at Whidbey Is-land, Washington, after shooting an FBI agent and escaping an at-tempt to arrest him in Portland, Oregon. Mathews held off SWAT teams for several days before being killed in a fire initiated by the agents. He was heavily armed, and wore body armor and a gas mask.[10] Numerous other member of The Order were convicted of federal racketeering charges and sentenced to prison for their par-ticipation in the robberies and murders.

Although Mathews and The Order raised the profile of militant anarchists, they were not the first such individuals to experience confrontation with federal law enforcement agencies. In 1983, United States marshals attempted to arrest Gordon Kahl, a North Dakota tax resister, for violation of Internal Revenue laws. Kahl was accompanied by his son and several other sympathizers when he was confronted by the marshals and local officers. In the resulting confrontation, two marshals died, and Kahl escaped. Kahl died, after killing a local sheriff, in a subsequent confrontation with the FBI and local authorities in Arkansas. In his account of the confrontation with the marshals, Kahl makes it clear that he believed he had the right to resort to deadly force to resist what he believed was illegal government action.[11]

The Covenant, Sword and Arm of the Lord

Even before the investigation of The Order, ATF had begun investi-gating the activities of an associated Christian Identity group in Arkansas. Known as the Covenant, Sword and Arm of the Lord (CSA), the group was led by self-proclaimed minister and white separatist Jim Ellison.[12] The CSA had established a fortified com-munity on several hundred acres at Bull Shoals Lake in northern Arkansas, where they engaged in extensive military training. Elli-son preached that the United States was facing a massive civil war that would be triggered by black riots and would result in anarchy. When his predictions did not materialize, the group began a series of crimes to bring it about.[13] In one scheme, the CSA bombed a natural gas pipeline that supplied gas to the Chicago area. Ellison predicted that this would result in a loss of heat in the inner city and subsequent riots. Fortunately the bomb was inadequate to rupture the pipeline.

The group's most violent member, Wayne Snell, killed the proprietor of a pawn shop in Texarkana during a robbery and later murdered an Arkansas state trooper, who stopped him shortly after he left the CSA compound.[14] When captured after a gunfight with Oklahoma police, Snell possessed a firearm silencer that matched a silencer previously seized in Missouri. The second silencer was traced back to the CSA compound by ATF. The subsequent investigation provided probable cause for an arrest warrant for Ellison and a search warrant for the CSA compound.

The CSA compound was occupied by more than a hundred people and fortified with bunkers, land mines, machine guns, hand grenades, and a LAW rocket.[15] The occupants engaged in regular military training, conducted armed patrols, and prepared for the coming of Armageddon. In April 1985, agents obtained a federal search warrant for the compound and a federal arrest warrant for Ellison. Because ATF lacked adequate personnel and equipment to serve the warrant, they requested the assistance of the FBI Hostage Rescue Team (HRT) and the FBI became full participants in the investigation.[16]

On April 19, 1985, an Arkansas state trooper who had established rapport with the CSA notified the occupants of the compound that ATF and the FBI had the location surrounded and that a search warrant had been issued. After three and a half days, the occupants finally surrendered. The search of the compound revealed numerous machine guns, explosives, land mines, and grenades. Ellison was convicted of federal racketeering, arson, and firearms charges and sentenced to twenty years imprisonment. Numerous other members were also convicted of a variety of charges stemming from arsons, bombings, and weapons possession.[17] Snell was sentenced to death and executed for the murder of the trooper. Another associate, David Tate, later was convicted of killing a Missouri highway patrolman on April 15, 1985. A member of The Order, Tate killed the trooper after being stopped for transporting firearms from Idaho to the CSA compound.[18]

Although the situation at the CSA compound in many ways paralleled the later situation at Waco, it received far less press attention.[19] Ellison, like David Koresh, took multiple wives, preached a message of Armageddon, defied the law, and amassed illegal arms in preparation for the coming conflict. Yet, there were key differences. Bill Buford, who directed the CSA investigation and assumed a key role in planning and executing both tactical operations, viewed the two events as differing in one significant aspect. Ellison's vision required that his followers survive the conflagration, while David Koresh's vision required the death of his followers.[20] It was for this reason that Buford believed a siege approach was appropriate for the CSA but not the Branch Davidians.

While the CSA operation generated less national attention than events at the Branch Davidian compound at Waco, the potential for disaster was equally great. The defenses at the CSA compound were far more formidable than those at Waco, and the potential for loss of life was even greater. Knowledgeable participants estimated that a direct confrontation at the CSA compound would have required the government to use a reinforced infantry battalion to clear the compound forcefully.[21] Many in ATF were frustrated by the agency's inability to conduct the CSA operation without FBI tactical assistance, which generated additional internal pressure to develop tactical capability.[22]

Most importantly, the CSA case revealed the potential for future situations that would not correspond to the capabilities, procedures, and tactics available to civil police in a democratic society. The potential danger and complexity of armed separatist groups became more obvious if one examined the violent confrontations that occurred during efforts to arrest Robert Mathews and Gordon Kahl. Taken together, these events indicated the potential for a far larger and more violent confrontation between an armed separatist group and law enforcement. However, no organized effort was undertaken to analyze the potential for such events or possible responses within ATF or elsewhere.[23] Outside ATF and the FBI, the CSA case attracted little interest or attention. Within three years the two agencies would again find themselves facing armed religious separatists in a fortified compound.

Bombing at Marion

Early in the morning of January 16, 1988, a bomb severely damaged a Latter Day Saints (LDS) church in Kamas, Utah. Investigation by ATF and local authorities quickly identified the suspects as occupants of the Singer home in Marion, Utah.[24] John Singer, a German immigrant and breakaway, polygamist Mormon, had resided at that location until January 18, 1979, when he was shot to death by Utah state law enforcement officers. He had been involved in an extended armed standoff that began with his refusal to send his children to public school or to comply with home schooling laws. When officers, disguised as journalists, attempted to arrest him, he drew

a gun, and they shot him. Subsequent to Singer's death, two broth-
ers, Jonathan and Addam Swapp, moved into the compound, and
Jonathan Swapp assumed the mantle of the deceased John Singer.
The Swapps and the Singer family believed John Singer would be
resurrected and return to lead the group. The church bombing had
been carried out to avenge the death of Singer and precipitate his
resurrection, and the perpetrators left a clear trail.[25]

The Singer residence was occupied by a number of armed
adults and several children. The house was fortified, and occupants
threatened to shoot any law enforcement officer who approached.
ATF agents from throughout the West and four FBI SWAT teams
were rushed to the scene. For eleven days agents attempted to ne-
gotiate a surrender with the occupants of the residence. After several days the agents cut off electricity and later used loud speakers
and lights to disrupt the occupants' sleep. The occupants responded
by routinely directing rifle fire at the speakers and lights and dan-
gerously close to agents. Eventually the agents obtained two armored personnel carriers from the National Guard. The aged
M113s, however, were potentially vulnerable to rifle fire if hit from
the side, and on-scene commanders feared that using the personnel
carriers to batter the house could expose occupants of the carriers
and the house to injury.

Although ATF exercised primary jurisdiction over the case, a
joint command team consisting of ATF, the FBI, and the Utah Highway Patrol was set up. As one agent later stated, "We were in
charge but never in control."[26] ATF lacked the equipment, training,
and command structure to manage the scene. The FBI brought in
their HRT after the first few days, thus exercising almost total tactical control over the scene.[27] Both the FBI and ATF were under constant direct pressure from the governor of Utah, whose overriding
concern was the safety of the children.

Early on the morning of January 28, a trap was set by placing
speakers outside the residence and rigging them with trip wires and
flash-bang grenades. Previously, the occupants had come out under
cover of darkness and destroyed speakers whenever they were utilized. The plan was to utilize two dogs from the Utah Department
of Corrections to overcome the suspects, who then could be captured without using deadly force. When the trap was sprung, the
Swapps fired on the dogs, and the plan went awry. One dog turned
away, and a second bit an HRT member.

Toward daylight on January 28, the on-scene commanders devised a plan to again try to capture suspects using a dog. HRT members and a dog handler hid in a small, vacant house close to the goat
pen. When the Swapps came out to milk the goats, as they had each

morning, the dog handler would set the dog on the Swapps, and the HRT members would take advantage of the diversion to affect the capture. The Swapps did come to the goat pen as expected, but when the dog was released, gunfire erupted from the house, killing the dog handler. An HRT sniper asked for authority to return fire at the shooter, but the FBI special agent in charge ordered him not to fire.[28] HRT members on the capture team did shoot Jonathan Swapp, striking him once with a 9-mm bullet. The Swapps both retreated into the house but soon surrendered. Subsequent investigation of the event identified a fifteen-year-old boy, who was confined to a wheelchair, as the shooter who killed the state officer.

The Marion case attracted far more media attention than the CSA case had.[29] It was also more frustrating for ATF. The lack of specially trained and equipped personnel had forced ATF to surrender operational control to the FBI, the last thing most ATF agents or managers wished to do.[30] Again, events and trends provided both a reason and a justification for increased tactical competence. The events at Marion very likely influenced the FBI as well as ATF. Many in ATF, and likely in the FBI, felt that an overly cautious approach had cost the life of the dog handler. On numerous occasions, the occupants exited the residence under arms. At no time was consideration given to using gunfire against them, even though snipers could have inflicted disabling wounds, with little chance of killing the suspects. In addition, gas was not used because of the presence of children, and the armored vehicles were not used to breach the house. All of these options were apparent to individual agents but never seriously considered by management.[31]

Randy Weaver and Ruby Ridge

For many Americans who are highly distrustful of government, the Randy Weaver case has taken on symbolic importance equal to that of David Koresh and the Branch Davidians.[32] In 1983, Weaver and his family had moved from Iowa to an isolated cabin in northern Idaho after developing apocryphal Christian beliefs. After arriving in Idaho, Weaver associated with members of the Aryan Nation and became a firm believer in Christian Identity. In 1987 he was introduced to "Gus," an Aryan Nation associate from Spokane, through a mutual acquaintance and kindred spirit, Frank Kumnick. Gus, who purported to be both an outlaw biker and a firm believer in white supremacy, was actually Kenneth Fadley, an ATF informant. Weaver, Kumnick, and Fadley discussed the need for a more active agenda to bring down what they saw as a corrupt government.

Fadley showed little interest in Weaver, and the two had only occasional contact between their first meeting in 1987 and a discussion in 1989 about the purchase of sawed-off shotguns.

In October 1989, Weaver sold Fadley two shotguns, both less than the twenty-six inches in length required by federal law. Fadley and Weaver discussed more purchases, but Fadley never followed through. ATF was not interested in Weaver himself, but in using him as an unwitting agent to conduct an undercover investigation of other militant separatists. When Weaver failed to take Gus to these people and Gus's identity was compromised for other reasons, the ATF case agent decided to utilize the threat of prosecution to obtain Weaver's cooperation.[33]

When agents attempted to contact Weaver at his cabin in June 1990, Weaver's children met them carrying weapons and asking their business.[34] Weaver refused to cooperate with the agents or even to meet with them at the Spokane ATF office. At this point, ATF forwarded the report on the criminal case to the United States attorney, who presented the case to the federal grand jury and obtained an indictment of Weaver for the unlawful manufacture and sale of the sawed-off shotguns. Although ATF's actions would later be the center of considerable controversy, the sequence of events was fairly routine. During the period that Randy Weaver associated with militant antigovernment individuals and groups in northern Idaho, several members of these groups were involved in violent crimes, including bombings. The Aryan Nation had been the recruiting ground for The Order, which had committed numerous crimes including premeditated murder. Weaver did sell an ATF informant illegal firearms and discussed selling more. When given the opportunity to cooperate with law enforcement, he refused. Such scenarios were everyday occurrences in the much lauded "war on drugs."

Believing that an attempt to arrest Weaver at his cabin would endanger both the agents and Weaver's children, ATF agents set a trap to arrest him as he drove to town. They arranged to be notified by neighbors, who had a grievance with the Weavers, when Randy and his wife passed the neighbors' cabin. In December 1990, the Weavers stopped to assist a couple whose disabled pickup blocked the road. As soon as the Weavers were out of their vehicle, they were arrested by agents and the local sheriff. Both of the Weavers carried handguns and Randy Weaver had to be overpowered.[35] Released by a United States magistrate after posting his cabin as bond, Weaver failed to appear for his next scheduled court date. Subsequently, the Weavers notified the United States attorney by letter that Randy would not cooperate with the court.

Over a period of eighteen months the United States Marshal's Service negotiated verbally and in writing with Weaver through intermediaries. Although given every opportunity to peacefully surrender, Weaver and his wife both made clear their intention to defy the courts and clearly implied willingness to use force to repel government agents.[36] The marshals were advised that the Weavers would not surrender and that they were likely to use force to repel the marshals.[37]

Eventually the Marshal's Service brought in members of their Special Operations Group (SOG) in an effort to apprehend Weaver. On the first day of surveillance, the Weavers' dog detected the SOG team and began to pursue them. The marshals retreated, and the dog followed. Weaver, his fourteen-year-old son, Sammy, and Kevin Harris, a friend and sympathizer of Randy's, all carrying firearms, followed the dog. Although the Weavers later contended that they thought the dog was pursuing a deer or elk, the marshals interpreted their actions as a pursuit.[38] Eventually the dog overtook the marshals, who were hiding in heavy cover attempting to avoid detection.

What happened next is still the subject of some dispute. However, all accounts concur that one of the marshals shot the Weavers' dog, Kevin Harris shot and killed Deputy Marshal William Degan, and a marshal shot and killed Sammy Weaver. The marshals and Harris, however, report the sequence and nature of events differently.[39] The Weaver family and Harris retreated to the house and the marshals eventually withdrew with Degan's body. The FBI HRT was immediately requested and took control of the scene by the next day. Based on the FBI's interpretation of events prior to the HRT arrival, the normal rules of engagement were modified to allow deadly force to be used against armed adults.[40] An FBI sniper subsequently wounded Kevin Harris and Randy Weaver and killed Vicki Weaver. Again, the events are interpreted differently by different parties. The sniper acknowledged trying to shoot the two men, but he contends Vicki, who was behind the cabin door, was accidentally struck by a bullet fired at Harris, who was diving through the door.[41]

An eleven-day siege ensued, during which antigovernment activists from throughout the country congregated at the roadblocks and checkpoints established around Ruby Ridge. As the numbers of antigovernment sympathizers, many sporting swastikas and shaved heads, increased, angry confrontations developed between the protesters and the ATF, HRT agents, and Idaho State Police manning the barricades. Ironically, the ATF agents, who had not been involved in either of the shootings, found themselves the most visible federal agents on the scene. After the eleven-day siege, the Weavers and Harris finally agreed to surrender to Bo Gritz, a retired special forces colonel and antigovernment activist. Unable to establish a dialogue with Weaver, the FBI accepted Gritz's offer to act as an intermediary.

A federal court jury in Idaho found Randy Weaver and Kevin Harris not guilty of murdering Deputy Marshal Degan. The same jury acquitted Weaver of firearms charges for making and selling the sawed-off shotguns but convicted him of failing to appear for trial. The government subsequently settled a lawsuit with Weaver and his children for the death of Vicki, agreeing to pay $3.1 million. Weaver's acquittal on the firearms charges stemmed from an entrapment defense, although subsequent events and actions by the government likely influenced the jury's decision on this charge as well.[42] Legally, entrapment occurs when an agent of the government originates the intention to commit the crime and entices an otherwise innocent person into the crime. In fact, a jury can utilize this finding when they object to the behavior of law enforcement and sympathize with the defendant.

The Impact of Militant Separatism

The rise of militant anarchist and religious separatists, primarily in rural settings, has placed federal law enforcement in a new and difficult role for which there are few precedents. Urban riots and separatist groups, such as Move in Philadelphia, primarily have been the problem of large city police. These agencies did not seek out federal law enforcement to solve their tactical problems, although they did look to the military in some riot situations. Rural law enforcement was far less equipped to act and more willing to defer to federal action. In addition, groups such as The Order and the CSA operated over a wide variety of jurisdictions in their criminal actions and were beyond the capacity of state or local agencies to investigate. Thus, the federal agencies found themselves placed in an unfamiliar police role. Also, ATF was engaged in an inevitable competition with the FBI over jurisdiction. The FBI viewed these cases as domestic terrorism and, thus, solely within their jurisdiction.[43] In many cases, however, firearms and explosives violations were the most available avenue for action. ATF viewed these as their sole jurisdiction.

Events at Waco, Texas, would parallel, in many ways, events at the CSA, Marion, and Ruby Ridge. In each instance, ATF exercised initial jurisdiction, with the FBI HRT eventually assuming operational control of the scene.[44] Although the exact impact of each case on the subsequent action of both agencies cannot be precisely established, some must be assumed.

These events brought both agencies into confrontation with lawbreakers, who behaved very differently from what law enforcement had generally experienced. Law enforcement officers had assumed that persons involved in intentional violations of the law usually attempted to avoid detection. If detected, they either surrendered or attempted escape. In these cases, the suspects defied authority. Instead of making a rational calculation regarding the utility of forceful resistance as a means of escape, they resisted when their action offered no hope for escape. Unfortunately, neither the public nor law enforcement fully appreciated the potential for violent confrontation that these cases had demonstrated. Even within ATF and the FBI, where awareness should have been greatest, there was no systematic effort to develop strategic responses for future events.

Notes

1. Interview with Daniel Hartnett, former associate director for law enforcement.

2. For an in-depth discussion of Christian Identity beliefs and history see Michael Barkun, *Religion and the Racist Right: The Origins of the Christian Identity Movement* (Chapel Hill: University of North Carolina Press, 1994).

3. For an in-depth discussion see Barkun, above, and James Aho, *The Politics of Righteousness: Idaho Christian Patriotism* (Seattle: University of Washington Press, 1990).

4. Aho provides substantial detail regarding the distinctions in the underlying beliefs of separatist groups and individuals. Although he focuses primarily on the underlying beliefs of Idaho residents, his work captures the essence of separatist militancy among whites in general. He also devotes substantial attention to explaining the links between Idaho movements and those elsewhere.

5. A notable example is the loosely organized community established by William Potter Gale, a retired army officer and Identity believer, in Mariposa County, California. Although Gale and some of his followers were convicted of federal crimes emanating from tax resistance, no significant confrontation with law enforcement has occurred in over twenty-five years.

6. Aho, 57–61.

7. Ibid., 61–67.

8. Ibid.

9. Barkun, 228–233.

10. Based on an interview with the FBI SWAT agent present at the scene.

11. Barkun, 228–233.

12. The details of the CSA investigation are drawn primarily from interviews with Resident Agent in Charge Bill Buford.

13. Ibid.

14. Ibid.

15. Ibid.

16. Ibid.; interview with former associate director Phillip McGuire.

17. *Arkansas Democrat,* "CSA Leader Gets 20-Year Sentence for Racketeering" (September 5, 1985).

18. Buford.

19. See the *New York Times,* April 20, 21, and 23, 1995.

20. Buford.

21. Interviews with Kenny King and Bill Buford, both of whom are experienced combat veterans of Vietnam.

22. Phillip McGuire, who cited the operation to the author as a superb example of interagency cooperation and the high point of good relations between ATF and the FBI, was not among those distressed by the lack of ATF tactical teams.

23. For a more extensive discussion of the problems presented by such situations, see William J. Vizzard, "Reassessing Bittner's Thesis: Understanding Coercion and the Police in Light of Waco and the Los Angeles Riots," *Police Studies* (18:3 and 4, 1995) 1–18. The only immediate and direct innovation made in response to the CSA operation was to purchase new raid jackets with *ATF* displayed in large gold letters. Steve Higgins directed this after observing similar jackets on FBI agents and realizing that they were much more visible on television.

24. Kamas is an unincorporated settlement adjacent to Marion. For simplicity's sake the location will be described as Marion. Events are reconstructed from interviews with ATF agents Allan Galyan, Steven Bauer, Nolan Douglas, and numerous conversations with other agents.

25. Bombing the church, or more precisely the LDS stake center, was a symbolic act of repudiation of mainstream LDS beliefs. As with most breakaway cults, this group viewed the larger church as corrupt and in need of cleansing.

26. Interview with Special Agent Steven Bauer.

27. A full-time tactical team developed by the FBI to respond to terrorist incidents, the HRT selects members from volunteer agents after a grueling field evaluation. The team trains constantly, except when deployed, and has a wide variety of weapons and equipment not available to most SWAT teams. In this case, the HRT possessed extensive cold-weather clothing, which ATF lacked.

28. The dominant concern throughout the operation was an inadvertent injury of one of the children in the house.

29. The *Washington Post* had only three short items on CSA in the "Around the Nation" section on April 20, 21, and 23, 1985. There was some television coverage, but the remote location, lack of view of the compound, and short duration reduced visual potential. Most television coverage of the event shows police and agents at roadblocks. Marion was more open to television coverage and lasted far longer. Although it did not generate extensive coverage in national newspapers, it received extensive television coverage and inspired a television movie.

30. Unlike his predecessor, Phillip McGuire, Associate Director Daniel Hartnett did not approve of depending on FBI expertise. In an interview with the author, he cited the lack of capacity in this incident as a primary influence in convincing him to develop specialized tactical teams within ATF.

31. The author had extensive conversations with Nolan Douglas, the ATF scene commander, regarding the events, as well as with several agents and supervisors on the scene.

32. *Newsweek*, "The Echoes of Ruby Ridge" (August 28, 1995) 26–33.

33. These events are condensed from Jess Walter, *Every Knee Shall Bow* (New York: HarperCollins, 1995); U.S. Congress, Senate report, *Ruby Ridge*, 1996; interviews with the ATF case agent, Herb Byrley.

34. Walter, 114.

35. Ibid., 120–121.

36. Senate report, *Ruby Ridge*, 25–30.

37. Surveillance and investigation revealed that both the parents and the older children were routinely armed; see Walter, 153.

38. Walter, 164–166.

39. Because the details are in dispute and relate to the actions of the United States Marshal's Service and not ATF, the author has chosen not to attempt a reconstruction of the events of the shooting. For additional details see Walter and the Senate report, *Ruby Ridge*.

40. This change in rules of engagement has become the most controversial event in the Ruby Ridge case. There are differing accounts from within the FBI regarding who made the decision and what information was used. See Walter and the Senate report for discussion.

41. As with the details of the first shooting, the author has chosen not to attempt a detailed discussion of the events, because they relate primarily to an agency other than ATF. See Walter, 195; Senate report, 70–75.

42. According to Walter, the failure of ATF to record the initial conversation about purchasing firearms with Weaver and the fact that the informant was paid by the government were critical to the jury's verdict. The case agent, Herb Byrley, explained that the first conversation was not recorded because there was no expectation of negotiating for guns with Weaver and he was not the focus of the investigation. He also testified that the informant would be paid for his actions regardless of whether Weaver was convicted. Both of these explanations are consistent with normal ATF practice; however, the jury did not, apparently, accept this. Weaver presented no defense and did not take the stand.

43. For a discussion of the issue as it related to Ruby Ridge, see Walter.

44. The one exception is the CSA case, where ATF and the FBI exercised joint control.

CHAPTER 10

Clouds on the Horizon

While ATF experienced both growth and a lull in political conflict, the outside political environment was undergoing changes that would soon impact the agency. The NRA had laid the groundwork for the McClure-Volkmer Bill, later passed as the Firearms Owners Protection Act, by demonizing ATF and personalizing the "victims" of firearms laws.[1] However, this effort lost much of its momentum as a result of the NRA opposition to the merger of ATF with the Secret Service and the incorporation of ATF into the administration's war on drugs and violent crime. ATF also benefited from the NRA's strategy, which was to shift emphasis from orchestrating hearings and publicity to establish a record of alleged abuse under existing law, to focusing on passage of McClure-Volkmer.

Attention Shifts to Congress

Republican Senator James McClure of Idaho had introduced bills in every session of Congress from 1975 on to abolish the entire GCA. In 1981 McClure and Democratic representative Harold Volkmer of Missouri jointly introduced a bill to make far-reaching changes in the existing GCA without revoking the entire law. Popularly know as McClure-Volkmer, the bill was crafted with significant input from the NRA, which became its chief advocate. The bill as originally proposed had two primary goals: It sought to substantially reduce the restrictions on firearms commerce and to severely restrict ATF's authority to enforce the remaining restrictions, particularly with criminal sanctions. Among other changes, the bill, as originally drafted, proposed eliminating the prohibition on all out-of-state purchases and mail-order sales of firearms. These provisions formed the central core of the GCA, and their elimination would have altered the entire logic and purpose of the law.[2] It also limited ATF's authority to inspect dealer records to once per year and required prior notice before the inspection to prevent surprise or repeated inspections of dealers, including those with poor records of compliance. The bill altered the definition of a felon under the firearms laws from the generally accepted federal definition of any person convicted of a crime punishable by more than a year imprisonment to the definition utilized by the state in which the conviction occurred, thus recognizing all state actions to reduce or expunge felony convictions after the fact. The net effect of the proposed bill would have been to create substantial confusion regarding the application of federal restrictions to firearms possession and to substantially decrease the number of persons restricted from firearms possession, as many states retroactively reduced felonies. The bill also allowed all felons to apply for restoration of their privilege to possess firearms, removing the restriction from those convicted of violent or armed crimes. Denial of the restoration of privilege was to be subject to court review.

The proposed bill also impacted litigation of firearms cases by raising the standard of proof for conviction on most firearms violations to willfulness, thus requiring the government to prove specific knowledge and deliberate intention to violate the law, a standard not applicable to most federal crimes. It also restricted the government's authority to seize and forfeit property, including firearms, used in violations of the firearms laws, thus establishing procedures and standards for firearms violations not applicable to other federal criminal laws. Another requirement, unique to firearms prosecutions, was a requirement that the government pay the attorneys' fees of persons charged with firearms violations but not convicted.

In a direct attack on ATF's authority to control trafficking in firearms, McClure-Volkmer redefined "engaging in the firearms business" to exclude those who did not devote time and attention for the principal purpose of livelihood and profit, regardless of how many guns they sold. It also reduced the charge of falsification of firearms records by licensed dealers to a misdemeanor, eliminating the most effective criminal sanction against unscrupulous dealers. To assure that ATF did not institute a requirement for dealers to report purchases of firearms, the bill prohibited such a requirement as well as that for any central record of firearms purchasers. Finally, the bill guaranteed the right to transport firearms interstate, even if prohibited by a state, so long as they were unloaded and locked in a vehicle trunk.

The bill did not pass in its original version and conflict developed within the NRA over whether to compromise on some provisions or pursue passage of the law in undiluted form. As a result of this conflict, Neal Knox was forced out as director of the Institute for Legislative Action (ILA), the lobbying arm of the NRA, when he opposed all compromise. Two years later Knox lost his seat on the NRA board when he testified against an NRA-backed version of the bill.[3] Knox had been one of the key leaders of the 1977 revolution that placed intractable opponents of gun control in the NRA leadership. An unfailingly polite and gentlemanly individual, Knox represents the extreme libertarian position on firearms. Knox does not phrase his opposition in terms of pragmatic difficulties with an administration or the impact on crime. He clearly is focused on what is described as the sovereignty paradigm (see Chapter 2).[4] Knox was replaced by Warren Cassidy, who would later ascend to the position of executive secretary, the operational head of the NRA. ATF found that some accommodation could be reached with the NRA leadership after the Knox faction lost power.[5]

In 1986, a compromise version of the McClure-Volkmer Bill finally passed both houses of Congress under the title of the Firearms Owners Protection Act. As enacted, the bill retained the restriction on interstate sales of handguns. Some of the restrictions on ATF operations and requirements for heightened levels of proof were also modified. The politics of the bill were complex because the bill cut across party lines, fracturing Democratic solidarity. The administration avoided an official position on the bill but provided symbolic support when President Reagan addressed the 1983 NRA convention. Although not allowed to publicly oppose the bill, ATF and Treasury quietly presented arguments against some of the most objectionable sections to congressional staffs.[6] Senator Robert Dole, who previously had not been associated with opposition to gun control, became a key factor in obtaining Senate passage of the bill.[7] Although a Democratic-controlled House Judiciary Committee, chaired by Peter Rodino, attempted to bottle up the bill, it passed after a successful discharge petition moved it from committee to the floor. Rodino's lack of popularity and a perception by members that his actions in blocking the bill were highhanded apparently played as large a role in these events as the power of the NRA.[8]

The enactment of the Firearms Owners Protection Act in 1986 after a protracted political battle generated both benefits and costs for ATF. Inflexible resistance to compromise had temporarily cost Neal Knox and his extremist supporters key positions of influence in the NRA and shifted the organization toward a more moderate position. The bill's enactment eliminated the NRA's political and organizational focus since the 1970s, thus eliminating much of the momentum from the organization's efforts. Changes made in the bill before passage somewhat lessened the impact on ATF's regulatory and law enforcement operations. In addition, a last-minute effort to sink the bill by attaching a total prohibition on manufacturing machine guns for other than government use had passed with the bill, sparing ATF the problems of dealing with a budding market in new machine guns.[9] Although the Firearms Owners Protection Act did restrict ATF's ability to control gun trafficking by licensed and unlicensed dealers, it opened new enforcement opportunities by imposing mandatory sentences on violent felons and drug traffickers for possession of firearms. Politically, the battle over passage solidified ATF support from organizations representing state and local law enforcement and further alienated these groups from the NRA.[10]

Cop-Killer Bullets

The process of separating the NRA from police organizations had been developing incrementally. The NRA had long courted the police through firearms training programs, and the organization counted many police officers among its ranks. Police organizations had generally supported the GCA. Direct conflict between police organizations and the NRA had not developed over the GCA because the then more moderate NRA leadership had used a strategy of backing alternative bills and not directly attacking the GCA or its supporters. The NRA had drawn some negative law enforcement attention for its attacks on ATF in the late 1970s, but no direct confrontation had occurred with police organizations. The real division between the NRA and police organizations began with the unlikely issue of restrictions on ammunition.

Beginning in the mid-1970s, bullet-resistant vests became standard equipment for most of the uniformed police in the United States. The vests became practical with the development of Kevlar, a synthetic fabric that when layered could resist penetration by bullets. The rising violent crime rate of the period ensured demand. None of the vests would stop the penetration of rifle bullets unless metal or ceramic plates were added, thus making the vests too heavy and bulky for routine use. Vests could be constructed to protect against most handgun and shotgun rounds and still be worn under the officer's uniform shirt. Armor-piercing handgun rounds had been available for many years, but their popularity was never great.[11] Since the bullet resistance of soft body armor results from the number of layers of fabric and the penetration characteristics of different cartridges varies, there is no absolute point at which a cartridge could be dubbed "armor-piercing" in a definitive sense.

Technological advances have alternately favored offensive weapons and defensive protection throughout recorded history.[12] Advances in offensive technology have often been viewed as threatening.

The penetration of a bullet depends on its mass, velocity, shape, and composition. No soft body armor provided protection against all small arms, although some body armor provided protection against most handgun bullets. Although the Teflon-coated pistol bullets were not unique in their ability to penetrate soft body armor, the commercial availability of this ammunition generated widespread attention. The bullets became symbolically important, particularly to the police.[13]

In 1981 Representative Mario Biaggi, a former New York police officer, became the most visible advocate of federal legislation to outlaw what became known as "cop-killer bullets." The actual originator of the strategy to use armor-piercing ammunition as a wedge issue is in dispute, but Handgun Control Incorporated (HCI) was clearly at the forefront in advancing it.[14] They pursued legislation to ban the ammunition, hoping to bring police organizations to their support and to force the NRA either to give tacit support to a gun control measure or to oppose the legislation and alienate law enforcement. Unable or unwilling to ignore the issue, the NRA responded by attempting to frame it in rational and technical language. The so-called cop-killer bullets were not an issue of much substance.[15] The availability of this ammunition would not significantly increase the risk to police nor would the lack of such availability deny gun owners anything useful. Unfortunately for the NRA, their effort to invoke a rational analysis of a symbolic issue proved unsuccessful. Although they had successfully manipulated the facts relating to firearms enforcement for years, they failed at defining the issue when the facts favored their position. Their opposition to the bullet ban defined them as unwilling to accept reasonable compromise on even the smallest issue. The wedge had been set, but the NRA would now drive it deeper.[16] The cop-killer bullet controversy was soon followed by the "plastic gun" controversy. Again, the NRA's analysis was largely correct, but they lost more public relations ground.[17]

ATF played almost no role in these events. The issues were of little interest to enforcement personnel, who saw no means of applying these particular laws to their primary interest of pursuing criminals. The agency's firearms technicians reacted negatively to what they saw as a political issue that did not lend itself to technical definitions. Few in ATF understood the issue's importance in shaping future coalition, although Higgins and McGuire capitalized on the heightened police interest in firearms issues to further enhance ATF relations with police organizations.

The cop-killer bullet issue opened a new phase in the tactical battle between control advocates, centered around HCI, and opponents, centered around the NRA. Advocates had learned that pursuit of very narrow and innocuous proposals, symbolically perceived as gun control measures, allowed them to out-maneuver the NRA. By restricting proposals to innocuous actions that created little impact on firearms users, advocates could force the NRA to either capitulate to gun control or make a public stand that cast them as extremists. Given the internal politics of the firearms lobby, in which more extremist elements were always pushing the leadership, compromise was virtually impossible. The NRA leadership thus could not avoid costly battles over non-issues. Later, both the Brady Law and assault weapons restrictions would follow this pattern.

The Impact of McClure-Volkmer

The most significant impact of McClure-Volkmer on ATF was to further discourage development of a comprehensive firearms policy and particularly to discourage any policies intended to control licensed and unlicensed dealing in firearms. Until its passage, the bill loomed as a threat to ATF's operational discretion. ATF responded by limiting those types of investigations that generated support for the bill and opposition to ATF (see Chapter 7). Once passed, the law presented ATF with constraints on its use of regulation or criminal prosecution to control licensed dealers and greatly restricted its ability to control gun trafficking by unlicensed dealers. It also served as a warning that Congress was hostile to any activity that could be characterized as controlling firearms rather than criminals.[18]

In the case of unlicensed dealers, the constraints directly resulted from the potential defenses against a charge of unlicensed dealing created by the new law. In an effort to preclude the prosecution of anyone who might be a collector, the law required proof that one was engaged in dealing for livelihood and profit and exempted sales intended to upgrade one's collection. Even under the GCA, "engaging in the business without a license" had proven a difficult charge to substantiate to the satisfaction of a jury. With the addition of multiple new defenses, United States attorneys became very unwilling to prosecute these cases. No one knew if livelihood meant principal livelihood or something less, although profit was somewhat clearer. The permitted activity of collecting and upgrading collections was even harder to define than dealing, since no case law existed. Prosecutions for dealing in firearms without a license virtually ceased. It was not until the mid-1990s that the development of case law encouraged United States attorneys to begin filing a small number of these cases again.

The reduction of falsification of records by a dealer to a misdemeanor would not, at first examination, seem to have significant consequences. In fact, the change made prosecution of disreputable dealers far more difficult. Although the law prohibited dealers selling to anyone they had reasonable cause to believe was a prohibited person, such as a felon or an illegal alien, the records-keeping violations had historically been far more useful. The courts had ruled that sales by dealers to undercover agents, posing as prohibited persons, did not constitute a violation of law since the recipient of the firearm was not, in fact, prohibited.[19] Thus, agents were required to utilize informants who were actual felons. Such persons are reluctant to testify and often are not reliable to stay available and out of trouble for the extended period between the investigation and trial.[20] A second problem was the discovery through audits that dealers had not entered large numbers of firearms in their records. In some cases, dealers who sold hundreds of firearms without records went undiscovered until their inability to account for guns traced from crimes placed them under suspicion. In these cases, prosecution for failure to keep records was not difficult. Few reasonable explanations existed for the failure to record large numbers of firearms shipped by wholesalers and received by the dealer. After 1986 this violation became a misdemeanor, regardless of the volume of firearms, and United States Attorney's offices seldom prosecute misdemeanors.

Most field agents followed the course of least resistance and pursued other types of cases, thus pushing ATF further away from their traditional focus on firearms and toward the war on drugs. At the headquarters level, ATF associated itself with every available initiative directed at drugs or violence but avoided discussion of initiatives directed at firearms alone. The restriction to one compliance inspection per year had limited consequences, since resources were so limited in relation to the large and growing number of dealers that multiple inspections in a single year would have been rare. Many dealers held licenses for years without ever being inspected.

The lack of regulatory control and shift of law enforcement focus away from dealers interacted with changing dynamics in the firearms market to significantly influence the culture of the firearms business. Between the passage of the GCA and the mid-1990s, market demand shifted significantly. The sale of handguns as a proportion of all gun sales increased steadily from the mid-1960s onward. By the 1990s, in excess of two-thirds of all new firearms sold were either handguns or assault rifles or shotguns.[21] During the same period, large discounters began to dominate most retail markets, including hardware and sporting goods, reducing profit margins and forcing small retailers out of business. The profit margin in firearms was never high and competition was increased by the large number of gun enthusiasts who pursued the business part-time.

Firearms dealers thus faced small profit margins coupled with a declining demand for sporting firearms and competition from both discounters and hobbyists. Unlicensed dealers operated in open competition with them, selling firearms without any records, and large gun shows increased the visibility of these activities. At the same time, a weakening regulatory environment encouraged the boldest among them to push the margins of the law. All of these factors functioned to push dealers toward catering to clientele interested in other than sporting arms and in some cases to engage in transactions that were questionable, if not openly illegal. Although many legitimate dealers resisted the trend, many did not. As the market became more undisciplined, scrupulous dealers found themselves at an increasing disadvantage. ATF focused only on the most grievous violations, which were easily prosecuted. Ironically, the Firearms Owners Protection Act, crafted to prevent the prosecution of dealers, had helped to create an environment in which previously legitimate dealers were being prosecuted for criminal violations of the gun laws.

Notes

1. William J. Vizzard, "The Evolution of Gun Control Policy in the United States: Accessing the Public Agenda," DPA dissertation, University of Southern California, 1993.

2. The central purpose of the GCA had been to restrict commerce in firearms across state lines and thus allow states to establish their own standards for firearms ownership and purchase. See Vizzard, 1993; Franklin Zimring, "Firearms and Federal Law: The Gun Control Act of 1968," *Journal of Legal Studies* (475, 1975).

3. For more detail see Roger Davidson, *The Postreform Congress* (College Park: University of Maryland Press, 1992) 182–183; Josh Sugarmann, *National Rifle Association: Money, Power and Fear* (Washington, D.C.: National Press Books, 1992) 61–64; Vizzard, 1993.

4. This analysis is based on extensive conversations with Knox, his published writings, and interviews with those who know him.

5. Steve Higgins perceives ATF's ability to function in the political environment as tied directly to the nature of NRA leadership. Although ATF never received NRA support, the focus of NRA resources on seeking out, supporting, and publicizing individuals who claimed to have been wronged by ATF ceased during the period that Knox's influence was reduced.

6. Interviews with Steve Higgins and Richard Cook, former chief of the Firearms Division.

7. See the statements of Senator Robert Dole in *Congressional Record*, V. 132, Part 7, 9559, May 6, 1986.

8. Vizzard, 1993.

9. Although approximately half the states prohibit possession of machine guns, the others do not. In these states, machine guns registered with ATF can be possessed legally by private individuals. The $200 transfer tax, import restrictions, and the unwillingness of major domestic manufacturers, such as Colt, to risk the negative public relations from such sales had limited the traffic in machine guns until the 1980s. Inflation had, however, reduced the $200 to a mere fraction of its 1934 worth and new small manufacturers were coming on the scene. These manufacturers were intent on specifically filling the civilian market, and a much larger market in machine guns was around the corner.

10. See letter from the Law Enforcement Steering Committee Against S. 49, dated April 21, 1986, in the *Congressional Record—Senate*, May 6, 1986.

11. Although listed in catalogs, armor-piercing ammunition was generally not available in sporting goods stores. A few police officers alternated the ammunition in their revolver cylinders for the purpose of penetrating vehicles. The ammunition was expensive and the pointed bullet was inefficient at producing trauma. Police, shooters, and ammunition manufacturers were more interested in the production of soft-point handgun bullets that would produce enough trauma to disable humans. These bullets also generated some political attention. Although the state of New Jersey banned so called "dum-dum" bullets, the symbolism of the issue resonated primarily with people who disliked all guns and soft-point pistol bullets never became an issue with the public or politicians.

12. The same problem arose with penetration of armor in the Middle Ages, along with the bombardment of fortified walls by cannon and later the use of antitank weapons against armored vehicles.

13. Davidson, 87.

14. Michael Beard, longtime gun control advocate and founder of the National Coalition to Ban the Handgun (NCBHG), told the author that Sam Fields, formerly of NCBHG, first described this ammunition as cop-killer bullets and saw the potential for an issue that would bring organized police support. Mary Louise Cohen, former counsel for Handgun Control Incorporated (HCI), credits Charles Orison of HCI with the idea.

15. Virtually every gun control advocate interviewed by the author acknowledged there was little substance to the issue but asked not to be quoted. No documentation exists that the ammunition resulted in police deaths or injuries; see Gary Kleck, *Point Blank: Guns and Violence in America* (New York: Aldine de Gruyter, 1991) 82. The technical staff at ATF consistently advised that no workable definition existed for armor-piercing pistol ammunition.

16. For an in-depth review of the issue see Davidson, 85–95.

17. Davidson, 98–99; the controversy was over allegedly plastic guns not detectable by airport magnetometers. The guns were actually not plastic and were detectable.

18. Violence Policy Center, "Gun Shows in America: Tupperware Parties for Criminals" (Washington, D.C.: Violence Policy Center, 1996).

19. *U.S. v Plyman,* 551 Fed 2nd 965.

20. In one case supervised by the author, the dealer sold without records only to persons who spoke Spanish and appeared to be illegal

aliens. Under ATF direction, an informant, who was a convicted felon, made multiple illegal purchases of firearms from the dealer. Before trial time, however, the informant was arrested for murder and ceased to cooperate. His attorney advised that the purchaser could not testify while he was in custody without subjecting himself to serious injury or death. Without this key witness the case could not proceed.

21. The reasons for the market expansion and change are complex and not well documented, but likely include consumerism among baby boomers, media attention to firearms, and fear of crime. See Vizzard, 1993, for a more in-depth discussion.

CHAPTER 11

Changing Political Stakes

Although the elevation of ATF to the status of an independent bureau raised its profile with Congress and the executive branch, it remained largely ignored by the national media for two decades. ATF's regulatory function generated very little interest and controversy, and its law enforcement operations often were overshadowed by the FBI. Typically, the press described ATF agents as "federal agents" to avoid the need to explain what ATF was or did to a public that seemed little interested. In a world in which favorable media coverage translated into legitimacy and political support, this lack of attention galled both individual agents and management. At the most basic level, agents have always been frustrated by the need to explain who they were and what they did. They have longed for the universal legitimacy that provided recognition to the FBI from even the most uninformed of citizens. During ATF's entire history, it has labored to obtain equality in salary, equipment, and support with the FBI, and to a lesser extent, with Customs, the DEA, and the Secret Service. [1] Within ATF, favorable media attention has been perceived as the most effective means of establishing an identity in the public consciousness. In fact, ATF largely attained equity with other Treasury agencies and substantially reduced the disparity between it and the FBI during the period when it received favorable media coverage as a result of the abortion clinic bombing investigations, the Miami task force, the ACES, and the war on drugs. Thus, the perception that favorable media attention was critical to agency health was reinforced, eventually leading to the appointment of full-time "public information officers" in every law enforcement division. As with most agencies, these public information officers appear to occupy the majority of their time seeking favorable press attention.

Ironically, ATF's enemies have been as devoted as its management in trying to focus press attention on the agency. In general, however, the media not only ignored ATF's accomplishments but also its mistakes. This lack of press and public interest largely explains the reticence of administrations to expend political resources rushing to the agency's defense against such powerful opponents as the NRA. Although the NRA has remained a constant adversary for most of the bureau's history, it specifically focused attacks twice prior to the Waco incident. The first attack was precipitated by the Ballew case (see Chapter 1), but evolved from the passage of the GCA and the subsequent introduction of far more restrictive bills in its wake.[2] The administration responded by moving ATF out of the IRS and making it a bureau, allegedly to improve supervision while expending no political capital defending ATF. The national media took little note, although the firearms press devoted considerable attention to the issue. The administration managed temporarily to pacify the gun lobby and avoid negative media attention.[3]

The NRA campaign against ATF began in the late 1970s, following the passage of Saturday Night Special legislation by one house of Congress, organization of lobbies advocating strict gun control, and efforts by the Carter administration to implement new regulations.[4] The administration responded by appointing a new director, who placed emphasis on guaranteeing no future abuses rather than attacking the validity of the allegations. Again, the national media paid little attention and the administration avoided the expenditure of political resources to defend a second-tier agency. The next attack would occur in a different political environment, and the stakes for the administration would be far higher.

The 60 Minutes Ambush

ATF's first experiences with the national media spotlight were of a very different character than what the bureau sought. In 1984, the television program 60 Minutes presented a segment on ATF's restoration of firearms possession rights to an individual who subsequently shot a youth to death. The segment made an appealing exposé, but the facts were far less interesting than the television segment. A middle-aged, African-American businessman from Indiana had been granted relief from the federal prohibition against possession of a firearm. Through an unusual feature of Indiana law, the state automatically removed firearms possession restrictions from felons granted relief by ATF, thus removing all restrictions to their possession of firearms. Subsequent to being granted relief, the applicant shot and killed a teenage boy, who allegedly threw a brick through the window of the man's car. Though charged, the man was acquitted for the killing and the events received considerable local press attention.

At that time, ATF denied relief to about half of those who applied. In addition, applications from those convicted of violent or armed felonies and applicants who had not been off parole or probation for at least two years were returned to the applicant and not processed, thus increasing the actual proportion not approved.[5] ATF conducted a background investigation on every applicant processed, contacting neighbors, employers, local police, and references. The investigation on this applicant revealed no current criminal activity, positive references, and a dated criminal history. Thus, relief was granted. Unfortunately for ATF, the television professionals displayed far more skill than bureaucrats at manipulating images. The camera panned the subject's FBI rap sheet, showing numerous "arrests." Like many black males of his age, the applicant had numerous entries while young, but most did not reflect convictions.[6] When confronted by cameras, the applicant's references, including a staff member for a U.S. senator and a police sergeant, stated that they did not mean to recommend him for the possession of firearms, even though this had been the expressed purpose of the investigation.[7] The interviews aired by *60 Minutes* implied that ATF had overruled local police and that the state had no option but to allow the possession of the firearm. The most devastating portion of the segment was an interview with Director Steve Higgins. Higgins's background in regulation had not versed him well in the routines of the relief process, which was managed by enforcement. In addition, his folksy style seemed awkward and evasive in the face of hostile questioning. Most important, the producers controlled the editing process, which was used ruthlessly to portray Higgins as a bumbling bureaucrat in the act of covering up incompetence.

Although the experience produced dismay and anger within ATF, where the perception was that *60 Minutes* had deliberately misrepresented the circumstances in pursuit of a story, there was little impact outside the agency. Few people understood the issue, and the NRA had little interest in attacking the agency for being too lenient in the administration of firearms laws. The experience, however, revealed the agency's vulnerability as a target for television exposés. Higgins, who was generally well liked within ATF, at Treasury, and in the enforcement community, lacked two key skills. He did not understand the inner workings of law enforcement, the more controversial component of the bureau, and he did not perform well on television, particularly in an adversarial environment where quick responses were required.[8]

Apparently, the staff of *60 Minutes* recognized ATF as an easy target because it struck the agency again in 1992. This time the issue was of interest to far more people in and out of government and the potential for damage to ATF much greater. A segment was aired in which three female agents accused the agency of systematic gender discrimination and characterized the work environment as being rife with sexual harassment. With his first experience with *60 Minutes* in mind, Steve Higgins initially refused an interview. But, as pressure built, he reluctantly agreed to discuss two cases that were no longer being litigated.[9] One of these involved a female inspector in California and the second an agent in Missouri. During the interview, which lasted about an hour, no questions were asked about the first case. The second, which had occurred several years before, was discussed. However, all references to the two-grade demotion, removal from management, and transfer of the perpetrator were edited from the broadcast version of the interview, thus giving the erroneous impression that no action had been taken by ATF. Two other cases were raised by the interviewer, both of which were still unresolved. When Higgins protested that these could not be discussed because of privacy issues, signed releases from the two female agents in question were presented.[10] Although the presentation of the releases made for dramatic television, they were of less importance than they appeared, as they did not alleviate concern for the privacy of other individuals involved in the cases or the impact on pending litigation.

Unsure of the specific details of the cases, his legal position with regard to the privacy of other parties involved, and the potential impact on future litigation, Higgins refused to discuss the cases.[11] Although he appeared evasive and awkward in the edited version of the interview, the unedited version revealed a distinctly different picture. In his usual low-key, Midwest style, Higgins tried repeatedly to explain his predicament. This style, which could be so disarming in person, was a disaster on television, particularly when the interviewer controlled the editing. Neither Higgins nor the interviewer made the point that one of the cases involved a female manager accused of becoming involved with a male subordinate.[12] It is clear that *60 Minutes* had no interest in diluting the impact of its exposé, and Higgins apparently just missed an opportunity. The other case, involving accusations of harassment against a Chicago supervisor, later resulted in the supervisor being terminated.

Issues of Gender and Race

The issue of sexual harassment was highly topical in 1992. In addition, the opportunity to open the show with pictures of three attractive women dressed in snug T-shirts, combat boots, and utility trousers and firing weapons made the segment appealing in a ratings-driven business. At the time of the *60 Minutes* broadcast, most federal law enforcement and many other federal agencies were the targets of discrimination suits by various protected classes. Within ATF, a group of black agents was pursuing a class action suit that alleged discrimination in hiring and promotion, while numerous white male employees perceived that they were the victims of overt discrimination in the promotion of Hispanics, blacks, and females. The dominant assumption among ATF and other federal managers, however, was that backlash from majority employees presented far less risk for them than accusations of discrimination by members of any protected group.

ATF, like many agencies, had a clear history of discrimination, both de facto and de jure. Until 1971, women had not been considered for appointment to agent positions in ATF or any other major federal law enforcement agency. Although ATF had long employed both black and Hispanic agents, the Southeastern Region remained entirely white into the 1970s. With this region constituting over half of all the bureau's enforcement employees until 1971, and with minorities underrepresented in other regions, the result was an almost totally white, male work force in enforcement. Although women were not excluded from the position of inspector, few women or minorities were hired. This pattern was typical of federal agencies until the 1970s and not unique to ATF.[13]

Several factors mitigated against a rapid change in the professional workforce in ATF. Staffing for the compliance function was largely static with little growth or turnover, providing limited opportunity for quick change in the composition of the work force. Although law enforcement expanded rapidly during the period between 1968 and 1972, only modest changes occurred in the composition of the agent force. Most of the hiring was completed before women were accepted into agent positions. Conservative managers did not aggressively pursue minority candidates, and some very likely discriminated against them. The practice of primarily hiring former police officers, who quickly could become functional agents, mitigated against women and minorities, who were underrepresented in these ranks. Educational requirements proved a barrier to minorities and veterans-preference quotas favored males. Even where concerted efforts were made to seek minority and female candidates, applicants were not numerous.[14] Subsequently, ATF was far more successful in recruiting minorities than women into its law enforcement ranks, a pattern that is reflective of law enforcement in general.[15]

As with most federal agencies, ATF's affirmative action efforts intensified steadily through the 1970s and 1980s in response to changing national values, executive mandate, and fear of court intervention. By the mid-1980s, special agents in charge were directed to consider only women or minority males for a substantial portion of their open positions. Headquarters also intervened in some instances to assure that SACs selected specific candidates from the "best-qualified" lists for supervisory positions.[16] These strategies have had significant impact on the profile of ATF's work force. By 1996 ATF had the most racially, ethnically, and sexually diverse agent work force in all of Treasury law enforcement.[17] The current agent work force is 88.4 percent male and 81.1 percent white. The largest minority representation is African-Americans, who compose 9.8 percent of the agent staffing. ATF currently has two African-American and one woman special agents in charge.[18] The trend can be even more clearly detected when one examines new hires and promotions. Analysis of the inspector profiles for fiscal year 1996 reveals that females are being hired at more than four times the rate of males, and blacks at almost three times their proportion of the labor pool.[19] Although new hires of agents have been too few for meaningful analysis since 1991, analysis of management positions reveals that nonwhites and women have been promoted to management positions at a rate higher than their representation in the agent work force. ATF has been least successful at recruiting women into its agent ranks. Although this is likely due in part to a virtual moratorium on agent hiring since 1991, the causes run far deeper. As of 1993, women composed less than 9 percent of the police in the United States.[20] For reasons that are open to debate, women continue to compose a distinct minority of applicants for law enforcement positions.

For ATF management, the most difficult issue relating to race and gender, however, has not been the underrepresentation of women in its law enforcement ranks but a class action suit by African-American agents.[21] The suit alleges that the agency has systematically discriminated in hiring and promotion against black agents. It is primarily based on an analysis of hiring and promotion figures that reflects lower levels of hiring and promotion of blacks than their representation in the labor pool. This evidence is buttressed with anecdotal evidence from the plaintiffs. Curiously, some of ATF's affirmative action strategies have become issues in the case. The plaintiffs charge that ATF routinely hired black agents under Schedule A authority, and that this disadvantaged these agents in competing with their counterparts. Schedule A hiring bypasses normal civil service requirements and is intended to allow agencies to hire a limited number of individuals with the skills necessary for accomplishment of the agency mission. ATF and other agencies have routinely used this authority to hire members of underrepresented classes that could not be hired under normal civil service procedure. Once hired, these employees must be converted to career positions to be eligible for promotion to management and are thus at some disadvantage.

Many of the actions charged by the plaintiffs, such as arbitrariness of promotions and promoting primarily those persons known to management, were also common complaints among white agents. But, while black agents interpreted these actions as being rooted in racist attitudes, whites saw them as discrimination at a more personal level.

The driving force behind the black agent suit has been Larry Stewart. Hand-picked by Associate Director Phillip McGuire for rapid advancement, Stewart was selected as the supervisor for the Long Beach, California, office in 1985.[22] McGuire made a conscious decision to push Stewart rapidly up the promotion ladder in an effort to develop him as a top-level manager.[23] Once in headquarters, Stewart lost McGuire's confidence, and it became clear that he was no longer favored for rapid promotion. Stewart's failure to internalize ATF's law enforcement culture may have been the key element in this development and the key to generating the class action suit.[24] McGuire had demonstrated a significant capacity to adapt to social and political change. Originally employed to work liquor violations in an openly racist and regionalized organization, McGuire had survived and prospered as the organization nationalized, changed mission, and delegitimized racism. He was the only southern manager able to move almost seamlessly into the new reality. But in the end, diversity generated more changes in organizational culture than even McGuire could manage. In 1990, Stewart and Mark Jones filed the class action suit, which was later joined by additional plaintiffs.

Prior to the filing of the suit, Stewart, accompanied by several other black agents and an attorney, engaged in discussions with ATF. At the time of the discussions, McGuire had retired and had been replaced by Daniel Hartnett. Hartnett designated his deputy, Daniel Conroy, and Division Chief Richard Cook as the ATF negotiators, but exercised almost total control from behind the scenes.[25] Hartnett, in turn, reported to Higgins, who did not become involved in the details of the discussions.[26] Hartnett's position was that ATF would agree to affirmative action goals, including target goals for promotion and hiring. The negotiations reached an impasse over the issue of guaranteeing promotions for specific individuals, including Stewart.[27] Stewart has since been promoted.

Allegations of race or gender bias represent a threat to any agency. ATF is particularly vulnerable for several reasons. Its historic southern roots make it suspect in all issues of race, and the male domination of law enforcement makes it suspect in issues of gender. It also has enemies, who would be unlikely to focus on issues of race or gender in other agencies, but find them welcome opportunities for attacking ATF. Unlike many other law enforcement agencies, when the issue was raised, ATF could not be assured of support from the political right that was beholden to the NRA. The agency thus faced potential attack from the left on issues of affirmative action and individual rights, without full support from law enforcement's traditional political allies. Without deep residual political support within Congress and with limited external support, the agency was an appealing political target that generated a strange coalition. When right-wing extremists provided the press with information that ATF agents had organized and participated in a law enforcement gathering in Tennessee known as the Good O' Boys Roundup at which openly racist symbols were displayed, demands for investigation came simultaneously from liberal Democrat John Conners and conservative Republican Orrin Hatch (see Chapter 13). After the *60 Minutes* segment was aired, issues of race and gender discrimination suddenly dominated the attention of ATF management. Steve Higgins, who had presided over an almost decade-long effort to hire and promote women and minorities, found himself the personal target of accusations of racism and discrimination.

With a new Democratic administration coming into office in January of 1993, the timing of the controversy could not have been worse for ATF management. Although Steve Higgins and his chief subordinates were career bureaucrats with no real party identity, they were viewed as holdovers from the past twelve years of Republican rule.[28] Normally, ATF would have attracted little attention from a new administration. The environment was beginning to change, however. Gun control had escalated as an issue during the campaign, and the Democrats were beginning to openly identify with the issue again. Democrats were also committed to affirmative action and sensitive to allegations of discrimination. Although both of these factors would have prevented ATF from being entirely invisible to the new administration, it would not likely have been of primary concern but for one fateful event.[29]

Notes

1. Treasury agents lagged several grades behind the FBI for many years; by the mid-1960s the Secret Service had reduced this to one grade,

while ATF remained two behind. IRS and Customs agents were somewhere between ATF and the Secret Service. By the late 1970s, ATF reduced the difference to one grade, and by 1990 the Treasury agencies had almost matched the FBI. In general the salaries, equipment, training, and other resources available to the various Treasury enforcement agencies has been fairly uniform, with the exception of those resources provided to the Secret Service for their protective function.

2. William J. Vizzard, "The Evolution of Gun Control Policy in the United States: Accessing the Public Agenda," DPA dissertation, University of Southern California, 1993.

3. "ATF Becomes a New Federal Bureau," *American Rifleman* (May 1972) 45.

4. Vizzard, 1993.

5. Congress has transmitted mixed messages on the granting of relief. Authorized as a part of the GCA in 1968, eligibility was expanded in 1986 by the Gun Owners Protection Act, which also recognized state expungement of felony convictions and extended appeals for those denied relief. Subsequently, Congress effectively ended the granting of relief by inserting a prohibition on the use of funds to conduct relief investigation.

6. For African-American men who grew up in the 1940s and 1950s, an arrest record with numerous entries was neither unusual nor indicative of a criminal career. Arrests for vagrancy, gambling, intoxication, and other minor offenses were common. Even arrests for more serious crimes were sometimes little more than pretext arrests for being on the street. In addition, one arrest often generated numerous entries as an individual could be fingerprinted by arresting, transporting, and receiving agencies. Sometimes a single arrest could result in half a dozen entries and a person could be arrested numerous times without a single conviction.

7. The references also included a former Indianapolis chief of police and a United States marshal. Among the routine questions asked of applicants was, "Do you know of any reason that this person should not be allowed to possess a firearm?"

8. The experiences of regulatory managers provided very little preparation for such situations. They seldom dealt with the press, almost never testified in court, and routinely dealt with an industry with which they shared a symbiotic relationship.

9. Interview with Steve Higgins.

10. Based on the author's review of both the broadcast version and an unedited videotape of the interview.

11. Interview with Steve Higgins.

12. At this writing the case is unresolved.

13. In the Western Region, the first two black agents were hired in 1968. ATF received two positions specifically for this purpose and recruited only black candidates. Several Hispanic agents were already employed at this time. The Western and North Atlantic Regions were clearly the leaders in moving toward a representative work force. They also hired the first female agents.

14. The author served on interview panels during the period 1970 to 1972 and was the college recruiter for northern California.

15. Women constituted less than 9 percent of local police in the United States as of 1993. See U.S. Department of Justice, Bureau of Justice Statistics, *Local Police* (Washington, D.C., April 8, 1996).

16. Former associate director Daniel Hartnett denied directing the promotion of specific candidates. However, former special agents in charge report being denied selection authority until they voluntarily chose the proper candidate. Although they were never told the reason that other choices were refused, the acceptable candidate was always a woman or a minority. Although SACs were the selecting officials for supervisors, there had been a long tradition of informal direction and intervention by associate directors. This usually took the form of a telephone call from the chief of the Planning and Analysis Division advising the identity of the candidates and suggesting that one particular candidate should receive strong consideration. Although affirmative action appears to have become the most common reason for these suggestions in the late 1980s and 1990s, it was not the exclusive reason.

17. Department of the Treasury, *Report of the Good O' Boys Roundup Policy Review* (Washington, D.C., April 1996) 19–30.

18. Bureau of Alcohol, Tobacco and Firearms.

19. Employment figures provided by ATF.

20. U.S. Department of Justice.

21. *Larry Stewart, et al. v. Robert E. Rubin*, United States District Court for the District of Columbia, docket 90–2841.

22. David Troy, who was assistant special agent in charge of the Los Angeles Division in 1985, stated that McGuire, and not the special agent in charge, selected Stewart for the Long Beach position. Troy also stated that McGuire selected Stewart for promotion to headquarters approximately one year later, although both the special agent in charge and Troy advised that Stewart was not yet experienced enough for promotion. McGuire confirms this account with minor variations.

23. Interview with Phillip McGuire.

24. Interviews with both Phillip McGuire and Larry Stewart reveal an evolution of events that appear to be driven more by generation than race. Stewart reports going directly to McGuire with a proposal that McGuire would have perceived as inappropriate for such a junior staffer. Both of these individuals were highly sensitive to status. McGuire expected his protégés to be humble and appreciative; Stewart tended toward the presumptuous and showed little deference. Some observers have raised serious questions regarding the level of experience, knowledge, and skill displayed by Stewart during his headquarters tenure. Whether or not he was lacking in any of these areas was most likely not the most critical issue. McGuire had promoted the less-than-competent, but not if they failed to display loyalty or deference, two traits that were absolutely expected of agents in the Southeastern Region from which McGuire sprang.

25. Interview with Richard Cook, former ATF division chief.

26. Interviews with Steve Higgins and Daniel Hartnett.

27. Higgins, Hartnett, and Cook all report that this was the key issue that could not be resolved. Stewart advised the author he was unable to discuss the negotiations in detail because of a gag order on the case issued by the district court.

28. Interview with Steve Higgins.

29. During the House Waco hearings, former secretary of the treasury Lloyd Bentsen testified that he had never met with Higgins in the month between taking office and the Waco raid. That the secretary of the treasury paid little attention to ATF came as no surprise to ATF insiders, who know that ATF had never been a part of Treasury's primary agenda.

CHAPTER 12

Waco

On the morning of February 28, 1993, near Waco, Texas, ATF agents attempted to serve a search warrant on Mount Carmel, a compound housing the religious sect commonly referred to as Branch Davidians, and an arrest warrant on the sect's leader, Vernon Wayne Howell. The attempt resulted in a gun battle in which four agents and six Davidians died and twenty-eight agents and four Davidians, including leader David Koresh, received injuries.[1] Forced to withdraw and leave the compound in the hands of the Davidians, ATF surrendered primary control of the scene to the FBI within days and withdrew to a supporting role. The subsequent fifty-one-day standoff ended on April 19, 1993, when agents of the Federal Bureau of Investigation's Hostage Rescue Team injected tear gas into the compound and the occupants responded by initiating multiple fires. The fires and self-inflicted gunshot wounds resulted in the death of over seventy occupants, including a number of children. Both the Departments of Justice and the Treasury conducted extensive investigations, as did the Texas Rangers, who were requested to conduct the investigation of the shootings by the United States Attorney's Office to avoid a conflict of interest. A subsequent trial in United States District Court resulted in the conviction of several Davidian survivors on weapons and manslaughter charges but acquittal on murder and murder conspiracy charges.

To date, three congressional hearings have been conducted on the raid and siege. The most extensive of these, by a joint House of Representatives subcommittee, extended over nine days during the summer of 1995.[2] These later hearings were believed to have resulted, at least partially, from pressure from the NRA and others opposed to ATF and gun laws. The Treasury report determined that there had been significant errors in the command and control of the ATF raid and that some managers had attempted to distort the fact that an undercover agent had warned that secrecy had been compromised but that the raid commanders still had proceeded with the raid. This was particularly critical because the tactics employed were dependent upon surprise. As a result, two ATF managers were dismissed, and the director, associate director of law enforcement, and deputy associate director of law enforcement all retired prematurely under pressure. The administration moved Secret Service Director John Magaw to the position of ATF director, which apparently served the dual purpose of placing a high-profile director in charge of a beleaguered ATF and removing from a sensitive post, with access to White House activity, a person closely associated with former president Bush.

Background

The community of Mount Carmel was originally established by Victor Houteff and a small group of followers who left the Seventh Day Adventist Church.[3] Although the group remained isolated from much of the larger society and focused their attentions on preparing for the imminent second coming of Christ, it was neither militant nor armed. Upon Houteff's death, the group divided between followers of Houteff's widow, Florence, and those who accepted the leadership of another member, Ben Roden, who referred to his followers as The Branch. After Florence Houteff's 1959 prediction of the slaughter and resurrection of all the believers failed to materialize, many of her followers drifted away and Roden's faction predominated. After Roden's death in 1978, his widow, Lois, assumed leadership of the group.

In 1981, Vernon Wayne Howell, a twenty-two-year-old high school dropout and sometimes rock musician, came to live at Mount Carmel. Howell came to exercise substantial influence on Lois Roden and was engaging in a sexual relationship with the seventy-one-year-old Roden by 1982.[4] A contest for control of the group developed between Howell and George Roden, Lois's son, and in 1984 Howell left Mount Carmel with a group of followers. Lois Roden died in 1986, and in 1987 Howell and a group of armed followers fought a gun battle with Roden for control of the Mount Carmel compound.[5] Although Howell and the seven who accompanied him on the raid were charged with felony assault, Roden made a very poor victim and witness and the jury failed to reach a verdict on Howell and found the others not guilty. Howell and his followers obtained control of the property by paying back taxes, and Roden was later placed in a mental institution.

For nine years, Howell, now known as David Koresh, functioned as the unquestioned spiritual leader and absolute potentate of the community at Mount Carmel, as well as among followers elsewhere. During this time, Howell-Koresh decreed celibacy for all the male residents and claimed all the female residents as his wives, in some cases engaging in sexual intercourse with girls as young as ten.[6] Koresh also acquired numerous firearms in preparation for a prophesied coming conflagration and rejected the jurisdiction of secular government and law over his actions.[7]

In May 1992 local authorities requested assistance from ATF in investigating the activities of Koresh and residents of the compound relating to the production of explosives and illegal firearms.[8] The subsequent investigation established probable cause that members were making and possessing unregistered NFA firearms, specifically machine guns and hand grenades, in the compound. The investigation also revealed allegations of child abuse, child sexual molestation, and holding persons against their will, as well as indications that the Davidians might resist lawful authority by force.

ATF's investigation included the infiltration of an undercover agent into the compound and the establishment of an observation post that could watch the compound. Operating on the belief that they could overwhelm the Davidians with a show of force and the use of surprise, ATF developed a plan to serve search and arrest warrants on the compound. On February 28, 1993, a force of seventy-six ATF agents dressed in dark blue utility uniforms and protective vests, distinctively marked with large gold badges and the letters *ATF*, moved to the scene hidden in two large cattle trailers pulled by pickups. As the agents burst from the trailers and raced for the front door and rear windows, they were met with automatic weapons fire and grenades. After an extended gunfight between the agents, who were pinned down in a hopeless position, and the occupants, a cease-fire was negotiated by telephone and the agents withdrew with their dead and wounded. Before the day ended, Treasury officials had decided to surrender control of the scene to the FBI to avoid any future allegations of bias by ATF and to capitalize on the resources of the HRT. The weeks and months following the Waco incident proved the most trying in ATF history. Every aspect of the operation proved controversial, and the initial ATF decision to make a dynamic entry and the FBI decision to use tear gas to attempt to precipitate a surrender proved the most controversial issues. To understand how and why Waco occurred requires that the events be viewed not through the benefit of hindsight but with an understanding of ATF history, culture, structure, and experience.

The Decision

Given both the physical risk to agents and the potential political risk to the organization, why did ATF proceed with the raid on

Mount Carmel? The organization had historically displayed an aversion to risk consistent with its precarious political position. No bold new leaders had assumed control. The political environment had not undergone significant change. What then explains ATF's actions? Viewed in the context of organizational routines formed by structure, culture, environment, and task and as a series of interrelated but distinct decisions by individuals within ATF, the raid becomes understandable, though not essentially defensible. Although the personality and nature of key actors also played a critical role in the Waco decisions, the factors of structure, culture, environment, and task had influenced both the placement and outlook of these key actors.

The process began as a routine investigation after a referral of information and request for assistance made to the Austin ATF office by the McLenan County Sheriff's Department, regarding shipments of explosives components, inert grenade hulls, firearms parts, and large quantities of firearms to a location called the Mag Bag, a small building near the Davidian compound used by the Davidians.[9] Subsequent investigation by Special Agent David Aguilera revealed that the Davidians were ordering numerous kits of replacement parts for M-16 machine guns. Represented as repair parts for legally registered machine guns, these kits have primarily been used to convert semi-automatic AR-15 rifles to fully automatic M-16 machine guns.[10] The Davidians also had obtained explosive components and grenade hulls that could serve as components to manufacture grenades. Agents coupled the orders with statements from former members and reports of machine gun fire from the compound to establish the probable cause required to obtain a search warrant to examine the compound for machine guns, grenades, and evidence of their manufacture.[11]

With some exceptions these constituted routine events for ATF agents. An information referral and request for assistance from a local law enforcement agency precipitated an investigation by ATF agents that revealed probable violations under ATF jurisdiction. In addition, the investigation revealed evidence of probable child abuse and sexual abuse of minors by David Koresh. The United States Attorney's Office concurred with the evaluation of the probable cause and the need to proceed with federal action. This satisfied the usual standard for further ATF action. The normal questions asked of an agent were: Is there evidence of a crime? Is the crime within ATF's jurisdiction? Do the actions justify prosecution? And does the United States attorney concur? ATF's standard for prosecution had long required more than just a violation of law to generate enforcement action. Even before the passage of the GCA, the official orders had recognized something called a "nonwillful violation." Cases that did not involve convicted felons, large-scale commercial violations, or other crimes were not to be pursued unless the violator had been previously warned and persisted. This standard applied only to firearms violations and not to alcohol violations. Although the official policy of not prosecuting isolated firearms violations ceased after 1968, it remained as an unofficial standard.

Much has been made by some critics, particularly in academia, of law enforcement's efforts to portray the Davidians as engaged in child molestation and abuse, when these were not the crimes charged in the warrants.[12] ATF actions were rooted in years of experience and conditioning. Critics have repeatedly attacked the agency for not pursuing real criminals and for using the gun laws to harass innocent citizens. Congressional investigations have repeatedly focused on this issue and United States attorneys have used other criminal activity as a key element for deciding which firearms violators to prosecute. Both the press and the public have displayed far more support for pursuit of firearms violations when the violator has been perceived as a criminal. ATF has interpreted these events as evidence that the importance of a firearms violation is largely dependent on the other criminal activities of the violator. Prosecution of firearms violations become important when directed at a person or persons whose activities are otherwise objectionable or dangerous. Thus illegal possession of a machine gun is of little consequence unless the possessor is a criminal or otherwise demonized. Likewise, illegal sales of firearms are of little consequence unless the purchasers are criminals or other violent persons. This constitutes a far different standard than the one applied to drug laws, but it is similar to the attitude toward gambling and liquor laws.

As a result of these experiences, ATF has focused as much on who violated the law as what law they violated. It has become both a formal and informal component of the investigative routine to consider this issue. Thus, the attention agents gave to information that Koresh molested young children, had been involved in a past violent confrontation, held people against their will, and talked of future violent confrontations was consistent with normal working routine that evolved from past experience. Virtually any police agency would have focused on the same information in evaluating the public safety aspects of the case. ATF agents did not see themselves as gun regulators, whose job was to stop Koresh from obtaining machine guns. They saw themselves as protectors of public safety, whose job was to investigate Koresh and bring to light all his crimes. The firearms jurisdiction was their legal justification for doing so. Federal agencies, particularly the FBI, have followed this same practice for years and been afforded widespread acclaim. The very nature of federal laws that utilized the marginal interstate nexus to allow federal jurisdiction over hate crimes, kidnapping, carjacking, gun possession, and bombing reveal that Congress has assumed this to be a legitimate federal role since the passage of the Mann Act at the beginning of the century.[13]

The symbolic and political importance of additional criminal acts was apparent in the 1995 House hearings on Waco. Widely assumed to be engineered by the Republicans to embarrass the administration and pacify the NRA, the hearings quickly changed course with the testimony of Kiri Jewel, who described her rape by Koresh when she was ten years of age.[14] As it became apparent that parents routinely allowed their children to be sexually assaulted by Koresh, both Koresh and the parents lost status as victims. Soon Republicans found it necessary to begin every session with the caveat that they did not seek to support Koresh or attack law enforcement, and the political dynamic of the hearing changed direction.

Thus for ATF, the decision to investigate Koresh reflected the application of organizational routine in a classic sense. This investigation was exactly what the agency existed to do. Had the investigation revealed no criminal activity, other than firearms violations, and no evidence of a threat to public safety, the decision would have been far more problematical, and management might have forced the agents to back away from a law enforcement approach.[15] The decision to use a search warrant flowed directly from the decision to pursue a criminal investigation. Prosecution required seizure of the evidence, in this case the converted firearms and grenades. In addition, the arrest of Koresh and service of a search warrant very likely would aid in revealing other crimes on the premises. Because firearms are difficult to hide or destroy quickly and are routinely retained for very long periods of time, search warrants have proven a very effective tool for obtaining evidence in firearms investigations. The tendency to retain firearms has resulted in ATF being able to obtain warrants and seize evidence using probable cause that would be considered stale in other types of cases.[16]

Why the Raid?

The raid on the Branch Davidian compound by a large number of uniformed, armed agents shocked a significant portion of the public. Their reaction is typified by Representative Henry Hyde,

Republican chairman of the House Judiciary Committee. During the 1995 hearings, Representative Hyde repeatedly expressed shock that seventy-five armed agents wearing helmets and ski masks attacked the compound. Even after being repeatedly told that there were no ski masks and that the agents were uniformed for identification and wore helmets for protection, Hyde seemed unable to comprehend any possible justification for what he apparently viewed as an armed attack on a religious community. ATF agents and other law enforcement officers across the country found Hyde's response as bewildering as Hyde found the raid procedures.

For veterans of the wars on crime and drugs and for those who live in the neighborhoods where these wars are waged, the scene was unusual only in its scope. Similar scenes, in fact, appeared regularly on the local news in urban areas across the country. ATF had consistently received congressional and administration support for similar actions during the implementation of the ACES and the ACES II, both of which received extensive favorable coverage in the Washington media. What, then, prompted the strong reaction to ATF's tactics at Waco from individuals and organizations who had paid little heed to similar actions by ATF and numerous other agencies in the war on drugs? The differences in reaction apparently derived from three separate causes. For the NRA and its followers, the use of coercive force to enforce firearms laws lacked legitimacy because the firearms laws lacked legitimacy. In addition, criticism of the raid and increased fear of ATF served their political agenda.[17] For a portion of the population who saw the raid as a conflict between the power of the secular state and unpopular religious views, the raid was an unacceptable repression of religion.[18] Finally, civil libertarians, typified by the American Civil Liberties Union, and radical libertarians, such as militia members, objected to virtually all uses of coercive force by the government. Representative Hyde appears to represent this final view, which recoils when confronted with the unmasked use of force, except in narrowly construed circumstances of self-defense.[19] U.S. culture has displayed a dichotomous pattern with regard to use of coercive force by government. In general, government authority and coercive means of enforcing it have been distrusted, yet this pattern has reversed when the subjects of the action are perceived as evil or alien.[20]

The agents investigating the case invoked organizational routine and proceeded to obtain a search warrant. Their actions constituted standard practice given the existence of probable cause of a crime under their jurisdiction, related criminal activity, interest from the United States attorney, and the need for physical evidence to establish proof of a crime. Although the involvement of a religious sect distinguished this case from others, the investigation had followed familiar patterns that invoked familiar technology and routines.[21] The next phase of the investigation also involved familiar technology and routines, but the magnitude of the operation exceeded anything ATF had previously undertaken with the exception of the CSA search warrant (see Chapter 9). The organizational failure began as a failure of management to comprehend the implications of this change in magnitude, thus management made only incremental adjustments to adapt.[22]

The evolving nature of ATF's mission and task environment combined with promotion patterns to produce a top level of management with little or no applicable experience for overseeing the Waco operation. Aggravated by the common bureaucratic pattern of assigning authority based on position rather than experience, knowledge, or skill, this lack of managerial experience resulted in a severe lack of overall command and control.[23] Conversely, the Special Response Team commanders, who were experienced supervisors with extensive experience in police and military tactical operations, enjoyed substantial credibility.[24] The result was an operation in which the operational level was far more qualified than the management level. This was not unusual in ATF and normally would have had only limited implications. In this case, however, command and control capacity was necessary, particularly in assuring that intelligence was gathered, analyzed, dispersed, and utilized. The entire Department of the Treasury report is critical of command and control, with particular emphasis on poor intelligence support.[25]

Functions such as intelligence, operational security, and overall command and control had not been well developed in ATF because normal ATF operations could not justify the expenditure of resources for training specialists. Therefore, managers had very little opportunity to develop command and control skills. These are essentially military concepts, although law enforcement, firefighting, and civil defense require command and control in circumstances such as riots and natural disasters. Maintenance of command and control capabilities requires an organization to either engage actual experience or practice under realistic simulation utilizing all the organizational components. The military maintains these skills at substantial cost in training and simulation, but law enforcement historically does not. For instance, the Los Angeles Police Department's failure to respond effectively and rapidly to the 1993 riots reflected a failure in command and control. Law enforcement agencies commit virtually all their resources to routine daily operations. Budgets have not allowed for the overstaffing necessary to conduct large-scale tactical training operations or maintain reserve forces for emergencies. At the federal level, only the FBI maintains a full-time tactical team with full logistical support. Even that team, which represents less than 1 percent of the FBI's agent staffing, did not exist prior to the mid-1980s.

Many of the problems might still have been avoided if ATF managers had been innovative thinkers who recognized the potential risks, asked hypothetical questions, or invoked different paradigms.[26] This was not the case. ATF law enforcement had cultivated managers and staff for their loyalty and dependability, not for their innovation and intellect.[27] Associate Director Daniel Hartnett was well known throughout the agency as a person uncomfortable with change and dissent. He did not seek out alternate points of view nor cultivate hypothetical discussions.[28] The operational plan for the raid, for instance, was not reviewed or critiqued by ATF's Headquarters Enforcement Staff. Although they were briefed by the Houston SAC and others regarding the investigation, the raid briefing was given to only Hartnett and Conroy.[29] Higgins, who had come up through the regulatory side of ATF, had no expertise or background in tactical operations. This, no doubt, reinforced his tendency to delegate operations to those who, in his mind, had the expertise.

In spite of the fact that the operation appeared on the surface to be similar to past ATF operations, it was not. Excepting the Marion and CSA cases, this situation was not like anything ever faced by ATF. It was, in fact, more dangerous than any operation conducted by a law enforcement agency in the history of the United States.[30] The level of danger was not fully evident to the Special Response Team (SRT) supervisors who planned the raid, utilizing intelligence information that was not properly collected, analyzed, or disseminated. The planners never accepted the worst-case scenario, that is, that the occupants would resist en masse, using firearms.[31]

The Decision to Use Dynamic Entry

Critics of ATF and the Waco raid have repeatedly characterized it as some sort of poorly planned publicity stunt directed by ATF management for the purpose of enhancing the agency's image.[32] This characterization reflects a misunderstanding of both ATF's structure and procedures. ATF's management has never successfully controlled the field activities of its law enforcement personnel. ATF's law enforcement component displays the combined traits of what James Q. Wilson calls craft and coping organizations.[33] These organizations are characterized by very limited management control of operators. Although headquarters originated the concept for some projects, such as Project CUE and the ACES, individual agents always initiate the actual investigations. ATF management has attempted to capitalize on visible activity, as has the management of most agencies.

In the case of Waco, much of the criticism has focused on the actions of Sharon Wheeler, the public information officer for the Dallas Division.[34] Wheeler has stated that she was directed by Dallas SAC Ted Royster to obtain weekend contact telephone numbers for Dallas television news organizations.[35] Wheeler told the contacts at the stations that she wanted the numbers because something important might be happening in the area over the weekend.[36] This evidenced an effort by Royster to capitalize on an expected success at Waco to obtain favorable publicity, not a headquarters-directed plan to concoct the Waco raid for publicity.[37]

Ironically, the Waco operation did turn into the biggest press event in ATF's history. The disastrous mistakes in planning, command and control, intelligence, and postraid response resulted in the press quickly dubbing the operation as the "bungled Waco raid." A combination of sloppy research and outright fabrication have received wider acceptance than otherwise might have been the case had the mainstream press not laid the groundwork through the repetition of stories characterizing the raid as bungled, without more detailed explanation.[38]

The attempts to characterize Waco as the bungling of an incompetent agency, or worse, as a deliberately illegal attack on peaceful citizens, serve only to conceal the very serious issues raised by the events. The command and control and intelligence failures that plagued this operation would very likely reoccur in most law enforcement agencies, given a similar problem.[39] Although extensive planning and preparation had preceded the raid, a close examination of the planning process reveals a very fundamental dilemma. Even with adequate intelligence, planning, and command and control, there may be no legally and socially acceptable means of dealing with situations like those confronted at Mount Carmel. A review of the testimony given at the 1995 House hearings reveals a curious pattern. Numerous witnesses are critical of ATF's choice of tactics, but no alternative that allowed for all known difficulties was offered. Each alternative had its own potential risks, and calculating the risk level requires substantial speculation.[40] Although a siege-and-wait option appears to be favored by agencies after Waco, this strategy forfeits all initiative to the violators, establishes a precedent of rewarding the threat of forceful resistance, creates immense costs, and risks mass suicide.

Once the probable cause for a warrant had been developed and the decision made that no other course was available, the issue was how the warrant should be served. Two other options were available to ATF, although both so violated the values and routines of the field agents that top-level management would have had to invoke them. ATF could have ignored the violations, and taken no action. This could have been done by simply closing the case and ignoring the evidence of violations or by making the very questionable assumption that Koresh had not intentionally violated the law and by negotiating a voluntary surrender of the firearms.[41] ATF has done both in the past when political risk appeared unacceptable.[42] None of the factors that would support such approaches were present, however. Koresh appeared to constitute a potential threat to public safety and to be engaged in other criminal activity, precluding the argument that the violations were innocent mistakes by a law-abiding citizen. The magnitude and nature of the violations also invalidated such an interpretation. The United States attorney showed interest in the case, thus depriving ATF of any justification for dropping it due to lack of prosecutive potential. Finally, the referral of the case to local authorities would have been difficult, given the earlier request by those authorities for ATF assistance. Had ATF failed to take any action and had Koresh and his followers taken some violent action similar to the Jonestown massacre or the Tokyo subway gassings, the agency would likely have been the focus of intense criticism from many of its current critics.

A far more professionally and politically prudent approach would have been to request the FBI HRT to effect the service of the warrant. The HRT was clearly the most highly trained and best-equipped law enforcement tactical group in the United States. Although the operation might well have been beyond their capabilities and likewise ended in disaster, ATF would have been politically buffered. Although this would have been a politically shrewd move, and the FBI hardly could have avoided accepting the challenge, it would have met a firestorm of resistance within ATF. At both the management and operational levels, ATF had spent twenty years attempting to differentiate itself from the FBI. Even when ATF actions were critical to an investigation, joint participation with the FBI assured that ATF would be relegated to a minor role in the eyes of the press and public.[43] ATF Special Response Teams had been created largely to preclude the need to turn to the FBI. There is no indication in the official record or in any informal discussion that this alternative was ever considered, though it might have been the best option for ATF.

Four SRT team leaders, each with substantial tactical experience, planned the raid.[44] The planners had information from local officials, former Davidians, neighbors, and an ongoing undercover operation. ATF had placed several agents, posing as students enrolled in a nearby technical college, in a house adjacent to the compound. One of the agents, Robert Rodriguez, had established contact with Koresh. This residence provided a surveillance post to observe the compound but afforded the agents a view of only one entrance.[45]

The planners considered three options: a siege, the arrest of Koresh away from the compound combined with a raid or siege, and a dynamic entry.[46] Initially favored, the siege option faced the problems of a lack of cover for agents and the presence of .50-caliber weapons. The range of these weapons required a parameter beyond ATF's capabilities.[47] The most influential of the raid planners, William Buford, shifted from a position favoring a siege to one advocating dynamic entry.[48] Buford stated that he changed his position primarily in response to information from former Davidians that convinced him the group might engage in mass suicide and that adequate supplies existed on the compound to hold out for at least three months and likely longer.[49] The planners also believed that a siege would result in the destruction of most of the evidence, nullifying the purpose of the search. Finally, the planners faced the possibility an assault might still be necessary if a siege failed, albeit against a far more prepared target.

Based on information that the men in the group usually worked outside during the day in a large excavation, referred to as "the pit," and that weapons were locked in an arms room, a dynamic entry became the favored option. This is not surprising in light of the fact that SRTs were created primarily to engage in dynamic entry. Originally designated "entry control teams," their primary role consisted of making initial entries on arrest and search warrants. Dynamic entry constituted their core technology, their reason for being. Team members had experienced great success with this methodology as had members of tactical teams across the country.[50]

Unfortunately, the decision was predicated on faulty information.[51] Apparently, the men did not work in the pit regularly, and the arms were sometimes distributed and stored in the members' rooms. Numerous other intelligence oversights occurred, thus providing an inadequate and undependable information basis for planning the operation.[52] Planners did not seriously prepare for the contingency that the women might forcefully resist.[53] The plan also lacked adequate checks to assure that no changes had taken place.[54] Finally, no contingency plan was developed to extract the agents and secure the compound if there was an ambush.[55] In retrospect, it appears clear that in spite of the awareness of the large number of weapons and the apocalyptic rhetoric of Koresh, the planners just did not contemplate that they would face armed resistance by a significant number of occupants.[56] The Treasury report attributes this to an assumption that the ATF presence would intimidate the Davidians.[57]

The truth is likely even more complex. Although the planners accepted the concept of risk as an abstract reality, they had never observed or experienced such massive armed resistance in a domestic law enforcement setting. It was simply not an internalized reality.[58] Similar assumptions had cost the lives of two FBI agents in Miami several years before.[59] Similar inability to foresee risk appears in international relations, despite the availability of extensive intelligence and large planning staffs. To explain the inability to comprehend such risks is to explain why the United States was surprised at Pearl Harbor, the Soviets by the Nazi invasion, or the United Nations Forces by the intervention of the Chinese in Korea. To some extent, the operation of a civil law enforcement function requires the assumption that citizens will rationally respond to authority and submit. Without such an assumption, police would routinely have to strike first.

An effort to enlist the aid of the Texas Department of Protective and Regulatory Services to lure Koresh out of the compound failed when managers at that agency refused cooperation.[60] Having been advised by former members and the case worker from Protective and Regulatory Services that Koresh seldom left the compound, and having failed to confirm his departure through surveillance from the undercover residence near the compound, the planners concluded that arresting Koresh away from the compound was not practical.[61] This conclusion now appears to have been reached prematurely without adequate intelligence collection and analysis.[62] Although the planners may have reached their conclusions prematurely, their decision may not have been incorrect. Subsequent reports that Koresh left the compound on several occasions do not essentially imply he could have been arrested away from the compound. Arresting a potentially violent person away from a fortified stronghold and weapons is clearly a desirable tactic. Use of this strategy requires some predictability in the subject's departure, however. Random occasional forays present planners with the need to keep an arrest team on constant alert without being detected. Because the search warrant service would have to be coordinated with the arrest, this team would also have to be ready to act on a moment's notice. A mistake in the identity of the individual leaving the compound would have compromised the entire operation, as would detection of the arrest or search teams by the press or others.

The Plan

Convinced that no alternative means allowed the entry team to avoid or easily overcome resistance, the planners turned to the technology most familiar to the them, dynamic entry. Once committed to this option, they followed a common pattern by both attempting to perfect the plan and ignoring its most troubling potential weaknesses. The failure to plan for contingencies, such as the evacuation of the raiding party in the case of an ambush, likely reflects the fact that admitting such contingencies would have undermined support for the plan. Such a contingency was beyond ATF's ability to respond to, both practically and politically. For instance, providing for intense covering fire or aggressive use of armor to allow a withdrawal would have raised questions that could not have been answered. To plan for such contingencies would have constituted an admission that the operation presented a higher risk than ATF management would have accepted.[63] Combined with weak management oversight and poor intelligence, the tendency to avoid facing worst-case scenarios resulted in underestimating the downside risks of the raid plan. In spite of the tactical competency of the planners, intense preparation for the raid, and dedicated personnel, the raid turned into a disaster for ATF.

The final plan was to serve the arrest and search warrants at 10:00 A.M. on Monday, March 1, 1993. The planners expected that most of the men would be working outside in the construction area known as the pit, thus separated from the women and children, and more importantly from the weapons. The plan called for the use of three SRT teams, from Houston, Dallas, and New Orleans, to make the entry along with additional agents, who would function as arrest teams. In all, the raiding party would number seventy-five agents. Although the special agents in charge from each of the three field divisions would be present, the Houston SAC would exercise overall command, since Waco was in the Houston District. Although a veteran agent and former police officer, Houston SAC Philip Chojnacki had no special expertise or training in tactical operations. He delegated planning oversight to his assistant special agent in charge (ASAC), Charles Sarabyn. As the supervisor of the SRT, Sarabyn had received SRT training but was relatively young and had only limited tactical experience. As had been the ATF pattern, position and not specific knowledge or background drove the selection of key personnel, a practice that received harsh criticism by the Treasury review.[64]

Raid planners made advance arrangements for a command post and a separate assembly point for the agents, both several miles from the compound. New Orleans ASAC Jim Cavanaugh was assigned to the undercover house for the purpose of exercising overall command there. The plan also called for advance placement of several forward observer, or sniper, teams on two sides of the compound. All the agents involved were required to wear blue tactical uniforms with badges and the letters *ATF* in gold clearly visible on them. Each agent would also wear a bullet-resistant vest and helmet. A small number of agents were assigned to carry AR-15 rifles, and several others would carry MP-5 carbines or submachine guns. Only the AR-15 rifles assigned to the forward observers had the capacity to effectively penetrate walls. The MP-5s and the pistols carried by all agents utilized a low-velocity, 9-mm cartridge and were useful only in a direct confrontation and not for returning fire against barricaded opponents. The arms allocated reflected the planners' assumption that agents would make entry quickly and face risk only from isolated individuals inside the compound.

Assigned to secure the arms room, the New Orleans SRT would first have to scale the roof and enter the second story through the windows. The primary entry team, consisting of agents from the Houston and Dallas SRTs, would sprint for the front door, announce their identity and purpose, and make entry.[65] Other teams were designated to control the men in the pit and control the dogs.[66] In the service of any search warrant, officers must first locate and control all the occupants to assure the safety of the officers and occupants and prevent the destruction of evidence. This is normally accomplished by sweeping the premises quickly, searching, disarming, and moving all occupants to a central location. Although occupants may leave, officers have authority to control any who do not. The search of Mount Carmel did not differ from other warrants in this regard, except that clearing a complex of this size and locating and controlling approximately a hundred people presented tactical problems exponentially more difficult than those normally encountered when clearing a house or apartment.

Planners made extensive preparations for emergency medical care of any injured persons. Agents designated and trained as emergency medical technicians received additional training from Army Special Forces medics, and emergency supplies were stockpiled. In addition, ATF arranged to have ambulances available on standby for the morning of the raid, a preparation that would contribute to the ultimate disaster. After assembling in Waco, the entire raid team engaged in a series of rehearsals at the army's urban warfare training facilities at nearby Fort Hood, Texas. Army Special Forces advisers critiqued and advised the rehearsals and made suggestions for improvements.

The Execution

One of the agents residing in the residence near the compound, Robert Rodriguez, had established contact with Koresh. Rodriguez went to the compound regularly and talked with Koresh about religion and biblical teaching, and they sometimes went shooting together. As the raid became more imminent, the undercover agent's role was transformed from investigation to collection of tactical intelligence. Ultimately, Rodriguez played a critical role, not only in the investigation but also in the aftermath that shook ATF to its roots.

Although the raid was originally scheduled for Monday, March 1, 1993, external events accelerated the date. The local Waco newspaper, the *Tribune-Herald*, had been pursuing a story on Koresh and the Davidians since the spring of 1992. In October 1992, a reporter contacted the office of the United States attorney for information on Koresh, and the United States attorney informed ATF of the request.[67] Subsequently, ATF and the United States Attorney's Office received information that the paper had prepared a feature story titled "The Sinful Messiah" for publication. The story included much of the information that had been gathered during the ATF investigation including allegations of child molestation and abuse and information regarding acquisition of firearms. On February 1, 1993, ASAC Sarabyn and Group Supervisor Earl Dunagan met with the managing editor of the paper and requested a delay in the publication of the article, offering "front-row seats" to the paper in any upcoming law enforcement action.[68] ATF representatives continued to meet with the paper in efforts to secure a delay in the publication of the article on the assumption that its publication would alert Koresh and heighten security at the compound. In so doing they compromised operational security, although this may have been worth the risk if they had been successful.[69]

As the raid date approached, ATF personnel became convinced that the "Sinful Messiah" article would be published on Sunday, February 28. In fact, the article was scheduled for Saturday, February 27.[70] Special Agent in Charge Chojnacki pushed his tactical commander, Sarabyn, to move the raid up to Saturday; however, Sarabyn indicated that Sunday was the earliest possible date. The date of the raid could not easily be altered. Almost a hundred agents had to be brought to Waco, equipped, briefed, and rehearsed. Once set in motion, the mechanics of the operation largely dictated the timeline.[71] Thus, through a series of unfortunate circumstances, the agents would arrive the day after Koresh became agitated and alarmed by an article that accused him of criminal activity and implied strong law enforcement interest in his activities. The efforts to serve the warrant before the publication of the story resulted in scheduling for the day on which Koresh would be most focused on and agitated by the article.

While the teams assembled and prepared for the operation, ATF headquarters notified the office of the assistant secretary of the treasury for enforcement of the pending operation in a one-page memorandum.[72] The notification arrived at Treasury on the afternoon of Friday, February 26, 1993. On the same date, ATF was notified by the *Tribune-Herald* that the "Sinful Messiah" story would run the next day.[73] Events were beginning to move beyond the capacity of the ATF managers to evaluate and respond to them.

After receiving notification on Friday afternoon, Acting Assistant Secretary John Simpson contacted Director Higgins and notified him that ATF should not go forward with the operation at this time.[74] Higgins subsequently recontacted Simpson after conferring with Associate Director Hartnett, who, in turn, conferred with Chojnacki. Higgins provided additional information on the raid and assured Simpson that the plan would allow ATF to avoid the danger of the Davidians' weaponry and protect the children present. Higgins also assured Simpson that the undercover agent, Rodriguez, would reenter the compound before the raid and assure that no preparations were being made by the Davidians to resist ATF.[75]

Unknown to Higgins and others in ATF, who were focused on making last-minute preparations and satisfying Treasury concerns, an even more critical element in the unfolding events had already taken place. Word of the pending action by ATF had leaked from the newspaper to a local television news reporter. Another employee of television station KWTX had determined from a friend, who was employed as a dispatcher by a Waco ambulance service, that ATF had requested that ambulances be placed on standby for Sunday morning. On Saturday the newspaper article appeared and local attention was specifically focused on the Branch Davidians and any potential law enforcement action. By piecing together their knowledge of an ongoing ATF investigation with the request for ambulances, the local television news staff and newspaper reporters had both concluded that some sort of action was scheduled for Sunday.[76]

All components for a disaster were now on an intersecting course. Momentum had taken over the ATF operation, which could not be delayed, only canceled. Local news staffs had correctly concluded the location and approximate time for ATF activity. Publication of an article accusing Koresh of crimes and implying imminent law enforcement action had raised awareness and suspicion at the compound to a peak. And finally, ATF had divided its command structure across several layers, with no single person in a position to exercise overall control.[77] Worse yet, it appears that at least some in that chain of command conceptually focused solely on overt preparations by the Davidians as the criteria for aborting the operation, while others believed that any compromise of the element of surprise would precipitate an abort order. This resulted in a fragmentation in command without even those involved fully comprehending that this had occurred. Any decision to abort was made even more difficult by the lack of any alternative options and by the fact that those actively involved in and overwhelmed by the operational details were the only ones who were positioned to make the final call. The pending disaster resulted as much from faulty structure and planning as any error in execution of the operation. An operation of this magnitude has immense inertia. To terminate such an operation requires organizational and moral authority, self-confidence, reliable information, courage, and detachment. Although key participants collectively possessed these elements, they were not concentrated in a single individual.

Saturday, February 27, 1993

On Saturday, February 27, 1993, the final elements of the raiding party came together in the Waco area with intensive activity, including establishing a command post at the Texas State Technical College campus, housing personnel in over 150 motel rooms, and moving ATF bomb trucks and National Guard helicopters into the area. Although ATF made an effort to maintain operational security, the sheer size of the operation rendered this effort largely ineffectual.[78]

On Saturday morning, Rodriguez attended a worship service at the compound and reported that Koresh preached about the "Sinful Messiah" article and told his followers that "they" were coming after him. He did not specify who "they" were, but told the followers to remain calm and do what he had told them to do. What actions might be taken by Koresh were not clear to Rodriguez.[79] That afternoon Rodriguez met with SAC Chojnacki and reported this information. Chojnacki's specific questions related to preparations for combat by the Davidians, and Rodriguez reported that he had seen none.[80] The role of analyzing intelligence was clearly being commingled with command.[81] The planners lost much of the value of their inside source by focusing exclusively on overt preparations by the Davidians for armed resistance as indicators of danger. Rodriguez returned to the compound at 5:00 P.M. and remained until midnight. Assistant Special Agent in Charge Sarabyn instructed

Rodriguez to return to the compound the next morning to make a final check on conditions and to exit the compound by 9:15 A.M. Rodriguez, concerned for his own safety, reluctantly agreed to return but expressed concern that his actions were likely to arouse suspicion and that he might have difficulty exiting on time.[82]

Sunday, February 28, 1993

At 5:00 A.M. seventy-six agents consisting of the three SRT teams and the supporting entry teams assembled at Fort Hood. They then traveled by vehicle to the designated assembly point, the Bellmead Civic Center. The large collection of agents, dressed in distinct blue uniforms with *ATF* in large letters on the front and back, and the numerous vehicles created a very conspicuous scene. At 8:00 A.M., Sarabyn briefed the raid personnel inside the center. Three Texas National Guard helicopters arrived at the Texas State Technical College, and Division Chief Andy Vita opened a command center at ATF headquarters in Washington.[83] Concurrent with the last-minute ATF preparations, news personnel from both the *Tribune-Herald* and KWTX Television, who had collectively analyzed their information to conclude activity was likely on Sunday, set out for the compound. Amazingly, no evidence has emerged from either the Treasury review or the subsequent congressional hearings that the extensive movement of agents compromised the operation. This was most likely the result of accident than any action by ATF, as the size of the operation made it impossible to conceal.

If fortune favored ATF on the one hand, it revoked the favor with the other. ATF had arranged for police to isolate the compound with roadblocks immediately before the raid on Sunday morning. The decision to hold off the roadblocks until the last minute to avoid attracting attention allowed the reporters, who started early in the morning, to move very close to the compound before the roadblocks were established. At least one Texas Department of Public Safety officer and agents in the undercover house became aware of the reporters' presence. Although the agents relayed the reporters' presence to ASAC Cavanaugh, who was in command at the undercover house, no procedures existed to process and utilize this information.[84] KWTX cameraman Jim Peeler became lost. Although he requested directions from his office by cellular telephone, he was still unable to find the compound. He encountered David Jones, a rural mail carrier in a vehicle bearing a "U.S. Mail" sign, and asked for directions to the compound. Unknown to Peeler, Jones was a Davidian follower. During the ensuing conversation Peeler advised that some type of law enforcement action might be taking place there that morning and that there could be shooting.[85] Jones drove directly to the compound to report the information.[86]

At 8:00 A.M. on February 28, Rodriguez again went to the compound. Koresh invited him to join a Bible study session with Koresh and two other Davidians. Shortly after David Jones drove to the compound, his father, Perry Jones, called Koresh out of the Bible study group for a telephone call. Koresh initially ignored the request. Perry Jones then told him that the call was from England and Koresh left the room to take the call.[87] When Koresh returned, he appeared agitated, had trouble holding the Bible, and could not talk. When Rodriguez asked him what was wrong, Koresh responded that "neither the ATF nor the National Guard will ever get me." He then walked to the window, looked out, and stated, "They're coming, Robert. The time has come." He repeated, "They're coming, Robert, they're coming."[88] Rodriguez became alarmed for his own safety, noting that other Davidians had entered the room, effectively cutting him off from the door. He made an excuse that he had a breakfast appointment and left, driving directly to the undercover house near the compound.[89]

Warning Ignored

Rodriguez immediately reported the events at the compound to Cavanaugh at the undercover house, who instructed Rodriguez to call Sarabyn. Sarabyn asked a series of questions relating to the presence of weapons and specific preparations from a prepared list, to which Rodriguez responded in the negative. Sarabyn then asked what the people in the compound were doing when Rodriguez left, and Rodriguez responded that they were praying. Sarabyn and Cavanaugh discussed the situation at the compound, and Cavanaugh advised that he could see no overt signs of preparation there.[90] Sarabyn then went to the tarmac where Dallas special agent in charge Ted Royster and Chojnacki were preparing to board National Guard helicopters.[91] Over the noise of the helicopters, which were warming up, Sarabyn and Chojnacki held an impromptu conference that would decide the fate of agents and Davidians alike.

The exact content of the discussion remains in contention. Sarabyn and Chojnacki were subsequently dismissed from ATF employment over their actions and Royster was transferred to a far less important and desirable assignment.[92] Regardless of the exact words, the general focus can be reconstructed from events, statements, and the subsequent testimony of the participants. The discussion apparently focused on specific preparations for resistance by the Davidians and not on loss of the element of surprise. No doubt, momentum played a significant role, as did the fractured command structure, lack of preplanning for this specific contingency, the physical location of the discussion, haste, and some breakdown in communication as information was passed from Rodriguez to Sarabyn to Chojnacki. Regardless of the relative importance attributed to specific causes, this constituted the most critical moment of organizational and individual failure. Although circumstances and command structure contributed significantly to their mistake, the failure of Chojnacki and Sarabyn to cancel the raid at this moment constituted the most grievous error in the entire chain of events leading to the disaster at Waco.[93]

Chojnacki returned to the command post and called the ATF headquarters communication center. He notified them that Rodriguez was out and that the raid was going forward. He then returned to the helicopters and both he and Royster departed.[94] Sarabyn left for the staging area where he told agents that Koresh was aware ATF and the National Guard were coming and that they had to hurry.[95] Rodriguez subsequently arrived at the command post, but Sarabyn had already left for the staging area. Rodriquez testified at the House hearings that he was emotionally distraught and shocked that the raid had not been aborted.[96] What seemed clear to Rodriguez and to most that have examined the events subsequently was apparently not clear to Chojnacki and Sarabyn. They somehow focused exclusively on what actions Koresh took in response to his discovery of the pending raid. Others, including Rodriguez, understood the discovery alone was the critical piece of information.

At about 9:25 A.M., the raid team left the staging area, concealed in two large cattle trailers towed by pickups, a familiar sight in rural Texas. Sarabyn rode in the cab of the first truck and maintained constant contact with Cavanaugh at the safe house, who reported no signs of unusual activity at that location. Ironically, the raid likely would have been canceled if even a couple of armed sentries had been observed. However, the possibility of an ambush seems to have been outside the parameters considered by the raid commanders.[97]

Prior to the arrival of the two trailers, the plan called for the helicopters to create a diversion. However, the helicopters arrived concurrently with the trailers. When the helicopters were about 350 meters from the compound they began receiving fire from the compound and turned away. They landed in a nearby field and conducted an inspection that revealed two of the aircraft had been hit.[98] It has been alleged by some that the helicopters fired on the compound.[99] These were not attack helicopters. Thus they carried no armament other than the 9-mm pistols carried by the agents.[100] These weapons would have been highly ineffectual against a structure at any range and virtually useless firing from a moving helicopter at 350 meters. The rotor noise from the helicopters would have masked the sound from small-caliber weapons, making it virtually impossible for compound residents to hear gunfire from the helicopters. Aimed rifle fire from the ground, however, would have posed a threat to the aircraft.

The two trucks and trailers carrying the ATF agents pulled up along the southwest side of the compound. The first vehicle carried the Dallas agents, who were assigned the front door, and a portion of the Houston agents, who were assigned the pit area. The second vehicle carried the rest of the Houston agents and the New Orleans agents, who were assigned to move around the northeast side of the compound, scale the roof, and secure the arms room on the second floor. The first agents out of the vehicles were equipped with fire extinguishers to repel dogs, a common raid practice. As agents raced toward the front door, Koresh stepped outside and shouted, "What's going on here?" The agents, who were wearing helmets and distinct blue uniforms with badges and the letters *ATF* on the chest, responded by identifying themselves and shouting, "Freeze and get down." Koresh stepped back inside and closed the doors. Immediately thereafter, gunfire erupted through the front door, wounding one agent.[101] Cavanaugh later testified before the House Joint Subcommittee that the fire from inside was so intense that the door appeared to bulge out. The agents dispersed for any cover they could find as they were subjected to attack by automatic weapons fire and hand grenades.

The New Orleans SRT moved around the east side of the building and scaled the roof using a ladder. Seven agents climbed to the roof while an eighth provided cover from the ground. Kenny King, Conway LeBleu, Todd McKeehan, and David Millen went to the northwest pitch, where they came under heavy fire. McKeehan and LeBleu were killed outright, and King was shot six times. Badly wounded, King rolled off the roof into a courtyard, where he would remain for almost two hours, undetected by the Davidians.[102] Millen retreated over the ridge of the roof to the southeast pitch and joined agents Jordan, Buford, and Constantino, who had made entry through a window into what had been identified as the arms room. Millen positioned himself at the window.[103] The Davidians fired through the walls and floor of the room with automatic weapons, wounding Buford three times and Jordan twice. The bullets fired through the interior walls of the room exited the exterior wall near Millen, who also was being subjected to automatic weapons fire

through the roof from below. The combined fire forced him to retreat to the ground. This sequence of events was captured by television news footage, as was Jordan's earlier entry into the window.[103] The wounded agents escaped back out through the window
and dropped to the ground. Remaining behind to cover the exit of
the wounded agents, Constantino was confronted by a male subject
with an assault rifle, who entered the room immediately after the
two agents escaped. Constantino fired and the subject fell. Constantino then jumped through the window, striking his head as he did.
He subsequently fell from the roof and was severely injured in the
fall.[104] Both Constantino and Buford were pulled to safety by other
agents. Although it has received little attention in the aftermath of
Waco, ATF agents performed repeated acts of courage in rescuing
and treating injured comrades while under fire, returning fire in a
disciplined manner while in exposed and vulnerable positions, and
retrieving wounded and dead agents under the guns of the Davidians. Although television and movies often portray police performing heroically under fire, few actually experience exposure to gunfire and very few encounter sustained fire. The performance of the
agents is even more commendable if one understands that they
were not trained nor prepared for such eventualities. Their experience was more akin to Normandy or Iwo Jima than to policing.

The agents huddled behind any available cover outside the
compound and returned fire as best they could, although their
weapons were poorly suited to the task. The forward observers, or
snipers, kept up a steady fire against the windows. Although they
were firing from far greater distance and had a slower rate of fire,
their superior weapons actually posed the greatest threat to the
Davidians. Close observation of the films of the events reveals that
the Davidians utilized their volume of fire rather than exercising
fire discipline. This likely resulted from a lack of training and experience combined with the ATF return fire.[105] Had the Davidians
engaged in effective target identification and produced disciplined, aimed fire, ATF casualties would have been catastrophic.
As it was, fifteen of the agents on the ground suffered gunshot
wounds, of whom two, Steven Willis and Robert Williams, died. In
addition, seven agents were wounded by grenade fragments, and
several others received substantial injuries.[106]

Cease-Fire

At 9:48 A.M., within a minute of the raid's onset, the McLennan
County Sheriff's Department received a 911 call from Wayne Martin, a resident at the compound. Although the deputy could hear

gunfire, he could not get Martin to talk with him, and after fourteen minutes, someone at the compound hung up the phone. The Sheriff's Department called back, using the number that appeared automatically on their screen, and reestablished contact with the compound but was unable to reach their liaison officer at the ATF command post, whose radio had been turned off. For almost two hours, periodic contact was made between various compound occupants and the Sheriff's Department and ATF. It was during one of these calls that Koresh stated that they were under attack and demanded that everyone get off the property.[107]

Eventually, Cavanaugh established communication with Steve Schneider and negotiated a cease-fire.[108] No formal hierarchy designated positions for members, but Schneider functioned as a key assistant and spokesman for Koresh. Once both sides stopped shooting, negotiations continued over removal of the dead and wounded and withdrawal of the agents from their locations immediately around the compound. Schneider initially demanded immediate withdrawal, but Cavanaugh refused to do so until the dead and wounded were removed. Eventually, Schneider agreed to allow the seriously wounded King to be removed by four agents, who retrieved him from the rear courtyard utilizing a ladder as an improvised stretcher. A few minutes later, Schneider agreed to allow the removal of the remaining dead and injured agents, and there was a general withdrawal by ATF.[109]

Because there were no contingency plans for the events that occurred, there were no plans for controlling the scene in the aftermath. The perimeter around the compound was not secured. This was a direct result of several factors, including a combination of command breakdown, inadequate procedures, and efforts by the ATF management structure to direct events from Washington.[110] Local and state officers responded to the scene by closing all roads, but the Davidians could have walked away en masse. ATF agents did intercept Davidians attempting to enter the compound in two instances. In one instance, a group of Davidians attempting to make their way from a shop away from the main compound engaged in a gunfight with agents, and one Davidian was killed. Although individual agents did seek out and perform necessary tasks, the command structure essentially ceased to function.[111]

Although ATF management quickly dispatched three additional SRTs to Waco, a request for the FBI HRT was made immediately after the cease-fire. ATF, Treasury and the FBI reached agreement that ATF would relinquish control of the scene to the FBI if the HRT was deployed.[112] Ironically, a request for the HRT to serve the warrant might have spared ATF much of the political attack that subsequently was directed toward it. The HRT would have faced the same logistical problems encountered by ATF, and the results might have proved equally disastrous. The FBI, however, would have been far better positioned to weather the political and media storm. The FBI enjoyed a large reservoir of public recognition and support and lacked a well-organized opposition devoted to attacking their every action. It would, therefore, have offered a far less inviting target for ridicule by the media or politicians.[113] Turning to the FBI after the disaster, on the other hand, simply reinforced public perceptions of ATF incompetence among the media, politicians, and the public.

By March 2, 1993, the FBI had assumed operational control of the Waco scene. Cavanaugh, who continued negotiations after the withdrawal, continued his role as negotiator under FBI direction and succeeded in obtaining the release of some of the children in the compound.[114] Although ATF management's initial concern focused on the injured and dead agents, their attention soon turned to determining what went wrong and ultimately to providing a public explanation.

Notes

1. Department of the Treasury, *Investigation of Vernon Wayne Howell Also Known as David Koresh* (Washington, D.C., September 1993) 103–104. Physical evidence indicated that three of the Davidians who died were killed by persons inside the compound, after being wounded. These three died as the result of gunshot wounds to the head, fired from close range.

2. The first House hearing was conducted by the Committee on the Judiciary on April 28, 1993. The general tone of these hearings was supportive of ATF and the FBI and the only witnesses called were Director Higgins, Attorney General Janet Reno, and FBI Director William Sessions. The second House hearings, conducted during July and August of 1995 by a joint subcommittee of the Committee on the Judiciary and the Committee on Government Reform and Oversight, occurred after the Republican takeover of the House in the 1994 mid-term elections. This hearing was distinctly hostile to ATF and the Clinton administration. Senate hearings in April 1993, chaired by Democratic senator Dennis DeConcini, were far less hostile to ATF.

3. The history of Mount Carmel and David Koresh's ascendancy to control of the community is primarily condensed from Dick J. Reavis, *The Ashes of Waco* (New York: Simon and Schuster, 1995). Specific page citations have been omitted except for issues in contention.

4. Reavis, 75–76.

5. Ibid., 78–79.

6. Ibid., 112–116. Also testimony of Kiri Jewel, House hearings on Waco, 1995.

7. Reavis, 15–19.

8. Department of the Treasury, *Investigation of Vernon Wayne Howell*, 17.

9. The details of the investigation are condensed from the Department of the Treasury report, and are supported by the trial record and testimony before the House Joint Committee. They will therefore be footnoted only where critical.

10. Although any part or combination of parts solely for the purpose of converting a semi-automatic firearm to full automatic is controlled under the NFA, machine gun replacement parts do not fall under this restriction. Because they can be used to repair machine guns, they are not solely for the purpose of converting semi-automatic firearms to full automatic capability. Machine guns could be manufactured and obtained legally in about half the states prior to 1986, and those that were registered constituted a legal inventory. There were no registered machine guns at the Davidian compound, thus no purpose for the parts other than illegal conversion of semi-automatic firearms to machine guns.

11. This point has been strenuously contested by some critics. For one of the most detailed critical evaluations of the probable cause, see David B. Kopel and Paul H. Blackman, "The God Who Answers by Fire: The Waco Disaster and the Necessity of Federal Criminal Justice Reform," paper presented to the American Society of Criminology, 1994 (revised July 12, 1995). Kopel and Blackman attack the warrant by disassembling the affidavit and examining each statement in isolation. It is not the author's intention to evaluate and respond to each of their criticisms. However, it should be noted that an affidavit should be examined as a totality and not as a group of independent assertions that stand alone. It also should be noted that probable cause is not proof of guilt. The probable cause standard is met when enough information to convince a reasonable and prudent person is presented. In this case the assistant United States attorney and the United States magistrate believed that the standard had been met. Although some civil libertarians and defense attorneys would like to raise the standard for probable cause and litigate the appropriateness of the issuance of the warrant by the magistrate, the Supreme Court ruled in *U.S. v. Leon* (468 U.S. 897, 104, S.Ct. 3405, 82 L. Ed 2nd 677, 1984) that evidence seized under authority of a search warrant is not subject to exclusion, unless the affiant intentionally includes false information in the affidavit.

12. See Reavis; James D. Tabor and Eugene V. Gallagher, *Cults and the Battle for Religious Freedom in America* (Berekley: University of California Press, 1995); Daniel Wattenberg, "Gunning for Koresh," *American Spectator* (August 1993).

13. The Mann Act was a prohibition against interstate transportation of females for immoral purposes, passed to attack the so-called white slave trade.

14. *New York Times*, "Use of NRA Is Criticized in Raid Case" (July 19, 1995); "Examination of Waco Raid Goes Partisan" (July 20, 1995); Erik Larson, "ATF Under Siege," *Time* (July 24, 1995).

15. This is based on the author's personal experience as both a manager and member of the headquarters staff.

16. The author designed and instructed the section on search warrants in several firearms investigation courses for both federal and state officers. He has also obtained and served and supervised the obtaining and serving of hundreds of firearms warrants.

17. NRA criticism of law enforcement actions has primarily been restricted to cases involving firearms violations. Their literature has specifically described ATF agents as "jackbooted thugs." Although the NRA has not

shown a comparable concern for the tactics of drug enforcement by either local or federal agents, the organization did join with the American Civil Liberties Union, the National Association of Defense Lawyers, the Drug Policy Foundation, and other groups opposing gun or drug laws to demand an investigation of federal law enforcement actions. See "A Joint Letter From a Coalition of Diverse Organizations on the Issue of Government Violence and the Need for a National Oversight Commission," January 10, 1994, provided to the author by the NRA. Kopel and Blackman also express concerns beyond firearms enforcement; however, the official publications of the NRA, its resources, and its efforts have been directed at firearms cases. No comparable concern has been displayed regarding enforcement of drug laws or even overt brutality, so long as gun laws are not involved.

18. Tabor and Gallagher; Richard A. Shweder, "Why the Flames of Waco Won't Die," *New York Times* (April 17, 1994); Lawrence Criner, "Waco the Tragic Collision of Religious and Secular Mindsets," *Washington Times* (March 4, 1994).

19. For civil libertarians, Waco did not differ from the war on drugs, but did offer a more sympathetic audience. For radical libertarians, such as militia members, the raid represented both the power of government and the imposition of illegitimate firearms laws.

20. Examples can be found in the broad acceptance of government action against Native Americans in the last century and later against Communists. Most recently the wide support of the war on drugs and crime, as well as the popular genre of police avenger films, demonstrate a willingness to support very coercive government action against recipients viewed as criminals.

21. The case had been designated sensitive, requiring regular reporting to headquarters; see Department of the Treasury, *Investigation of Vernon Wayne Howell*, 24.

22. William J. Vizzard, "Reassessing Bittner's Thesis: Understanding Coercion and the Police in Light of Waco and the Los Angeles Riots," *Police Studies* (18:3 and 4, 1995) 1–18.

23. Department of the Treasury, 151, B 66 and B 110.

24. Department of the Treasury, 38.

25. Department of the Treasury, 152, 165–168, B 11–20, B 63–66, B 89, and B 100–102.

26. The Department of the Treasury report notes that managers never asked "what happens if" questions, p. 151, and assumed that this operation was essentially like past operations only larger, p. 156.

27. When asked by the author if any member of the law enforcement staff during his tenure would voice opposition to the position of the associate director, Higgins responded, "Do you mean would they tell the emperor he was naked? No, I don't think so; maybe Cook would have."

28. In fact Hartnett did not cultivate discussion at all. The author once observed Hartnett for four days at a large management conference, attended by at least fifty ATF field managers. During that time he was never once observed asking a single question of a manager and appeared to avoid all conversations relating to policy or operations. Other managers at the conference reported observing the same. Members of Hartnett's staff reported similar experiences in their meetings. The Department of the Treasury report makes specific mention of Hartnett's hierarchical style of management cutting him off from information.

29. Interview with David Troy, former chief of Intelligence Division, ATF.

30. With the exception of the CSA operation, the author is unaware of any instance in which domestic law enforcement has attempted to effect arrests or search warrants against this many armed and disciplined adversaries. The nature of their weapons, lack of protective cover, and presence of children all aggravated the situation. In its scope, this was a military and not a police operation, but it was not conducted as such. Other experienced reviewers have reached similar conclusions. See the statements of John A. Kolman at p. B 35 and Robert A. Sobocienski at p. B 123 in the Department of the Treasury report.

31. Department of the Treasury, 143–148, B 17, B 76, and B 89. Also, interviews with William Buford and Kenny King.

32. Kopel and Blackman devote much of their paper to this thesis. Reavis devotes most of chapters 2 and 3 to the same basic theme. For a more conspiratorial view, see Linda Thompson, *Waco, the Big Lie* (videotape copyright by Linda Thompson, Indianapolis, Ind., 1993).

33. James Q. Wilson, *Bureaucracy: What Government Agencies Do and Why They Do It* (New York: Basic Books, 1989) 165–175.

34. Kopel and Blackman devote substantial attention to this theory, referring to Wheeler as the ATF public relations director. In fact, Wheeler was the public information officer (PIO) for the Dallas Division, which did not even have operational control of the investigation. Public information officers in ATF were a relatively new phenomenon at the time, with poorly defined duties. PIOs regularly initiated press contacts in pursuit of publicity without consulting the agents and supervisors controlling the cases, a practice that angered field agents and supervisors, who viewed this activity as potentially damaging to the investigations and as intended primarily to justify the PIO position.

35. Sharon Wheeler's testimony before 1995 House hearings.

36. Dallas is 100 miles from Waco.

37. ATF had a headquarters public affairs operation. The highest ranking agent assigned to that operation, Jack Killorin, was not in Waco nor involved in any contact with the press.

38. Several publications have alleged that no evidence existed of any violations of the law by the Davidians prior to the ATF raid; see "Crystals in the Waco Crucible," *Washingon Times* (April 4, 1993); Gary Null, "Holocaust at Waco," *Penthouse* (April 1995). Null also alleged that the agents were dressed in black clothing that did not identify them as law enforcement officers, thus the Davidians had no idea who was attempting to enter the compound. The agents were in blue uniforms, clearly marked front and back with the letters *ATF* as well as with large gold badges on the front. Other publications such as *American Spectator, Soldier of Fortune,* and *American Rifleman* have made even more serious accusations. In her patently hostile and highly inaccurate video, Linda Thompson attempted to establish that the ATF agents were killed by other agents and not the Davidians; this same video purported to present evidence that the FBI used flame-thrower tanks against the compound.

39. Few law enforcement agencies have developed routines, procedures, and expertise to handle large-scale operations. The realities of daily operations consume the time, attention, and resources of most agencies in solving immediate problems with little remaining for preparing to deal with unusual and unlikely events.

40. For a more extensive discussion see Vizzard, 1995. In the Freemen confrontation in Montana in 1996, the FBI reverted to siege-and-wait. ATF's current director John Magaw told the author that this would be the only strategy used by ATF if faced with a similar situation to Waco in the future.

41. The first option would be both legally and ethically questionable. The second option required that agents make assumptions not supported by the evidence. It also required Koresh to cooperate. This seems to be the favored approach of critics; see Kopel and Blackman; Reavis. These critics do not explain why Koresh and the Davidians should be distinguished from other individuals or groups in this regard, although the implication is that firearms violations do not constitute serious crimes.

42. The author has personally observed both strategies being invoked.

43. Examples of ATF's relegation to secondary status by the FBI include the Marion siege, the World Trade Center bombing, the fatal bombing of a federal judge and a civil rights attorney in Georgia, and the Unabomber case.

44. One had Army Special Forces combat experience, two had Marine combat experience, and one had extensive police SWAT experience. All were experienced supervisors and tactical team leaders.

45. Department of the Treasury, 51.

46. Ibid., 43.

47. Ibid., 44. Note the testimony of FBI SAC Jeff Jamar and HRT supervisor Dick Rogers in the 1995 House hearings emphasizing these same concerns. Both stated that a parameter was impossible without the use of armor.

48. Ibid., 53.

49. Ibid., 53. Also, interview with William Buford.

50. The dynamic entry tactics are widely accepted in police tactical circles as being safer for both the police and the occupants of the target structure. The idea is to overwhelm and intimidate the occupants through speed and a show of force, thus avoiding any resistance and any need for force to overcome the resistance. Civil libertarians, advocates of armed home defense, and other critics are far less tolerant of this tactic. Since it depends on intimidation rather than voluntary compliance by the occupants, dynamic entry assures confrontation between police and occupants in every case. In practice, it often results in very short waits between knocking and announcing the police presence and purpose and the actual entry.

51. Department of the Treasury, 143–148.

52. Ibid.

53. Ibid., 147.

54. The plan did allow for calling off the raid until the final minute, when the pickups and cattle trailers carrying the agents could no longer turn around. Cancellation was tied to unusual activity, however, not a lack of usual activity. This would turn out to be the single most grievous error in the plan.

55. Department of the Treasury, 151. Buford told the author that there was a contingency plan for the agents being fired on as they approached in the vehicles. They would withdraw to a nearby block building and surround the compound. Arrangements had been made to bring in armored personnel carriers to facilitate such a siege, but it would take some time to bring the personnel carriers to the location.

56. Both Buford and King confirm this.

57. Department of the Treasury, 171.

58. Both Buford and King told the author that planners never truly considered the possibility of armed resistance by significant numbers of the compound occupants.

59. The agents surrounded two heavily armed bank robbers. Although the agents knew that these suspects had displayed extremely violent behavior in the past, they were clearly outnumbered by the FBI in this instance. Instead of surrendering, the suspects attacked. Two agents died and most of the others were disabled. A badly wounded agent finally killed the two wounded suspects in an exchange of shots at point-blank range.

60. Department of the Treasury, 64.

61. Ibid., 51, 54, and 64.

62. Ibid., 137.

63. Management was not entirely consistent in its reaction to risk and confrontation. Investigations of licensed firearms dealers had been discouraged to avoid conflict. At the same time, management had ventured into the margins of drug enforcement and developed SRT, both of which enhanced potential for violent confrontations by agents. In general, however, field agents knew that any predication of a controversial outcome would likely result in negative management reaction and often in cancellation of the proposed activity.

64. Department of the Treasury, 153.

65. Under the law, law enforcement officers with a search warrant must announce their presence and purpose and allow the occupants to open the premises before making forceful entry. The occupant has no legal right to bar the entry of the officers or to resist. Any occupant who does so acts at his peril because officers can and will use force to overcome resistance. These principles are well established in law and practice, but many commentators on Waco appeared to either be ignorant of them or to ignore them proposefully. The law affords no right of self-defense against lawful arrest or search, although Texas is unusual among states in codifying a right to resist unreasonable force by an officer. Critics have focused on the failure of ATF to rehearse a consensual entry. On one level this makes much of nothing. Consensual entries require little rehearsal. On a deeper level, however, these criticisms do address a real issue. Dynamic entries, as planned and conducted by ATF and many other agencies, assume a lack of cooperation and predicate all planning on the assumption that the value of surprise is too great to be risked by a patient, nonconfrontational effort at voluntary compliance. The author and numerous other experienced managers and agents have expressed reservations regarding these assumptions.

66. Dogs present a common hazard for officers during a raid. Normally, fire extinguishers are used to deter them. If the dogs persist in attacking they are usually shot.

67. Department of the Treasury, 67.

68. Ibid., 68–69.

69. Ibid., 158.

70. Ibid., 72.

71. This was the most complex tactical undertaking in the history of ATF and, with the exception of the CSA compound operation, very likely the most difficult and dangerous tactical undertaking ever attempted by a law enforcement agency in the United States. See Department of the Treasury, 72–73.

72. This was not a requirement under existing regulations but was both prudent and normal for such a large and public operation.

73. Department of the Treasury, 75.

74. Treasury was not yet staffed by the regular appointees of the new administration and those in decisionmaking positions had little or no experience directing ATF or any other law enforcement organization. The Office of the Assistant Secretary lacked the staff and resources to adequately plan a tactical operation or even evaluate ATF's plan in detail. The only options were to cancel the operation or take no action and let the raid go forward. Initially, they followed the instincts common to all politicians and high-level government administrators by postponing an action they did not fully understand.

75. Department of the Treasury, 76.

76. Ibid., 76–77.

77. Although Higgins, Hartnett, and Simpson all had authority to cancel the raid, none possessed the full information or was in an appropriate location to exercise control. Chojnacki had authority but lacked some information and was not placed properly to act on last-minute changes. Sarabyn and the team leaders had the most information, but they were too involved in directing the tactical operation to exercise detached control.

78. For a detailed discussion of the preparation details and their magnitude, see Department of the Treasury, 73–78.

79. Department of the Treasury, 79–80.

80. Ibid., 80.

81. No separate intelligence analysis took place. The commander simply interviewed the agent and applied his understanding of events without placing them in the context of all known information.

82. Department of the Treasury.

83. Ibid., 82.

84. Ibid., 84.

85. Ibid., 85.

86. Ibid.; Reavis, 47.

87. Department of the Treasury, 88.

88. Ibid., 89; Rodriguez testified to this same sequence of events before the House Joint Subcommittee.

89. It remains unclear from testimony at the subsequent hearings and from statements taken during the investigation whether Koresh knew or was suspicious of Rodriguez being an informant or an undercover agent. It appears that at least some Davidians had reached this conclusion. Given the level of suspicion exhibited by Koresh on other issues, it is unlikely that he did not at least entertain some suspicion regarding Rodriguez. Either he was unsure of Rodriguez's status or he believed that his persuasive powers were adequate to control Rodriguez. Reavis reports that other Davidians believed Rodriguez to be an undercover law enforcement officer and presumes that Koresh also reached this conclusion, 66–73.

90. Department of the Treasury, 90. Again, these accounts were confirmed during the House hearings, although Sarabyn's recollection of events sometimes is at variance with others.

91. Chojnacki's decision to place himself in a helicopter during the most critical period of the raid further fractured the command structure.

92. Both Sarabyn and Chojnacki were subsequently reinstated in non–law enforcement positions. ATF justified this on the grounds that the bureau might lose in subsequent administrative appeals and litigation. This was no idle concern. ATF, as well as other agencies, have routinely lost appeals when they have attempted to dismiss employees with long records of unblemished service.

93. The author has a long history of association with Chojnacki, with whom he worked closely in ATF headquarters, and Royster, who worked for the author for four years. In addition, he has known Peter Mastin, the third SAC at Waco, since 1967. In spite of this, and with a great sense of empathy for them and their families, this account has been based on the record, unofficial sources, and the author's knowledge of ATF procedures and routines. This analysis leads to only one conclusion, that at least some commanders committed grave errors in judgment and that a divided command structure and inadequate command and control preparations greatly facilitated their errors.

94. There have been persistent rumors circulated within ATF that Chojnacki not only informed the command center but that he personally informed higher authority and that this is the reason that he was reinstated. Although the direct allegation never arose during the House hearings, some of the questioning hinted that these rumors had reached committee members. The author's research revealed no confirmation of this information and there is no reason to assume that Chojnacki reported that Koresh knew ATF was coming. The nature of ATF and Treasury management has always been to avoid uncertainty. Based on the author's experience, either ATF headquarters or Treasury would have ordered the raid postponed if they believed the risk had increased. They were not subject to the operational momentum at the scene nor did they have a high stake in the raid. It has been this very tendency to intervene on the side of caution that has generated repeated conflicts between operational managers and headquarters.

95. Department of the Treasury, 91.

96. Numerous observers quoted in the Treasury report confirm Rodriguez's reactions and his expectation that the raid would not go forward after he reported to Sarabyn.

97. This becomes most apparent when one reviews their testimony before the House Joint Subcommittee.

98. Department of the Treasury, 95–96.

99. Although these allegations have been made by Thompson and others, the most complete review of the evidence supporting this position can be found in Reavis, 129–134. The majority of evidence presented by Reavis comes from statements by residents of the compound, who have been engaged in both civil and criminal litigation with the government. The most independent witness is Jack Zimmerman, an attorney and former Marine officer, who testified to the House hearing that he observed bullet holes in the ceiling that appeared to have been fired from above. Zimmerman appears to have developed strong identification with the residents and was dependent upon their reports that these holes were made by fire from the helicopters.

100. No witness in the hearings testified to the presence of any other weapons on the helicopters. All witnesses interviewed by the author also confirm this. All reports from agents at the scene confirm that AR-15 rifles were in very short supply and there is no report that any of these firearms were on the helicopters. Even these firearms would have been poorly suited to use from the helicopters.

101. Department of the Treasury, 96. It is this aggressive approach by armed and uniformed agents that appears to shock a number of critics. For ATF agents and most others in law enforcement, this reaction in unfathomable.

The use of clearly identified and armed personnel, moving rapidly and shouting distinct and decisive commands, is common practice. Years of such practices in drug enforcement had resulted in constant support and praise from legislators and the public. Ultimately, of course, both points of view were equally dysfunctional in this situation. Koresh showed no willingness to passively accept authority without coercion, and ATF's tactics proved inadequate to overwhelm the potential resistance.

102. Ibid., 98.

103. Some confusion has occurred because of the assumption that these two pieces of film footage were shot at the same time and of the same agent. Thompson uses this footage as "proof" that agents shot other agents at Waco.

104. Department of the Treasury, 100.

105. This pattern of indiscriminate firing can be seen regularly in combat photographs, particularly those of undisciplined militias. The practice of firing blindly over, around, or through walls with automatic weapons serves more to buoy the spirits of the shooters than to produce enemy casualties.

106. Department of the Treasury, D 102–103.

107. Ibid., 106. Critics have viewed this call as evidence that Koresh had no intent to resist lawful authority; see Kopel and Blackman. Given the prior statements by Koresh that ATF was coming to get him, the obvious preparations to forcefully resist lawful authority, the clear identification of the agents as law enforcement personnel, and the continued resistance by the Davidians on that and future dates, the telephone call seems more a reflection of Koresh's megalomania than any effort to request lawful intervention.

108. Department of the Treasury, 105.

109. Ibid., 106.

110. Ibid., 110–112.

111. Ibid., 112–113. Although the descriptions of ATF performance in the aftermath of the Waco disaster seem harsh, they should be tempered with perspective. Military organizations that train for years are often shattered by surprise events such as Pearl Harbor or the Chinese intervention in Korea. The Los Angeles Police Department was unable to organize and respond to the riots that followed the acquittal of police officers for beating Rodney King. The sort of events that ATF faced in Waco are not something that any law enforcement agency is fully prepared to handle through experience, training, or contingency planning.

112. Department of the Treasury, 114.

113. The targeting of ATF is evident in the congressional response to the investigation of the Ruby Ridge incident (see Chapter 9). Although ATF's action was limited to the initial investigation and the subsequent deaths were the result of confrontations between the Weavers and the Marshal's Service and FBI, Senator Spector's press release focused on the fact that ATF precipitated these events by pursuing the original prosecution, which he characterized as "virtually entrapment," and raised questions about the justification for ATF's future survival. See Robert Wells, "ATF Criticized for Action in Ruby Ridge Shootout," *Congressional Quarterly Weekly Report* (September 9, 1995) 2725.

114. Although trained as a negotiator, Cavanaugh had never previously functioned in that role. In one of the most difficult situations conceivable,

he displayed courage, self-control, skill, and dogged determination to save as many lives as possible. As with the many agents who performed courageously under fire, Cavanaugh displayed the source of ATF's strength: a determination to perform in spite of inadequate resources, training, policy, leadership, and political support.

Chapter 13

The Aftermath

Just as nothing in ATF's past had prepared it to deal adequately with the raid and the ensuing ambush at Waco, nothing had prepared it for the events that would follow. ATF's management faced several potentially hostile publics. The press coverage was beyond anything previously experienced by the agency and predictably was focused on "what went wrong."[1] ATF's law enforcement personnel, both at the scene and around the country, asked many of the same questions. In addition, they were shocked by the loss of the agents and humiliated by the surrender of the operation to the FBI. Most important to ATF managers was the potential reaction of political elites in the administration and Congress. ATF never had experienced a sense of security as an organization. All of those in key positions had distinct memories of the Reagan administration's effort to eliminate ATF and the hostile congressional hearings preceding these efforts. Although virtually a taboo subject among high-level administrators, this underlying insecurity hung over every management action. Finally, there was the public at large, many of whom had never before heard of ATF. The public mattered for two important reasons. First, they constituted the friends, neighbors, and relatives of ATF personnel. Second, they made up the working environment in which agents and inspectors worked daily. Loss of credibility with a large portion of the public thus impacted the personal pride and self-image of employees and their ability to conduct their daily business. Unlike the FBI, ATF could not fall back on a longstanding popular myth to support its legitimacy. In addition, ATF had powerful enemies that would exploit any opportunity to focus the rising public tide of antigovernment sentiment on ATF and the firearms laws they enforced.

This set of circumstances would have verged on the overwhelming for even the most seasoned of public persons. Unfortunately for ATF, its most critical actor was a very private person with none of the preparation or skills necessary to control the situation. Associate Director Dan Hartnett was diligent, conscientious, and unfailingly loyal, but he was anything but a public person. His strengths did not include intellectual flexibility, political instincts, or adeptness at public discourse. Even in the controlled atmosphere of management meetings, he resisted free-flowing discussion, responding to even complex questions with brief and often unresponsive answers that clearly communicated he did not welcome follow-up questions. It was not surprising that he followed the same pattern in the aftermath of Waco. It is also not surprising that the press did not respond with the same deference or resignation normally displayed by ATF managers, whose careers depended on Hartnett's favor.

Hartnett also did not understand that the majority of field agents did not share his loyalty to the formal organization. Unlike him, they were not good soldiers who would accept management actions on faith and keep their own counsel. Hartnett himself had both practiced and valued these traits, and his immediate subordinates, anxious to remain in his favor, learned to behave likewise in his presence.[2] Most field agents and many field managers displayed more independence in perspective and action than did Hartnett or his staff, for whom they felt little loyalty. Even Hartnett's immediate staff exhibited little personal loyalty for or identity with him when out of his presence. Most agents were shocked and saddened by Waco and eager for an explanation. Subsequently, their shock turned to anger, providing the press with a steady stream of inside sources.

In the aftermath, as in the raid planning, Steve Higgins surrendered total functional control to Hartnett, who both controlled the flow and interpretation of information to Higgins and occupied center stage in the early press coverage. Hartnett's disinclination to delegate authority or seek counsel from subordinates precluded moderation of his actions by the law enforcement staff. ATF's structure and Higgins's lack of enforcement background interacted to place Hartnett in total control of all follow-up actions. Thus, Higgins's future rested entirely in Hartnett's hands. Unfortunately, Hartnett was poorly suited in temperament and skill to perform the critical tasks at hand. The resulting events emulated the pattern of organizational behavior documented in studies of Watergate. Every effort to stonewall the press and gloss over mistakes would spur the press to dig deeper and reveal more, which would heighten the bunker mentality, narrow the inner circle, and exacerbate the problem. ATF could not avoid adverse publicity and revelations of serious management errors. Instead of quickly realizing this and confronting it, Hartnett simply refused to admit the existence of a problem. Mistakes thus began to take on the appearance of intentional misconduct.

Almost from the beginning, some agents at Waco began to focus their anger on Hartnett, the bearer of the news that the FBI would assume full control from ATF. FBI special agent in charge Jeff Jamar exacerbated this effect when he and Hartnett first addressed agents on March 1, 1993. Jamar's comments on that day, and subsequently, seemed to communicate a tone that the FBI was coming in to clean up ATF's mess. The courage and character of individual ATF agents was never recognized.[3] Although no offense may have been meant, ATF agents interpreted Jamar's actions and statements in light of past FBI actions that communicated an assumption that the least of their agents was superior to the best in any other agency.[4]

Within days after the raid, rumors circulated through ATF that there had been prior warning that Koresh knew ATF was coming but the raid had not been called off. Although this information moved freely through the enforcement ranks of ATF, it apparently did not reach the director, who lacked informal law enforcement sources of his own. Although Higgins lacked such sources, the press did not. As Hartnett repeatedly denied that there had been any loss of surprise or that raid leaders had been aware of this fact, leaks began to spring from among angry agents, many of whom had heard Sarabyn tell them that Koresh knew they were coming. Throughout the country, management's credibility plummeted among the rank and file at a time when the agency most needed to stand together. When David Troy, the popular chief of the Intelligence Division, was substituted for Hartnett as spokesman, some in ATF became hopeful. But when Troy, who later admitted he lied at Hartnett's direction, repeated the same explanations, the mood turned foul.[5]

On March 1, 1993, Hartnett directed Troy to lead a shooting review team, composed of Troy, Cleveland SAC Bill Wood, and fellow Headquarters Division chief Dave Benton. The criminal investigation of the shooting had been turned over to the Texas Rangers, with the concurrence of the United States attorney, to avoid charges of bias. A shooting review is an internal investigation to provide information to management regarding the details of any shooting in which ATF agents are involved. Shooting reviews were mandated for virtually any discharge of a firearm by ATF agents, other than on a firing range, or for shootings by others during any ATF operation. Reviews are potentially useful in evaluating supervisory and agent performance, dealing with liability issues, and developing information on tactical situations. The formality of the review varied somewhat with the level of damage, who fired the shot, and why. Waco represented the highest level of formality and urgency possible in ATF.[6]

The review team began on March 1, 1993, and interviewed the undercover agent, Robert Rodriguez, almost immediately. Rodriguez stated that he had informed Dallas ASAC Sarabyn that Koresh was aware of the pending raid, that he had talked of ATF and the National Guard and had said he "could only die once" and that "they are coming for me but they can't kill me."[7] The review team then interviewed New Orleans SAC Peter Mastin, who confirmed that Sarabyn had stated, "Koresh knows we are coming," as the agents were loaded in the staging area.[8] Troy immediately reported this information to Hartnett on March 1, 1993. Troy clearly understood the significance of the information at this point and was shocked that the raid had not been aborted. He assumed that Hartnett would have the same reaction.[9] Subsequent interviews continued to reinforce Rodriguez's story with two exceptions. Interviews with Houston SAC Phillip Chojnacki and ASAC Charles Sarabyn produced few clear details of events, except that Rodriguez had not explicitly warned Sarabyn that Koresh knew ATF was coming.[10] There is no evidence in the Treasury report, the House hearings, or in interviews with knowledgeable ATF personnel that this information was passed on to Higgins until early April.

Hartnett responded to press inquires about Koresh knowing of pending ATF action by denying ATF had any such knowledge.[11] On March 6, 1993, Higgins appeared on *Face the Nation* and denied that ATF had any information that Koresh was aware of the pending raid.[12] Both Hartnett and Higgins testified before an executive session of the House Subcommittee on the Treasury, Postal Service, and General Government on March 10, 1993, presumably testifying as to the details.[13]

On March 3 and 4, 1993, Texas Rangers met with Hartnett and communicated that they believed that Rodriguez had informed Sarabyn that the raid was compromised.[14] Later in the month, they informed Hartnett that Chojnacki's and Sarabyn's accounts were inconsistent with the rest of the evidence and that the two appeared to lack credibility.[15] The official statements of the agency continued to deny Rodriguez's warning, and Hartnett apparently did not inform Higgins fully of the magnitude of apparent conflicts between the investigations and the official versions of events.[16] Thus, all press releases and all official accounts released by ATF continued to deny any loss of surprise. Within ATF, word quickly spread that official accounts were untrue. Unfortunately, Higgins was in one of the poorest of positions to receive this unofficial information. On March 28, 1993, the *New York Times* printed a page-one article in which it quoted four agents involved in the raid, stating that the raid leaders knew the element of surprise had been lost. Agent hostility toward top management continued to escalate and could not be contained.

On March 29, Higgins appeared on the *Today Show*, again denying that raid leaders had knowledge of the loss of surprise. He subsequently heard directly from an agent who challenged this statement.[17] Higgins then requested a copy of Rodriguez's statement to the Rangers. Hartnett provided Higgins with the statement during the first weeks in April. From this point on, Hartnett's influence and credibility with Higgins declined substantially.[18] The situation, however, had progressed beyond Higgins's ability to assert control. The Treasury Department had lost confidence in ATF, and Assistant Secretary Nobel was engaged in an effort to distance the administration from Waco and ATF management. By the end of April, a formal investigation of ATF's actions was initiated at the direction of the secretary of the treasury.[19]

The Media and the Public Controversy

The Waco story combined several elements that assured a political and media disaster for ATF. The highly visual nature of the event assured continued television coverage. The dramatic footage of an agent trapped on the roof, agents under fire, and agents retreating was tailor-made for television news. The continuing drama generated by the standoff kept the story current and retained numerous reporters on the scene with little to do until events changed. The words "botched" and "bungled" became standard adjectives in virtually every journalistic reference to the raid. ATF's clumsy efforts to deny significant errors simply reinforced reporters' presumptions of the agency's incompetence and lack of credibility. Management denials that raid leaders had known of Koresh's forewarning of the raid assured that leaks from agents would be numerous. The final cataclysmic event, in which most of the Davidians died, assured that Waco would not be quietly forgotten and that there would be a search for some responsible entity to blame. Waco took on all the characteristics of a mythical drama, although different groups seemed to assign the roles of victim and villain to different parties.

The duration of the siege and lack of satisfactory closure proved as important as ATF management's actions in molding the political impact of the event or mistakes made by ATF management. A parallel can be seen when one compares the 1980 Iranian seizure of the United States Embassy and staff to the 1982 bombing of the Marine barracks at the Beirut airport. Although the results of the embassy seizure were far less disastrous than the bombing, the political impact on Jimmy Carter was much more devastating than that on Ronald Reagan. Apparently the public experienced more frustration from the inability to resolve the hostage crisis than from the death of the Marines. The bombing was only a story for a short time. Although the invasion of Grenada helped to divert public attention, the lack of any ongoing story proved equally as important. Had the Waco raid ended without a standoff, regardless of the errors made, prolonged public attention would not have been focused on the event. In addition, the cadre of reporters awaiting an outcome in Waco would have been elsewhere and occupied with things other than delving into ATF.

The religious overtones of Waco also engaged some groups and individuals who otherwise would have shown little direct interest. A number of persons were inclined to invoke an analysis of events that viewed ATF's raid as an attack on the religious freedom of the Davidians.[20] The negative focus of opinion elites, such as civil libertarians, religious scholars, and opponents of state coercion in general, placed ATF in the uniquely unfavorable position of being attacked simultaneously from libertarian elements on the right and the left. In a nation with a different political tradition, this might not have occurred. In the United States, however, deeply rooted suspicion of government, focus on individual rights, and distaste for coercive government authority combined to bring attacks from both flanks.[21]

Although press and media attention to ATF was not particularly favorable, the majority of the mainstream press was neither unfair nor totally negative. Over time, some reasonably balanced and insightful articles began to emerge.[22] One exception to this was the *Washington Times*, which continually featured articles that were totally negative in tone. Less mainstream press outlets paid less attention to factual detail, producing much more hostile accounts.[23] The most extreme accounts appeared in the firearms press and *Soldier of Fortune*, a monthly that caters to armchair mercenaries and others who pursue a martial fantasy life.[24] The most extreme allegations were made by attorney and self-proclaimed militia leader Linda Thompson in a video titled *Waco, the Big Lie*, in which she accuses ATF of killing its own agents and attacking peaceful Davidians without provocation.[25]

The actions of the NRA and its associates went well beyond articles in the pages of the official organizational organ, the *American Rifleman*. Paul Blackman, director of research for the NRA, and David Kopel, an attorney long associated with the NRA, produced a paper that characterized ATF actions as deliberately criminal.[26] The organization consistently characterized ATF agents as acting unlawfully, violating citizens' rights, and threatening all who owned firearms.[27] The charges were reminiscent of those made in a 1980 NRA-produced film *It Can't Happen Here,* which detailed alleged ATF abuses against law-abiding citizens. In the film, Representative John Dingell of Michigan, a longtime member of the NRA board of directors, characterized ATF agents as "jackbooted fascists."[28] In addition to the Waco raid, the NRA focused on the Randy Weaver case and the case of Louis Katona, a collector of machine guns and the subject of an ATF investigation. The NRA characterized the ATF search of Katona's residence as an outlandish abuse of authority by ATF against Katona, his family, and his property. *Time* subsequently characterized service of the search warrant on Katona as "the raid that wasn't" and directly challenged the truthfulness of Katona's and the NRA's account.[29]

Lessons of Waco

Unfortunately, most of what has been said or written about ATF's performance at Waco has been either an effort to castigate the agency or defend it. Neither of these approaches is likely to enhance understanding of how agencies and the people in them behave under such unusual situations. It is useful to first establish a few basic assumptions that appear to be well supported by the voluminous record.

ATF acted lawfully in conducting a criminal investigation within its jurisdiction. In addition to the child molestation, so graphically documented in the House hearings, the Branch Davidians engaged in numerous ongoing crimes, including the manufacture and possession of numerous machine guns and hand grenades in violation of the National Firearms Act, a law that ATF routinely enforced with the mandate of Congress. The agents raiding the compound acted under authority of a lawful search warrant, legally entitling them to enter the compound. They were distinctly identified as law enforcement officers and any effort to impede them constituted a crime. Citizens do not have a legal right to resist the service of a lawful arrest or search by police or to a claim of self-defense for doing so. ATF was not a rogue agency that routinely abused citizens. Agents had served thousands of arrest and search warrants without any incident. In addition, ATF did not target the Davidians because of their religious beliefs, but rather initiated an investigation at the request of local authorities and continued the investigation after discovering evidence of illegal acts. ATF would have investigated any individual or group engaged in these same illegal acts. Although the raid plan was seriously flawed, it might well have been successful but for unforeseen circumstances, and there may have been no truly safe and legal way to have served a search warrant on the compound. Individual ATF agents and supervisors displayed honor and courage by their performance under fire and their refusal to allow what they believed to be a distortion of the public record by ATF management. In spite of commendable actions by individuals, events at Waco and during the aftermath revealed significant organizational dysfunction within ATF, particularly at the management level.

This analysis begins with these conclusions and attempts to determine the role of structure, task, culture, and political environment in shaping ATF's actions at Waco and during the aftermath in an effort to develop a more general and universally applicable critique of ATF's actions than has prevailed to date.

Structure proved critical in every aspect of the Waco case. Because bureaucracies assign authority and responsibility on the basis of office rather than skill and experience, they become dependent on incumbents in key positions, even if those incumbents are not the most qualified for the task at hand. Thus, personnel decisions and allocation of tasks at some previous time can greatly constrain a manager. This makes circumstances like Waco extremely dangerous for organizations. Persons and structures that function adequately under normal circumstances can suddenly be required to perform far beyond their capacity. ATF's tendency to seek conformity in management and avoid internal dissent encouraged placement of persons in key positions who would not oppose the operation, once it appeared to have received the endorsement of the associate director. In addition, the placement of law enforcement and regulation as two equal components within a single agency had assured that no director could have adequate expertise to understand the intimate working details of both core tasks. This did not necessarily constitute an insurmountable burden. With an open and communicative associate director of law enforcement, Higgins could have accessed the wisdom of a large and potentially diverse staff. With the selection of Hartnett, he assured that negative information and dissenting opinions would not reach him. Although loyal and dedicated, Hartnett had thoroughly internalized the organizational culture of law enforcement, which discouraged criticism, dissent, and open interaction between management levels.[30] In the case of ATF, task and culture both interacted with structure.

The nature of ATF's tasks had been the driving force behind its structure. Higgins had attempted to move the operational branches toward more integration by espousing a one-bureau philosophy, by mandating co-location of field offices, and by placing managers in temporary assignments in other directorates. However, the structural divisions that derived from tasks remained. Structure and task also interacted in another way to set the scene for Waco. As tactical operations became a more important aspect of ATF's task environment, a number of positions began to be linked to these operations. Those assistant special agents in charge, who directed the SRTs, and SRT supervisors became the authorities on any field operation.[31] They also became advocates for the technologies that enhanced their prestige and authority. The desire to oversee a high-profile operational activity motivated the Special Operations Division to develop the ACES project, which institutionalized special operations. These operations became progressively more institutionalized at every level of the enforcement structure with the creation of the SRTs.[32] This, in turn, encouraged the development of an organizational culture influenced by tactical operations and, in the case of Waco, placed Sarabyn in the position of being the primary check on an operation with which he was totally identified. Finally, the political environment had enhanced the legitimacy of special operations with the war on drugs. Most important in the case of Waco, ATF failed to recognize that the task at hand was beyond its technology. Although the Waco operation had many of the characteristics of past operations, it was far different in scope, complexity, and political risk.

The organizational culture of ATF's law enforcement personnel, particularly its management, contributed considerably to organizational failure. Authoritarian attitudes reinforced the tendency of a highly hierarchical structure to concentrate all decisions in a very few individuals and exclude dissenting opinions. These cultures and structures have advantages during tactical law enforcement operations, firefighting, and combat, but they risk significant cost in other settings. The military has a long history of procurement debacles and cover-ups that emanate from just such a culture.[33] Likewise, the tactical operations culture, with its emphasis on quick and decisive action, contributed to organizational failure at Waco. So long as it can be compartmentalized and controlled, tactical capacity can be an asset for a law enforcement organization. But if a tactical mentality begins to dominate decisionmaking, prudence and caution are likely to be the first casualties. In ATF, the expansion of SRTs and the identification of numerous key personnel within them had the effect of normalizing and routinizing tactical operations. As such activities became more familiar and integrated with daily operations, naturally cautious career bureaucrats became more complacent about their implementation. In earlier years, Waco would not have occurred because ATF management would simply have been afraid to attempt anything of that magnitude.

The political environment contributed indirectly to the development of the Waco case by heaping benefits on the agency for moving into drugs and tactical operations. ATF's position with Congress and the administration noticeably improved with the widespread news coverage of ATF agents battering down doors in Washington during Project ACES. Through the later years of the Reagan administration and all the years of the Bush administration, ATF received more support than ever in its history. The gun lobby focused very little hostile attention during the same period and ATF felt an unprecedented level of confidence. Ironically, this confidence resulted in actions that eroded all the gains. Additionally, the election of 1992 brought in an administration with no personal or political links to ATF's management. Thus, when ATF became controversial the most expedient course for the political appointees in Treasury was to distance themselves from ATF and set the agency adrift to fend for itself in hostile waters.

As the aftermath of Waco developed, the very characteristics that had been the building blocks of ATF's management style and culture placed the agency and its managers at the greatest disadvantage. In an agency where cautious, conventional behavior constituted the norm for advancement, the only hope for survival lay in quick, decisive, and high-risk decisions. Among managers not accustomed to public candor, brutal candor became necessary. For career bureaucrats, who looked to political leadership for direction, independent political calculations were required. In a culture that valued taking care of its own, public sacrifice of loyal managers became necessary. The demands were too great. No one in ATF management recognized the gravity of the situation, nor were they capable of acting decisively enough if they did.

Steve Higgins's best hope would have been to seize direct control the moment the magnitude of the disaster was apparent. He might have taken decisive action within the first two or three days by overseeing an internal probe, independent of ATF's law enforcement management staff. Once it was determined that serious oversights and errors had been committed, key managers should have been suspended immediately. Unfortunately, Higgins lacked the staff, knowledge, or temperament for such action. He combined personal caution, orderly bureaucratic values, loyalty, and trust in his staff with basic decency. None of these characteristics were inclined to support a bold, high-risk, and ruthless action to save himself and the bureau.

Circumstances could not have been much riskier for Higgins. He was nominally in charge of a law enforcement organization that had powerful enemies and was under the direct control of semi-autonomous managers who did not have the skill, experience, or inclination to take decisive and drastic action themselves. Nor did they provide him information that would have inclined him toward such action, and he lacked his own independent sources of information. With exposé of government incompetence the stock in trade of successful journalists, numerous agents, feeling abandoned and betrayed, leaked information to the press. Antigovernment feeling dominated the public and political agendas. Finally, a new administration with a weak electoral mandate and no history of trust or identification with ATF was in power. Even if ATF's task and political environment had not produced a culture averse to decisive, independent, and politically risky action, it is questionable whether Higgins could have survived as director and protected the bureau from the coming wave of public ridicule.

The new administration's first introduction to ATF was the controversy over allegations of sexual harassment that emanated from the *60 Minutes* story. This attention provided an opportunity for disgruntled individuals and groups within ATF to access a public forum. On January 12, 1993, the *New York Times* ran an article that reported Treasury's inspector general would investigate charges of sexual harassment in ATF that emanated from the television exposé.[34] Although the article reported that ATF had received only five complaints of sexual harassment during the previous five years, the only details reported on the three alleged sexual harassment cases came directly from the *60 Minutes* segment. Before Waco, this controversy, based on rather dubious allegations, had placed ATF's management in a very defensive posture. Concern with these allegations appeared to occupy the attention of the director and his senior staff members during the early weeks of 1993.[35]

Other timing factors worked against ATF. The Neal Knox faction was again gaining control of the National Rifle Association.[36] Knox had long exercised leadership among those in the NRA opposing all laws governing the possession and transfer of firearms. The fragile peace that had existed between ATF and the NRA for almost ten years quickly unraveled.[37] The increased support for the Brady Bill and assault weapons restrictions had reinvigorated the more libertarian wing of the NRA. The election of a Democrat to the White House only served to add to this process. The entire political dynamic bore a significant resemblance to the events of the mid-1970s. Then, Saturday Night Special bills and the election of the

Watergate class to Congress, followed by the election of Jimmy Carter, spurred the NRA to mount a massive preemptive attack on coming gun control efforts by attacking ATF (see Chapter 5).

The Purge

By late April 1993, leaks from the Department of the Treasury indicated that Higgins's tenure as director was likely short.[38] In early May, the secretary of the treasury directed a team of lawyers and investigators to conduct an exhaustive review of ATF's actions before, during, and after the raid. While the investigation was still in progress, unofficial Treasury sources began to characterize ATF management as "at fault" and predict that Higgins, Hartnett, and Conroy would all retire as a result of the investigation.[39] On September 28, 1993, all three announced their retirements. Three days later Treasury issued what the press characterized as the "brutally detailed report."[40] On October 1, 1993, Secretary Bentsen named Secret Service Director John Magaw as acting director of ATF. Insiders speculated that this accomplished two objectives for the administration. Magaw, who was closely identified with George Bush, was removed from control of the agency with the greatest access to the inner lives of the first family, and visible action was taken to change ATF leadership.

Although the Treasury report spared no detail in documenting ATF's mistakes, it stopped at Treasury's doorstep, providing few details of Treasury's role or the impact of policy on ATF. Assistant Secretary Nobel did state that no federal agency was equipped to deal with operations of this kind, one of the few public recognitions that the problems of Waco ran far deeper than failure by ATF management.[41]

John Magaw, ATF's fourth director, had served almost thirty years in the Secret Service, most of them assigned to protection and all in Washington, D.C. Well over six feet tall, Magaw retains the athletic good looks that once placed him on an Ohio Highway Patrol recruiting poster. He displays adeptness with the press and exudes an air of confidence and assurance that no previous ATF director ever displayed. Although his former position as director of the Secret Service did not place him in Washington's inner power circle, it did allow him a close proximity that puts him at ease in the presence of real power. Symbolically, he was an ideal choice for ATF director. Although the Secret Service does not play a major law enforcement role, its highly visible protective function and an almost total absence of controversy have conveyed an image of importance and professional expertise. Magaw's greatest assets, image and confidence, mirrored the Secret Service perfectly. Unfortunately, Magaw also brought certain liabilities, reflective of his Secret Service background. He possessed little understanding of ATF's mission and history, and little experience in implementing ambiguous and controversial policy. The Secret Service has a homogeneous structure, dominated by agents, and a clear set of priorities, dominated by protection. Its organizational culture avoids public controversy and concentrates on appearances. Secret Service agents operate constantly in the public eye, yet few ever examine their mission. Their primary law enforcement function, counterfeiting suppression, generates virtually no controversy or turf conflicts. The more predominant protection function is virtually immune from political attack and is afforded almost unlimited resources and broad authority. The organizational culture has been forged in an environment of public and political support with clear tasks and missions.[42] Although the juxtaposition of the two agencies in the Department of the Treasury and the periodic need for protective manpower have forged a close working relationship, the two agencies differ greatly in history, culture, and environment.

Once again, ATF had been denied a director who understood the complexities of the firearms enforcement mission. As in the past, the new director perceived the solution to ATF's problems as managerial. He announced the intention to concentrate on structure, staffing, and training to correct the problems of ATF.[43] Magaw immediately began reorganizing the structure of the headquarters staff and placed his greatest emphasis on training.[44] He reestablished the position of deputy director, thus reducing the authority of the associate directors for enforcement and regulation, and announced a plan to reduce the twenty-three law enforcement field divisions to seventeen. By the summer of 1996, the regulatory regions have been eliminated and replaced by districts.[45] Magaw also acted quickly to place his personal selections in most of the key management positions within an expanded headquarters staff. None of these changes, however, addressed the underlying conflicts in ATF's mission or structure. Nor did they communicate much future change in the daily operations of the agency.

During Magaw's tenure, ATF has made one major effort at addressing its mission with the initiation of a new firearms enforcement policy. Although this would appear to communicate that Magaw intends to address policy as well as administration, ATF policy documents undercut this interpretation. ATF's own documents make clear that the impetus for change originated not with ATF management but with the Office of Management and Budget.[46]

The new policy, entitled Violence Impact Strategy, differs little from the interdiction strategy of the Carter years (see Chapter 5). Unfortunately, ATF is even more poorly equipped to impact firearms trafficking now than it was in 1977 because of the changes made to the GCA in 1986 by the Firearms Owners Protection Act (see Chapter 10). Although the new strategy purportedly intends to capitalize on information developed from expanded firearms tracing to allow agents to identify illegal sources providing guns to criminals, it ignores past experience. Adequate information exists from previous trace studies to construct a reasonably accurate picture of the firearms market. Although a few licensed and unlicensed dealers do provide firearms to convicted felons and juveniles on a regular basis, the majority of firearms move in individual transactions.[47] Congress has shown no inclination to provide the agency with the sort of authority that would be necessary to control such transactions. In fact, Congress has significantly limited ATF's administrative and legal options for controlling licensed and unlicensed firearms dealers. In addition, the penalties for criminal violations remain extremely lenient in this area. The sale of one ounce of crack cocaine will result in a far more serious federal sentence than the illegal sale of a thousand guns does.[48]

The 1994 Elections and the Hearings

The 1994 elections did not bode well for ATF. Both the House and Senate came under conservative Republican domination. The NRA aggressively supported numerous members of the new conservative class, particularly in the House. Many of these new members had campaigned on the issues of revoking the newly passed federal waiting period for handgun purchases and the restriction on some assault weapons. For the most libertarian, such as Idaho Republican Helen Chenoweth, ATF and the laws it enforced represented the ultimate threat to the American people, requiring drastic action by Congress.[49] The willingness of the new Congress to attack ATF was demonstrated by the House vote to exempt ATF and the IRS from House Bill 666, which allowed evidence unlawfully seized by law enforcement to be admitted into evidence in federal criminal trials.[50]

Spared from much attention during the early days of the new Congress dominated by the Republican "Contract With America," ATF suddenly became the focus after a powerful bomb destroyed the Federal Building in Oklahoma City, killing 168 people on April 19, 1995. Within days of the bombing, the FBI arrested suspects characterized as extremist libertarians upset over Waco, Ruby Ridge, and what they perceived as a dangerous and oppressive government. Much of the country viewed this event as a warning that the growth in militant militia and Christian Identity groups might be a far greater risk to social order and public safety than previously had been recognized. Curiously, Congress did not rush to investigate the growth in armed, militant, libertarian organizations, but scheduled multiple hearings of Waco and Ruby Ridge. Soon after ATF and the FBI had solved the World Trade Center bombing and as ATF agents worked around the clock beside local police and the FBI at the Oklahoma City bomb scene, Congress chose to investigate the actions of both agencies in a very hostile and public forum. This did not bode well for ATF.

The South Rises Again

In the summer of 1995, as ATF reeled from the Waco and Ruby Ridge allegations and hearings scheduled before hostile congressional committees, new allegations surfaced. ATF agents were alleged to have organized an event called the Good O' Boys Round-up, characterized as an openly racist gathering of law enforcement officers in rural Tennessee. The president and key members of Congress immediately issued critical statements, promising investigations of the event and its participants. The allegations provided support for critics of the bureau, who had previously characterized it as a racist organization as a result of the lawsuit by African-American agents.[51] Investigations of the Roundup were launched by the Justice and Treasury Departments, as it became apparent that the event had included assistant United States attorneys and agents from virtually every federal enforcement agency. Charges against participants grew to include drug use and sexual assault.[52]

Subsequent investigation by journalists linked the charges and alleged videotapes of racist banners at the event to Richard Hayward, an avowed supporter of David Duke. The *New York Times* reported that Hayward initially had offered the tape and the story to the National Rifle Association. NRA officials met with Hayward and subsequently put him in touch with a reporter from the *Washington Times*, which broke the story.[53] Although the initial allegations appeared damning, the subsequent investigative report did not substantiate any of the allegations of sexual misconduct or drug usage. In addition, the exhaustive investigations did not reveal a single instance of any ATF or other Treasury employee engaging in an act of racism.[54] The report did reveal that the event, which began as a

social event for ATF agents in 1980, had grown to a gathering of law
enforcement agents from throughout the South and had been regularly attended by police from as far away as Canada. During at least
three of these events, individuals identified as local police officers
engaged in overtly racist public conduct in the presence of some ATF
and other Treasury personnel. Although the organizer of the event, a
retired ATF supervisor, admonished the local officers not to repeat
their racist behavior, organizers took no other action.[55]

The Good O' Boys Roundup offers little insight into ATF as an
organization. Only a small minority of agents attended and many of
these were not aware of the racist behavior of some participants.
The Good O' Boys Roundup represented the last vestiges of a culture rapidly disappearing from ATF and other law enforcement
agencies. Since ATF's creation in 1972, law enforcement had evolved
from a homogeneous blue-collar, white, male institution to a far
more heterogeneous one. In ATF, this change had been exacerbated
by the end of the regional structure. The Good O' Boys Roundup
represented an effort by participants to retain some of the sense of
unity, belonging, and camaraderie that once pervaded the ATF's
Southern Region. For older agents who began their careers in an organization dominated by rural, southern, male values, the loss of
that culture has been difficult. The organization they joined has experienced radical change as a result of reorganization, transfers, and
mission change. In an organization that has become cosmopolitan,
urban, and heterogeneous, their exclusively white, male, rural culture has become illegitimate. Most have adjusted to reality, while retaining some nostalgia for the good old days, but a few have not.
The Good O' Boys Roundup reflects an effort to hold on to some of
that culture while accepting the reality of change. It also reflects an
unwillingness to publicly repudiate those who cling to an overtly
racist and sexist culture of the past. ATF is not unique among law
enforcement organizations in having to deal with these issues, but
its strong southern roots, vulnerable image, and powerful enemies
combined to give the Roundup a very high public and political
visibility.

The attention generated by the Good O' Boys Roundup produced pressures on ATF to settle the pending class action suit by
African-American agents. The pressure intensified with accusations
that ATF had not given high enough priority to investigation of fires
in African-American churches (see Chapter 14). In July 1996, ATF released a proposed settlement with the agents that still required
court approval. In addition to agreeing to award the plaintiffs $4.7
million in damages and $1.2 million in attorneys' fees, ATF agreed
to make systemic changes in its hiring, recruiting, and promotion

procedures. Pending adoption of those new procedures, every selection of a candidate other than an African American will receive
review at the level of a deputy assistant director or higher when an
African-American is on the eligible list. Because managers tend to
avoid review of their decisions whenever possible, this applies significant pressure to select African-American candidates whenever
they are eligible.

With this settlement and the completion of the Good O' Boys review by Treasury, John Magaw succeeded in extracting himself and
ATF from a difficult political situation. Whether this proves a temporary or long-term solution depends largely on the willingness of
other groups to follow the lead of the African-American agents. At
least two other groups within ATF are collecting funds for class action suits. One of these consists of female agents who are patterning
their strategy after that of the African-American agents. The other is
composed of white males intent on bringing action for discrimination against them in favor of minority and female agents.

A High-Tech Lynching Goes Awry

Magaw also appears to have survived the most serious political
threat to both himself and ATF, hostile congressional hearings. In
July and August of 1995, a joint subcommittee of the House Committees on Government Reform and Oversight and the Judiciary
held ten days of hearings on the events at Waco. House Republicans
appeared to have two specific objectives in mind for the hearings.
The first was to pay off the NRA and other opponents of gun control, who had demanded the hearings as a platform to investigate
ATF.[56] The second was to link the Clinton administration to embarrassing mistakes.[57]

The political dynamics of the hearings shifted against the Republicans even before they began when allegations came to light that
the committee's investigation was linked to the NRA and that NRA
employees had posed as committee staff members when contacting
potential witnesses.[58] The administration characterized the hearings
as hostile to law enforcement and supportive of radical paramilitary
groups.[59] The Democratic effort at political jujitsu was greatly benefited by one of the first witnesses to testify. Kiri Jewel, a fourteen-
year-old former resident of Mount Carmel, testified that David Koresh sexually molested her at the age of ten, with the apparent
consent of her mother.[60] At that moment, the hearings ceased to be
about government abuse of an innocent group of religious believers.
Majority members began disavowing Koresh and repeatedly stated

their support for law enforcement. The hearings provided mixed results for ATF. Both Chojnacki and Sarabyn testified at odds with
other witnesses, and Hartnett challenged the conclusions of the
Treasury investigative report. On the other hand, the testimony of
agents, several of whom had risked their lives in the operation, hu-
manized ATF. Cavanaugh's account of his tireless efforts to negoti-
ate the removal of first the wounded and later the children from the
scene did not evoke images of jackbooted thugs. Overall, ATF
emerged somewhat bloodied but not fatally wounded by the hearings. In an environment where inertia protects the status quo, a
draw was more required to preserve ATF.

The House Waco hearing was followed in September and October of 1995 by Senate hearings on the events at Ruby Ridge. Republican Arlen Spector of Pennsylvania, who chaired both the full committee and the subcommittee, was coincidentally involved in a
pursuit of the Republican nomination for president, in which one of
his primary weaknesses was a lack of conservative credentials. Although ATF played only a tangential role in the siege and shootings
at Ruby Ridge, the committee devoted a significant amount of time
to questioning ATF witnesses and made much of ATF's role in press
releases.[61] Senators Spector and Thompson, in particular, focused
hostile questioning on the conduct of the investigation of Randy
Weaver, which Senator Spector characterized as "extraordinary."[62]
Senators Spector and Thompson pursued the theory that prosecution of a person for selling two illegal firearms was inappropriate
and bordered on persecution. Senator Spector asked if ATF could
have proven beyond a reasonable doubt that Weaver was "an illegal
firearms trafficker," a profile he had been administratively assigned
early in the case.[63] The entire process was difficult for ATF agents to
understand. They had spent their lives pursuing criminal cases in
which the use of potential charges to motivate informants was routine. They had been told that the courts and prosecutors should exercise discretion over who should be prosecuted, not agents.

To comprehend the unusual nature of the senator's questioning,
one merely has to imagine that this case had involved narcotics
agents buying crack cocaine from a small-time dealer, then offering
him the choice between turning in his source or going to jail. For
veterans of the so-called war on drugs, this was routine. Agents
knew that many of these same members of Congress had supported
mandatory sentences that sent small-time drug dealers and minor
actors in large drug operations to prison for life. Carrying just one
of the guns sold by Weaver during any drug sale would have subjected the possessor to an additional ten years in prison. The agents
did not understand the senator's interpretation of intentional felony

violations of the firearms laws as innocent mistakes. Of course, they were not seeking political support from the gun lobby. The most damning information regarding ATF consisted of revelations that the ATF case agent had passed on inaccurate information about Weaver that might have influenced the actions of the Marshal's Service. Although this did not place the agent in a particularly good light, it is hard to imagine how this played an important role in the outcome. Weaver, after all, refused to surrender for well over a year, armed his children, and announced his intention not to comply.[64]

Notes

1. Department of the Treasury, *Investigation of Vernon Wayne Howell, Also Known as David Koresh* (Washington, D.C.: September 1993) 115–116.

2. The characterization of Hartnett is the author's, although it has been confirmed by interviews with former staff members and others who worked closely with him. Although some, such as David Troy and Richard Cook, have given the author permission to use their names, others have not.

3. Department of the Treasury, 117–118.

4. Many FBI agents do not believe this and say so privately. It remains, however, part of the FBI myth and has created resentment in numerous law enforcement agencies. To counter this, the FBI has made a point of emphasizing cooperation and dependence on other agencies, particularly state and local agencies. As with the Marines, however, perpetuation of the myth is a critical element in building loyalty and esprit de corps and is absorbed by the majority of new agents.

5. Troy was the first high-level ATF manager to make a clean break with the effort to deny that on-scene managers knew that the element of surprise had been lost and that Hartnett and Conroy were informed of this fact on March 1. Troy provided a full statement to the Treasury investigative team and has confirmed this to the author. As a result, Hartnett, who has never fully acknowledged the effort to cover up these events, immediately ceased speaking to Troy. Troy stated that Hartnett directed him to review videotapes of previous press conferences to determine the official bureau position on events. Troy did so and was then again told by Hartnett that this was the official position. Troy does not believe that Hartnett was consciously lying, but that he convinced himself that his position was the truth. After years of observing Hartnett, the author concurs that Hartnett would not be likely to intentionally lie but was quite capable of convincing himself of a favorable interpretation.

6. Shooting reviews by ATF and other agencies often get in the way of criminal investigations and are not popular with the investigators or prosecutors engaged in those investigations. In this case, ATF suspended the shooting review without interviewing most of the agents on the raid. The stated reason for the suspension was a request by the United States Attorney's Office, which was charged with prosecuting the shooters. This suspension was an issue of repeated interest during the Senate hearings. Majority members of the committee appeared incredulous that the United

States Attorney's Office would make such a request. Given the probability that statements of so many witnesses under great stress and viewing events from different perspectives would contain contradictions, it is predictable that the prosecutors would not want them interviewed twice. Any good defense lawyer would request discovery of the statements to the shooting review team and compare every detail to those made to the Rangers. Any discrepancies would be fertile ground for a defense that has only to raise doubt. Although prosecutors are duty bound to provide the defense with exculpatory material, they are not bound to create it and few appreciate parallel administrative investigations that do. That the several former prosecutors among the Republicans on the committee gave the appearance of finding this unusual raises the question as to their intent and credibility.

7. Department of the Treasury, 195.

8. Ibid.

9. Ibid., 196. According to Troy, Hartnett subsequently talked with Chojnacki and satisfied himself that there was not a serious conflict in information. Although this seems difficult to reconcile with the facts, it is not difficult for the author to accept in light of Hartnett's past patterns of behavior.

10. Department of the Treasury, 196–197.

11. Ibid., 198–199.

12. Ibid., 199. Higgins told the author that he counted on Hartnett for information.

13. Department of the Treasury, 200.

14. Ibid., 201.

15. Ibid.

16. Higgins stated to the author that Hartnett had advised him that there were some discrepancies between Chojnacki and Sarabyn's versions and those of Rodriguez. Higgins, in turn, made this known to Assistant Secretary Nobel. What appears to have been missing from Hartnett's report was any sense of the gravity of the situation.

17. Interview with Steve Higgins, who has not identified the agent.

18. Department of the Treasury, 203. Higgins stated to the author that, in retrospect, he has come to the conclusion that Hartnett was not capable of fully dealing with the crisis, although he continues to believe that Hartnett did not intentionally deceive him. He is far more receptive to the idea that Hartnett was able to delude himself and thus Higgins into believing that the situation was not as serious as it was. Hartnett lacked political insight and was apparently not able to grasp the unique nature of the situation.

19. Higgins contends that he requested, in writing, a Treasury investigation of the events in Waco in early March. He also contends that both the United States Attorney's Office and Treasury were restricting his ability to respond to accusations. He states that he requested authority to put all key parties before Senator DeConcini's committee in executive session but was denied authority by Assistant Secretary Nobel.

20. Gary Null, "Holocaust at Waco," *Penthouse* (April 1995); James D. Tabor and Eugene V. Gallagher, *Cults and the Battle for Religious Freedom in America* (Berkeley: University of California Press, 1995).

21. William J. Vizzard, "Reassessing Bittner's Thesis: Understanding Coercion and the Police in Light of Waco and the Los Angeles Riots," *Police Studies* (18:3 and 4, 1995).

22. Kim Masters, "Gunfight at the NRA Corral," *Washington Post*, National Weekly Edition (May 8–14, 1995); Erik Larson, "ATF Under Seige," *Time*

(July 24, 1995) 16–20; John Mintz, "Who Are the Bad Guys? The NRA and the ATF Duel Over the Truth in Accounts of Raids on Gun Owners," *Washington Post*, National Weekly Edition (May 22–28, 1995) 31; *New York Times*, "Questions Raised on Report of Agents at Racist Outing" (August 27, 1995) 8.

23. See Carol Vinzant, "ATF-Troop," *Spy* (March 1994); Null.

24. See *Soldier of Fortune* (June 1993).

25. Linda Thompson, *Waco, the Big Lie,* videotape, Indianapolis, Ind. (1993).

26. David P. Kopel and Paul H. Blackman, "The God Who Answers by Fire: The Waco Disaster and the Necessity of Federal Criminal Justice Reform," paper presented to the American Society of Criminology, 1983 (revised 1995).

27. Mintz. Also see Wayne LaPierre, *Guns, Crime, and Freedom* (Washington, D.C.: Regnery Publishing, 1994) and "NRA Backgrounder" (January 5, 1995). LaPierre is executive vice president of the NRA.

28. Erik Larson, "ATF Under Siege," *Time* (July 24, 1995).

29. Ibid.

30. Higgins stated to the author that the selection of Hartnett was clearly a mistake, given their management styles. He believes that he should have departed from convention and reached deeper into law enforcement for a more open and innovative manager. It is questionable whether Higgins would have had adequate knowledge to locate such a leader, given the long history within law enforcement management of advancing compliant and conformist managers in the image of their predecessors and Higgins's lack of intimate knowledge of law enforcement personnel.

31. Every SRT had a team leader and an alternate, who were field supervisors. In addition, an ASAC would oversee the team. In field divisions large enough for two ASACs, one would assume responsibility for the SRT and the other for NRT operations.

32. Originally called Entry Control Teams, SRTs steadily expanded their role beyond providing support for high-risk entries.

33. George C. Wilson and Peter Carison, "The Ultimate Stealth Plane," *Washington Post*, National Weekly Edition (January 6, 1996) 6–11.

34. *New York Times*, "Agency Checking Sexual Harassment" (January 12, 1983) A16.

35. During this period, the author was dealing with the office of the director regularly regarding research for a dissertation.

36. Masters, 11–12. Although Knox had long been the force behind the libertarian wing of the NRA, two of his protégés now appeared to rival him in power within the organization. Tanya Metaksa was the director of the Institute for Legislative Action and Marion Hammer was the president. Both are described by organization insiders as soul mates of Knox's, who shared his zeal and commitment but not his good humor and courtly nature.

37. Larson.

38. *New York Times*, "Bentsen Signals Official's Ouster Over Initial Raid on Cult in Texas" (April 29, 1993) A1.

39. *New York Times*, "Report to Fault Firearms Bureau for Raid on Cult" (August 30, 1993) A1.

40. *New York Times*, "With Waco Report Due in 3 Days Firearms Chief Says He Is Quitting" (September 28, 1993) A1; "Report on Initial Raid on Cult Finds Officials Erred and Lied" (October 1, 1993) A1.

41. Ibid., October 1.

42. The protective function expends millions of dollars every year for such questionable purposes as protecting Lady Bird Johnson and ex-presidents Jimmy Carter and Gerald Ford, with congressional blessing. The protection of a sitting president can generate costs of over a million dollars for one photo opportunity. The author has observed multiple limousines flown across country and driven to a remote backcounty location to transport the president a few hundred yards so that he could be filmed "encountering" campers and admiring a tree. This same event required days of preparation and the use of several hundred police, forest rangers, and federal agents. It is routine to fly Secret Service agents thousands of miles and incur both lodging and overtime expense to simply stand a post for a few hours, when police and other federal agents are available locally for the task. The Secret Service routinely inconveniences large numbers of people by closing down roads or blocking off foot traffic and subjects numerous persons to search to facilitate the protective function. The response of Congress, the press, local police, and the public to these actions has been almost universally supportive. There has been little or no complaint or public debate regarding the broad authority granted the Secret Service or its expenditure of resources. Within the Secret Service, the policy mandate is clear that protection takes priority over law enforcement. Field offices are virtually shut down and investigations suspended to support the protection function.

43. Interview with John Magaw.

44. One result has been to increase an already swollen headquarters staff.

45. This largely follows a pattern that began with the creation of the bureau in 1972 of shifting authority to headquarters.

46. A memorandum to all enforcement personnel from the associate director of enforcement titled "Enforcement Program Strategies," dated May 3, 1995, states clearly that ATF's policy is a direct response to Office of Management and Budget priorities, which call for agencies to perform functions that do not overlap state or local functions.

47. William J. Vizzard, "The Evolution of Gun Control Policy in the United States: Accessing the Public Agenda," DPA dissertation, University of Southern California, 1993.

48. It is not clear to the author how many in ATF higher management understand these basic contradictions. It appears that John Magaw does not. Although the author provided him several opportunities to address the issue, Magaw never seemed to understand the question. He cited the expanded use of tracing data, as though it would magically reveal some new strategy that had evaded ATF for almost three decades. It appears that Magaw is not conversant with the details of firearms policy and enforcement, which is confirmed by numerous sources within ATF. For those staff members who understand ATF's dilemma, no means exists to address the conflict between reality and policy. Any open discussion would contradict the director and administration policy and give comfort to the enemies of ATF. Those in Congress and elsewhere who oppose current policy have shown no interest in seeking remedies to the conflict between legislation and reality.

49. Sidney Blumenthal, "Her Own Private Idaho," *The New Yorker* (July 19, 1995) 27–33. Chenoweth specifically cited ATF as an example of why Congress should require federal law enforcement to obtain written permission from local authorities to engage in enforcement action.

50. Holly Idelson, "House GOP Crime Bills Win Easy Passage," *Congressional Quarterly Weekly Report* (February 11, 1995) 456–458.

51. *New York Times* (July 13, 17, and 19, 1995).

52. U.S. Department of the Treasury, Office of the Inspector General, *Report of Investigation: Good O' Boys Roundup* (Washington, D.C., 1995) 3.

53. *New York Times*, "Questions Raised on Report of Agents at Racist Outing" (August 27, 1995).

54. Department of the Treasury, Office of the Inspector General, 3–6.

55. Ibid. This is a condensation of the details from throughout the report.

56. Kopel and Blackman.

57. *New York Times*, "New Chapter in Whitewater and Waco" (July 17, 1995).

58. *New York Times* (July 13, 19, and 20, 1995).

59. *New York Times* (July 6, 20, and 21, 1995).

60. *New York Times* (July 20, 1996). Testimony of Kiri Jewel, July 19, 1995. All references to testimony are from observation of the televised hearings; official transcripts were not yet available at the time this account was written.

61. Robert Marshal Wells, "ATF Criticized for Actions in Ruby Ridge Shootout," *Congressional Quarterly Weekly Report* (September 9, 1995) 2725.

62. From the televised hearing on September 7, 1995.

63. The question makes little sense. This is an administrative category, not a legal one. It therefore has no statutory elements, and one can never establish its truth beyond a reasonable doubt. Moreover, the classification of suspects at the early stage of an investigation routinely is not very precise in any agency.

64. A review of the questioning raises doubts about either the integrity or the intellect of some committee members. Repeated questions were asked about why Weaver was seen as dangerous, when the record reflected that he had confronted agents while carrying a weapon, was often surrounded by armed family members, refused requests to come in to the Federal Building, and told associates that he would resist.

CHAPTER 14

An Uncertain Future

In the twenty-five years since ATF became an independent agency only one of the four primary forces that shaped it has appreciably changed. The agency's regional tradition and rural roots, inherited from the IRS and shaped by the task of liquor enforcement, have largely disappeared, leaving a national organization of heterogeneous composition and less distinct character. In the process, the agency has evolved away from a craft-guild model and toward a rational bureaucratic model. Although the agency has emerged from the influence of its earlier regional structure, it still retains a functionally divided structure in spite of all efforts by management to develop the agency as a single bureau. These efforts have largely been frustrated by the reality of two primary organizational missions and task environments that support distinct cultures. Merging two components that retain different employment standards, training, salary, and benefits, as well as different tasks and skills, would appear an impossible task.

In addition to the internal division by function, longstanding political and policy conflicts continue to challenge the agency's ability to define its mission. National policy on firearms regulation remains muddled, ill-defined, and controversial. Mandates from Congress and the executive branch continue to be ambiguous and subject to change without notice. While the policies relating to explosives enforcement and control lack the contradictions and ambiguities of firearms policy, ATF's role continues to be competitive with the FBI's. None of these forces are conducive to a rational management or effective leadership. Because criminal investigation remains substantially a craft, difficult to direct centrally or subject to standardized procedures, ATF's management finds itself caught between political leadership that will not define its mission or turf and field-level operators whose activities defy control. The strength of its opponents places the agency in a vulnerable political position, unable to seek legislative remedies to policy problems and constantly subject to attack for any mistake, real or perceived. In addition, its location in the Treasury Department, smaller size, and weaker public image place ATF at a great disadvantage in turf conflicts with the FBI.

Thus, management is denied a predictable environment in which to pursue planning, resource allocation, and mission definition. In addition, the environment mediates against delegation of authority, because the political risk from error is high. Equally if not more important is the inability to provide leadership. Leadership is a largely symbolic act that requires legitimacy among organizational members. In an agency that must inspire individual agent initiative to produce results, leadership is more important than management in shaping the actions of operators. A tenuous, unsure, and vulnerable environment denies potential leaders the capacity to build esprit de corps and symbolic authority in the eyes of operators. Although first-line supervisors may be able to develop authority through demonstrating mastery of the craft of investigation, higher level managers are too far removed from the process to effectively accomplish this. They are thus denied both of the traditional avenues to legitimization of leadership, superior craft skill and the ability to mediate and control external environmental forces.

Although none of the characteristics of its environment is unique to ATF as an agency, the combination of factors may be. ATF management is caught in a number of unusual positions. The agency cannot retreat to its former position of relative obscurity once it has entered the consciousness of the press and public, yet it faces constraints on its ability to enlarge its public recognition and prominence. The FBI domination of public awareness of federal law enforcement leaves only limited room for other federal law enforcement agencies. Although the Secret Service and DEA have not recently received the negative attention directed at ATF, they remain overshadowed by the FBI in the public perception. More fundamentally, the jurisdiction and authority of other agencies is limited by the FBI's presence. Any effort to move from a mission of enforcing law within a narrow jurisdiction to one of attacking major crime problems categorically places agencies in direct conflict with the FBI. Thus, ATF may pursue explosives or firearms violations but not organized crime, terrorism, or violent crime. In an era in which police agencies are progressively moving from a narrow law enforcement mission to one of attacking crime as a more systemic social phenomenon, this places ATF and other federal law enforcement agencies at a decided disadvantage.

Although ATF's revenue and compliance functions could very easily survive in a low-profile environment, they require linkage to the law enforcement mission to justify independent bureau status.

Precisely because these functions are more amenable to management, they are also vulnerable to incorporation with other similar functions. The marriage of regulatory and law enforcement functions, linked primarily by historical accident, is unique to ATF, as is the ambiguity of the task environment relating to the firearms mission. For ATF, neither the what nor the how of firearms control is clear.

Given these problems, the likelihood that ATF would eventually fall victim to merger or reorganization appears strong. Three of the last four administrations have announced major law enforcement reorganization plans, and every plan has included ATF. Yet these plans seldom reach fruition, a situation that may well continue. The structure and function of federal law enforcement are of little political import, and the potential barriers to any change are numerous. No powerful constituency or interest group would gain from a more orderly or rational organization of law enforcement or the elimination of ATF. Thus, politicians lack incentives to provide the sort of political stewardship and commitment necessary to move reorganization through the political mine field presented by a strong and independent bicameral legislature, in which opposition by even one subcommittee chair is adequate to block change.

Because the federal role in law enforcement and criminal justice is limited, agency stature with the politicians, the press, and the public tends to be shaped primarily by major, newsworthy cases rather than by overall performance. This limited federal role has allowed considerable latitude for presidents, Congress, and the agencies themselves to focus upon those issues that capture public attention and largely ignore those that offer little political advantage. Thus ATF's stature is not exclusively tied to the quality of its management or even to the majority of its work output. Just as the agency's image plummeted after Waco, it may rise precipitously with a visible success, such as the 1996 arrests of militia members in Arizona for plotting to bomb public buildings.[1]

Such radical shifts in public image and political support would be far less likely if federal enforcement agencies served large constituencies or could be tied directly to easily measured outputs or outcomes, but this is not the case. The relationship between law enforcement and crime is neither well understood nor easily documented. Given the potential for use of crime and law enforcement as political symbols and the latitude available in manipulating the federal role, both Congress and future presidents will likely continue to view the actions of enforcement agencies more from a political than a managerial perspective.

The politicized nature of the federal law enforcement role was highlighted during the summer of 1996 by the reaction of various interests to arsons of African-American churches in the South. Although many individuals surely desired that these crimes be solved and that future arsons be discouraged, the actions and public announcements of some individuals and groups appeared to be motivated far more by a desire to capitalize on the arsons as symbolic events useful for mobilizing opinion and marshaling support.[2] African-American political activists have insisted that somehow the failure of ATF and the FBI to find any conspiracy is indicative of either insensitivity or racism and have linked the investigations with the Good O' Boys Roundup and the class action suit by African-American ATF agents.[3] Politicians of both parties postured to demonstrate their concern, with Congress rushing through a bill creating the specific federal crime of church burning.

The burning of buildings as symbolic as churches, particularly African-American churches in the South, assures an emotional reaction. And there is rightfully some suspicion of law enforcement among African-Americans in the United States. Yet, the events in this instance seemed to go beyond either of these explanations. The rhetoric of some seemed to demand that law enforcement's role was to pursue only explanations that supported evidence of white racism and hate. The powerful symbolism of such events was apparently too appealing for community leaders and politicians to pass up. Unfortunately, to capitalize on such events, one cannot wait for the outcome of investigations or trials. The secret to political success is to capture the public attention when the opportunity avails itself. Thus investigators are placed in a position in which various interest groups and politicians have a vested interest in specific outcomes well before the facts are known. In this case, as an example, any consideration of church officials or members as suspects in any of the fires was assured to generate negative reaction for those who desired to use the events to highlight racism. Even the statements by investigators that there was no available evidence of a common conspiracy behind the arsons was treated by some commentators as evidence that the investigators did not take the crimes seriously. Repeated announcements by the president that additional resources would be committed to the investigations and action by Congress to create a new crime category were done in obvious haste, with little evaluation of need or utility. The entire event was reminiscent of the previous efforts to placate middle-class white constituencies through symbolic action in response to child pornography, carjacking, and crack cocaine use.

Firearms regulation and enforcement remain at the core of ATF's identity, and the majority of ATF's political problems emanate from its jurisdiction over the gun laws. Yet, without the firearms laws, there is little likelihood that ATF would continue to exist. Most recently, the agency has attempted to redefine its firearms mission by increasing the oversight of dealers and shifting from the prosecution of individual criminals to traffickers. It has also initiated extensive firearms tracing efforts. None of these strategies is new. They parallel policies initiated under the Carter administration and terminated after the election of Ronald Reagan.

As of the 1996 election campaign, the political dynamics of the firearms issue appear to have again shifted in favor of ATF. Despite rhetoric to the contrary, a Republican Congress failed to revoke either the Brady Law or the assault weapons ban, and Republican presidential candidate Bob Dole distanced himself from the gun lobby.[4] Dole apparently acted in response to President Clinton's effective use of firearms issues to present a strong anticrime image.[5] Ironically, the heightened news coverage of ATF, much of it engineered by the NRA and its supporters in Congress, has accomplished what ATF could not. The coverage has elevated ATF's public profile to a level at which the organization is known to the general public and routinely identified by the press, rather than being referred to merely as "federal agents." Director John Magaw and his staff appear to be rather skillfully capitalizing on every opportunity to build and enhance the agency's image.[6]

Although this all represents favorable political news for ATF and Director Magaw, it does nothing to address the underlying conflict in policy that has repeatedly frustrated ATF's ability to pursue a consistent and effective firearms enforcement policy. So long as the nation retains a contradictory and shifting attitude regarding the role of firearms and the appropriate means of regulating them, Congress and future administrations will continue to send mixed and contradictory signals to the agency. ATF will respond by attempting to widen its law enforcement mandate into as many other areas as possible and by periodically shifting between its two alternate firearms enforcement strategies, neither of which will offer much hope for impacting violent crime, given the current state of the firearms laws. The probability that either the president or Congress will address these more fundamental questions of policy remains slight. Unlike symbolic issues of little substance, fundamental policy change is difficult and politically costly.

Yet, ATF has demonstrated an ability to adapt and reinvent itself in the past. It possesses a cadre of well-trained and committed agents and inspectors who effectively collect immense revenue, provide valuable support to other law enforcement agencies, conduct numerous criminal investigations with skill, and occasionally perform heroically. The agency has also reached a level of administrative maturity that only comes with age and experience. These constitute valuable real and symbolic assets for the government and the nation.

Notes

1. Patricia King, "Vipers in the Burbs," *Newsweek* (July 15, 1996) 20–23.
2. Michael Fumento, "A Church Arson Epidemic? It's Smoke and Mirrors," *Wall Street Journal* (July 8, 1996); Michael Kelly, "Playing With Fire: Who Is Burning the Churches, and Who Is Exploiting the Issue?" *The New Yorker* (July 15, 1996) 28–35.
3. Jack E. White, "First the Flame, Then the Blame," *Time* (June 17, 1996) 35; "ATF Troubled by Allegations of Racial Bias," *Washington Post* (June 21, 1996).
4. *New York Times*, "NRA Unlikely to Endorse Dole, Official Says," (July 18, 1996); "Bob Dole vs. the NRA," editorial (July 21, 1996); "Dole Sends Message of Inclusion to Abortion-Rights Republicans" (July 22, 1996).
5. *New York Times*, "Clinton Challenges Dole on Assault Weapons Stance" (July 11, 1996); "Federal Program Will Track Sales of Guns to Youth" (July 8, 1996).
6. *Parade* magazine recently presented a favorable image of Magaw and the "new" ATF in a cover story by Peter Maas, "Can John Magaw Save ATF?" (May 19, 1996), and Magaw has also made several television appearances, at which he excels. Although the focus on church fires began with statements critical of ATF, coverage has turned far more positive and photographs of agents wearing ATF utility uniforms have been prominently featured in numerous articles. The president's decision to use an ATF firearms tracing initiative as a key element in his reelection strategy reflects the improvement in ATF's image since Waco. See *New York Times* (July 8, 1996).

Bibliography

Aho, James A. *The Politics of Righteousness: Idaho Christian Patriotism*. Seattle: University of Washington Press, 1990.

American Rifleman. "Gun Law Enforcers Shoot Surprised Citizen, Claim Self-Defense" (July 1971).

———. "Gun Act Caused a Shooting" (August 1971).

———. "Ballews Suing Over ATFD Raid" (September 1971).

———. "How the 1968 Gun Act 'Creates Criminals'" (October 1971).

———. "Prosecution in Ballew Raid Still a Question," "The 1968 Gun Control Act as a National Affliction," "29 Practice Grenades = 10 Years," and "What Happens to a Wife's Guns?" (November 1971).

———. "ATF Becomes a New Federal Bureau" (May 1972).

Arkansas Democrat. "CSA Leader Gets 20-Year Sentence for Racketeering." September 5, 1985.

Barber, Benjamin. *Strong Democracy*. Berkeley: University of California Press, 1984.

Barkum, Michael. *Religion and the Racist Right: The Origins of the Christian Identity Movement*. Chapel Hill: University of North Carolina Press, 1994.

Blumenthal, Sidney. "Her Own Private Idaho." *The New Yorker* (July 19, 1995).

Bruce-Biggs, B. "The Great American Gun War." *The Public Interest* (no. 45, fall 1976).

Colwell, William Lee. "An Examination of the 1982 Decision to Reorganize the FBI and the DEA." DPA dissertation, University of Southern California, 1985.

Committee to Elect Reagan-Bush. "Gun Control." Undated press release from 1980 campaign furnished by the Ronald Reagan Library.

Comptroller General of the United States. *Handgun Control: Effectiveness and Costs*. Washington, D.C.: The General Accounting Office, February 6, 1978.

Congressional Digest. "Should Semiautomatic Assault-Style Weapons Be Banned by Congress?" (69:11, November 1990).

Cook, Phillip J. "The Effect of Gun Availability on Violent Crime Patterns." *Annals of the American Academy of Political and Social Science* (no. 455, May 1981) 63–79.

Criner, Lawrence. "Waco, the Tragic Collision of Religious and Secular Mindsets." *Washington Times*. March 4, 1994.

Dahl, Robert. *Dilemmas of a Pluralist Democracy*. New Haven, Conn.: Yale University Press, 1982.

Davidson, Roger. *The Postreform Congress*. College Park: University of Maryland Press, 1992.

Derthick, Martha. *Agency Under Stress: The Social Security Administration*. Washington, D.C.: Brookings Institution, 1990.

Fumento, Michael. "A Church Arson Epidemic? It's Smoke and Mirrors." *Wall Street Journal*. July 18, 1996.

Gentry, Curt. *J. Edgar Hoover: The Man and the Secrets*. New York: W. W. Norton, 1991.

Hamilton, Alexander, James Madison, and John Jay. *The Federalist Papers*, ed. and foreword by Clinton Rossiter. New York: New American Library, 1961.

Hardy, David. Task Force to Investigate the Enforcement Policies of the Bureau of Alcohol, Tobacco and Firearms. *The BATF's War on Civil Liberties: The Assault on Gun Owners*. Bellevue, Wash.: Second Amendment Foundation, 1979.

Haughton, James G. "Doctors Should Be Fighting to Ban Guns." *Medical Economics* (66:16, August 21, 1989) 24–27.

Helco, Hugh. *Government of Strangers*. Washington, D.C.: Brookings Institution, 1977.

Hofstadter, Richard. "America as a Gun Culture." *American Violence: A Documentary History*, eds. Richard Hofstadter and Michael Wallace. New York: Alfred Knopf, 1970.

Idelson, Holly. "House GOP Crime Bills Win Easy Passage." *Congressional Quarterly Weekly* (February 11, 1995).

Jones, Jaurie. "MD Groups Support Semiautomatic Gun Ban." *American Medical News* (33:8, February 23, 1990) 11.

Kaplan John. "The Wisdom of Gun Prohibition." *Annals of the American Academy of Political and Social Science*. (no. 455, May 1981).

Kates, Don B. *Guns, Murder and the Constitution: A Realistic Assessment of Gun Control*. San Francisco: Pacific Research Institute for Public Policy, 1990.

———. "Toward a History of Handgun Prohibition in the United States." *Restricting Handguns: The Liberal Skeptics Speak Out*, ed. Don B. Kates. Croton-on-Hundson, N.Y.: North River Press, 1979.

Kaufman, Herbert. *The Administrative Behavior of Federal Bureau Chiefs*. Washington, D.C.: Brookings Institution, 1981.

———. *The Forest Ranger*. Baltimore: Johns Hopkins University Press, 1960.

Kelly, Michael. "Playing With Fire: Who Is Burning the Churches and Who Is Exploiting the Issue?" *The New Yorker* (July 15, 1996) 28–35.

Kennett, Lee, and James Anderson. *The Gun in America: Origins of an American Dilemma*. Westport, Conn.: Greenwood Press, 1975.

King, Patricia. "Vipers in the Burbs." *Newsweek* (July 15, 1996) 20–23.

Kleck, Gary. *Point Blank: Guns and Violence in America*. New York: Aldine de Gruyter, 1991.

Knox, Neal. "The Thirty Year War for Gun Ownership." *Guns and Ammo* (August 1988).

Kopel, David P., and Paul H. Blackman. "The God Who Answers by Fire: The Waco Disaster and the Necessity of Federal Criminal Justice Reform." Paper presented to the American Society of Criminology, 1993, revised July 19, 1995; furnished to the author by Paul Blackman.

LaPierre, Wayne R. *Guns, Crime and Freedom*. Washington, D.C.: Regnery Publishing, 1994.

Larson, Erik. "ATF Under Siege." *Time* (July 24, 1995).

Leff, Carol S., and Mark H. Leff. "The Politics of Ineffectiveness: Federal Gun Legislation 1919–38." *Annals of the American Academy of Political and Social Science* (no. 455, May 1981) 48–62.

Levi, Edward. Address to Law Enforcement Executives Narcotics Conference. Washington, D.C., April 6, 1975.

Liddy, G. Gordon. *Will.* New York: St. Martain's Press, 1980.

Lofton, Colin, et al. "Effects of Restrictive Licensing of Handguns on Homicide and Suicide in the District of Columbia." *New England Journal of Medicine* (325:23, December 5, 1991) 1615–1621.

Masters, Kim. "Gunfight at the NRA Corral." *Washington Post*, National Weekly Edition. May 8–14, 1995.

McWilliams, John C. *The Protectors: Harry Anslinger and the Federal Bureau of Narcotics, 1930–1962.* Newark: University of Delaware Press, 1990.

Millspaugh, Arthur. *Crime Control by the Federal Government.* Washington, D.C.: Brookings Institution, 1937.

Mintz, John. "Who Are the Bad Guys? The NRA and the ATF Duel Over the Truth in Accounts of Raids on Gun Owners." *Washington Post*, National Weekly Edition. May 22–28, 1995.

Moore, Mark H. "The Supply of Handguns: An Analysis of the Potential and Current Importance of Alternative Sources of Handguns to Criminal Offenders." An unpublished paper, undated.

Naifeh, Steven, and Gregory White Smith. *The Mormon Murders.* New York: Penguin, 1989.

Newsweek. "The Echoes of Ruby Ridge" (August 28, 1995) 26–33.

———. "Who Is He" (May 8, 1995) 40–41.

Newton, George D., and Franklin E. Zimring. *Firearms and Violence in American Life: A Staff Report Submitted to the National Commission on the Causes and Prevention of Violence.* Washington, D.C.: National Commission on the Causes and Prevention of Violence, 1969.

New York Times. "Agency Checking Sexual Harassment." January 12, 1993.

———. "Bentsen Signals Official's Ouster Over Initial Raid on Cult in Texas." April 29, 1993.

———. "Report to Fault Firearms Bureau for Raid on Cult." August 30, 1993.

———. "With Waco Report Due in 3 Days Firearms Chief Says He Is Quitting." September 28, 1993.

———. "Report on Initial Raid on Cult Finds Officials Erred and Lied." October 1, 1993.

———. "Why the Flames of Waco Won't Die." April 17, 1994.

———. "Administration Tries to Blunt Hearing on Raid on Texas Sect." July 6, 1995.

———. "Waco Inquiry Is Said to Use NRA Support." July 13, 1995.

———. "New Chapter in Whitewater and Waco." July 17, 1995.

———. "Waco Witness Says NRA Consultant Posed as a House Aid." July 17, 1995.

———. "Use of NRA Is Criticized in Raid Case." July 19, 1995.

———. "Clinton Assails Officers' Racist Event." July 20, 1995.

———. "Examination of Waco Raid Goes Partisan." July 20, 1995.

———. "Diametric Views of Waco: Federal Agents as Aggressors—and as Victims of Outlaws." July 21, 1995.

———. "Questions Raised on Report of Agents at Racist Outing." August 27, 1995.

———. "Federal Program Will Track Sales of Guns to Youth." July 8, 1996.

———. "Clinton Challenges Dole on Assault Weapons Stance." July 11, 1996.

———. "GOP Report Faults Reno in Waco Raid." July 12, 1996.

———. "NRA Unlikely to Endorse Dole, Official Says." July 18, 1996.

———. "Bob Dole vs the NRA," editorial. July 21, 1996.

———. "Dole Sends Message of Inclusion to Abortion-Rights Republicans." July 22, 1996.

Null, Gary. "Holocaust at Waco." *Penthouse* (April 1995).

Pesso, Tanna. "Gun Control (B): The Bureau of Alochol, Tobacco and Firearms." Unpublished case study prepared for the John F. Kennedy School of Government, Harvard University. Boston, 1981.

Price, James, Sharon Desmond, and Daisy Smith. "A Preliminary Investigation of Inner-City Adolescents' Perceptions of Guns." *Journal of School Health* (61:6, August 1991) 255–260.

Reavis, Dick J. *The Ashes of Waco*. New York: Simon and Schuster, 1995.

Rohr, John A. "Ethical Issues in French Public Administration: A Comparative Study." *Public Administration Review* (51:4, July-August 1991).

Reich, Robert, ed. *The Power of Public Ideas*. Cambridge, Mass.: Ballinger Publishing, 1987.

Shannon, Margaret. "Before Watergate: Randolph Thrower vs. the Nixon White House." *Atlanta Journal and Constitution Magazine*. April 7, 1974.

Sherrill, Robert. *The Saturday Night Special and Other Guns with Which Americans Won the West, Protected Bootleg Franchises, Slew Wildlife, Robbed Countless Banks, Shot Husbands Purposely and by Mistake, and Killed Presidents—Together With the Debate Over Continuing Same*. New York: Charterhouse, 1973.

Sloan, John, et al. "Handgun Regulations, Crime Assaults and Homicide: A Tale of Two Cities." *New England Journal of Medicine* (314:24, June 12, 1986) 1557–1560.

Sugarmann, Josh. *National Rifle Association: Money, Power and Fear*. Washington, D.C.: National Press Books, 1992.

Tabor, James D., and Eugene V. Gallagher. *Cults and the Battle for Religious Freedom in America*. Berkeley: University of California Press, 1995.

Thomas, Pierre. "ATF Troubled by Allegations of Racial Bias." *Washington Post*. June 21, 1996.

Thompson, James. *Organizations in Action*. New York: McGraw Hill, 1967.

Thompson, Linda. *Waco, the Big Lie*. Videotape, Indianapolis, Ind., 1993.

U.S. Congress. House of Representatives. Subcommittee of the Committee on Interstate and Foreign Commerce. *Hearings on the National Firearms Act*. 73rd Congress, 2nd Session, April and May 1934.

———. *To Regulate Commerce in Firearms, Hearings*. 75th Congress, 1st Session, 1937.

———. Committee on the Judiciary. *Events Surrounding the Branch Davidian Cult Standoff in Waco, Texas, Hearing*. 103rd Congress, 1st Session, April 28, 1993.

U.S. Congress. Senate. Committee on Commerce. Subcommittee on S. 885, S. 2258, and S. 3680. *To Regulate Commerce in Firearms, Hearings*. 73rd Congress, 2nd Session. 1934.

———. Committee on the Judiciary. Subcommittee to Investigate Juvenile Delinquency. *Federal Firearms Act, Hearings*. 89th Congress, 1st Session. 1965.

———. Committee on the Judiciary. Subcommittee to Investigate Juvenile Delinquency. *Federal Firearms Act, Hearings.* 90th Congress, 1st Session. 1967.

———. Committee on the Judiciary. Subcommittee to Investigate Juvenile Delinquency. *Federal Firearms Legislation.* 90th Congress, 2nd Session. 1968.

———. Committee on the Judiciary. Subcommittee to Investigate Juvenile Delinquency. *Handgun Crime Control—1975–1976.* 94th Congress, 1st Session. Vols. I and II, 1976.

———. Committee on Appropriations. *Oversight Hearings on Bureau of Alcohol, Tobacco and Firearms.* July 11, 1979.

———. Committee on the Judiciary. Subcommittee on the Constitution. *Gun Control and Constitutional Rights, Hearings.* 96th Congress, 2nd Session. September 15, 1980.

———. Committee on Appropriations. *Proposed Dissolution of the Bureau of Alcohol, Tobacco and Firearms, Hearings.* 97th Congress, 2nd Session. 1982.

———. Committee on the Judiciary. Subcommittee on Terrorism, Technology and Government Information. *Ruby Ridge.* 104th Congress, 2nd Session. 1996.

U.S. Department of Justice. Bureau of Justice Statistics. *Violent Crime in the United States.* Washington, D.C., 1991.

———. Bureau of Justice Statistics. *Local Police in 1993.* Washington, D.C., April 1996.

U.S. Department of the Treasury. *Report of the Good O' Boys Roundup Policy Review.* Washington, D.C., April, 1996.

———. Office of the Inspector General. *Report of Investigation: Good O' Boys Roundup.* Washington, D.C., 1995.

———. *Report on the Bureau of Alcohol, Tobacco and Firearms Investigation of Vernon Wayne Howell Also Known as David Koresh.* Washington, D.C., September 1993.

Violence Policy Center. "Gun Shows in America: Tupperware Parties for Criminals." Washington, D.C., 1996.

Vinzant, Carol. "ATF-Troop." *Spy* (March 1994).

Vizzard, William J. "The Evolution of Gun Control Policy in the United States: Accessing the Public Agenda." DPA dissertation, University of Southern California, 1983.

———. "Reassessing Bittner's Thesis: Understanding Coercion and the Police in Light of Waco and the Los Angeles Riots." *Police Studies* (18:3 and 4, 1995) 1–18.

———. "The Impact of Agenda Conflict on Policy Formulation and Implementation." *Public Administration Review* (55:4, July-August 1995) 341–347.

Walter, Jess. *Every Knee Shall Bow.* New York: HarperCollins, 1995.

Washington Post. "No Conspiracy Seen in Bombings." January 6, 1985.

———. "Call for Fed Investigation." March 1, 1985.

———. "Mayor Criticizes FBI for Not Leading Abortion Clinic Probe." March 3, 1985.

———. "ATF Called Experts Despite Low Profile." January 4, 1986.

———. Editorial of January 22, 1986.

———. "Abortion Foe Convicted in 10 Bombings." May 22, 1986.

———. "Practical Implications of Crafting the Compromise: The Case of Assault Weapons," paper presented to the Academy of Criminal Justice Sciences, Boston, 1995.

Washington Times. "Crystals in the Waco Crucible." April 4, 1993.

Webster, Daniel, et al. "Reducing Firearms Injuries." *Issues in Science and Technology* (7:3, spring 1991) 73–80.

Wells, Robert. "ATF Criticized for Action in Ruby Ridge." *Congressional Quarterly Weekly Report* (September 9, 1995).

White, Jack E. "First the Flame and Then the Blame." *Time* (June 17, 1996).

Wilson, George C., and Peter Carison. "The Ultimate Stealth Plane." *Washington Post*, National Weekly Edition. January 6, 1996.

Wilson James Q. *Bureaucracy: What Government Agencies Do and Why They Do It.* New York: Basic Books, 1989.

———. *The Investigators.* New York: Basic Books, 1978.

Winnie, Mark. *Postmark Terror.* New York: Scribners, 1995.

Wintemute, Garen, Stephen Teret, and Jess Kraus. "The Epidemiology of Firearms Deaths Among Residents of California." *Western Journal of Medicine* (146:3, March 1987) 374–377.

Yang, Bijou, and David Lester. "The Effects of Gun Availability on Suicide Rates." *Atlantic Economic Journal* (19:2, June 1991) 74.

Zimring, Franklin E. "Firearms and Federal Law: The Gun Control Act of 1968." *Journal of Legal Studies* (475, 1975) 133–198.

Zimring, Franklin, E., and Gordon Hawkins. *The Citizens' Guide to Gun Control.* New York: MacMillan, 1987.

Index

About the Book

In the aftermath of Ruby Ridge and Waco, the Bureau of Alcohol, Tobacco and Firearms (ATF) has become one of the most controversial of government agencies. Yet, despite the headlines and congressional hearings, little has been written about the history and organizational culture of the bureau.

William Vizzard draws both on his twenty-seven years of insider experience as a special agent and manager and on the tools of organizational theory to trace the creation, structure, and historical development of the bureau. With a perspective that is further informed by direct interviews with all the former directors of the bureau, as well as former Treasury officials and members of key interest and lobbying groups, he considers how the ATF has evolved as a product of its political environment, the tasks it has been assigned, and its organizational culture. In engaging prose, Vizzard explores the bureau's ups and downs, the conditions that were a prelude to Waco, the ensuing time of turmoil, and the prospects and problems that lie ahead.

William J. Vizzard is associate professor of criminal justice at the California State University, Sacramento. Before receiving his doctorate, he spent twenty-nine years in law enforcement, serving in ATF from 1967 to 1994 as an agent, supervisor, program manager, and special agent in charge.